Business Intelligence Techniques

Springer

Berlin
Heidelberg
New York
Hong Kong
London
Milan
Paris
Tokyo

Murugan Anandarajan
Asokan Anandarajan
Cadambi A. Srinivasan
Editors

Business
Intelligence
Techniques

A Perspective
from Accounting
and Finance

With 53 Figures
and 18 Tables

 Springer

Professor Murugan Anandarajan, Ph.D.
Department of Management
Drexel University
32nd and Chestnut Streets
Philadelphia PA 19104, USA
murugan.anandarajan@drexel.edu

Professor Asokan Anandarajan, Ph.D.
School of Management
New Jersey Institute of Technology
University Heights
Newark, NJ 07102, USA
anandarajan@njit.edu

Emeritus Professor Cadambi A. Srinivasan, Ph.D.
Department of Accounting
Drexel University
32nd and Chestnut Streets
Philadelphia PA 19104, USA

HD38.7
.B873
2004
13540408207

ISBN 3-540-40820-7 Springer-Verlag Berlin Heidelberg New York

Cataloging-in-Publication Data applied for
A catalog record for this book is available from the Library of Congress.
Bibliographic information published by Die Deutsche Bibliothek
Die Deutsche Bibliothek lists this publication in the Deutsche Nationalbibliografie;
detailed bibliographic data available in the internet at http.//dnb.ddb.de

This work is subject to copyright. All rights are reserved, whether the whole or part of the
material is concerned, specifically the rights of translation, reprinting, reuse of illustrations,
recitation, broadcasting, reproduction on microfilm or in any other way, and storage in
data banks. Duplication of this publication or parts thereof is permitted only under the
provisions of the German Copyright Law of September 9, 1965, in its current version, and
permission for use must always be obtained from Springer-Verlag. Violations are liable for
prosecution under the German Copyright Law.

Springer-Verlag Berlin Heidelberg New York
a member of BertelsmannSpringer Science + Business Media GmbH

http://www.springer.de
© Springer-Verlag Berlin Heidelberg 2004
Printed in Germany

The use of general descriptive names, registered names, trademarks, etc. in this publication
does not imply, even in the absence of a specific statement, that such names are exempt
from the relevant protective laws and regulations and therefore free for general use.

Cover design: Erich Kirchner, Heidelberg

SPIN 10955093   42/3130 – 5 4 3 2 1 0 – Printed on acid-free paper

The authors would like to dedicate this book to the memory
of Rajapoopathy Anandarajan. Her Love has been a constant source
of Encouragement and inspiration.

Preface

Modern businesses generate huge volumes of data and information on a daily basis. The recent advancements in information technology have given organizations the ability to capture and store these data in an efficient and effective manner. However, there is a widening gap between this data storage and usage of the data.

Accounting is fundamental to the success of a company. In today's environment, accounting has been revolutionized. If the accounting function cannot provide speedy, real-time data to business managers, the success of organizations in an increasingly competitive environment will be threatened. In order to stay competitive and develop far-sighted strategies, the accounting function must use business intelligence techniques for obtaining and processing relevant financial information quickly and cost effectively. These techniques include; the activities of decision support systems, query and reporting, online analytical processing (OLAP), statistical analysis, text mining, data mining, and visualization.

Our goal was to assemble chapters that would explain the fundamental concepts of business intelligence in the accounting arena. We have been fortunate to call upon expert contributors; all of whom have extensive practical and academic expertise in the field. While these chapters stand of their own, taken together they provide a comprehensive overview of how to exploit data in the business environment. This book is not purely technical in nature but is written from an accounting perspective.

The fourteen chapters of this book address many of the above-mentioned areas. Chapter One provides a broad sweep of accounting history and the technologies used throughout history. The second chapter identifies and discusses the importance of using all types of organizational data for decision-making. The third chapter describes the process of extracting, loading and transforming disparate data into the data warehouse. Chapter four discusses the concept of the accounting data warehouse.

The next five chapters discuss various types of business intelligence tools. Chapter five discusses the concept of XBRL and how it can be used to extract, analyze, publish, and then exchange information for financial decision-making. In Chapter six, on line analytical processing (OLAP) techniques as tools for multidimensional analysis of accounting data are discussed. Chapters 7 and 8 discuss how artificial neural network techniques can be utilized to mine accounting data warehouses. This discussion is followed by chapter 9, which discusses utilizing information visualization technology to comprehend and analyze vast volumes of accounting data.

While obtaining and analyzing information is vital, a fundamental prerequisite is to design systems that are optimal to an organization's needs. In chapter 10, the concept of alignment between information systems and requirements is discussed. Chapters 11 and 12 examine methodologies for effectively developing and implementing business intelligence systems.

Once the system is set up, have we truly obtained the benefits that the system was designed to achieve? It is difficult to evaluate the benefits of a business intelligence (BI) system. Chapter 13 uses a balanced scorecard approach for evaluating the effectiveness of a BI system. The final chapter focuses on value creation through the design of BI systems.

We would like to extend our thanks to many people who helped with this book. First and foremost, we would like to thank the authors for sharing their expertise through their contribution to this book. We would also like to thank Dr. Werner A. Mueller, Publishing Director and Ms. Ruth Milewski, Economics Editorial at Springer-Verleg for their patience and invaluable guidance. Special thanks to Ms. Kate Wilson for her superb editorial work, Mr. Efosa Oyegun for recreating the figures, and Mr. Balakumar Arulgnanam for his invaluable help throughout the process.

Murugan Anandarajan, Ph.D
Asokan Anandarajan, Ph.D
C.A. Srinivasan, Ph.D

Table of Contents

1 Historical Overview of Accounting Information Systems

Asokan Anandarajan[1], C.A Srinivasan[2], Murugan Anandarajan[3]

[1]School of Management, New Jersey Institute of Technology, New Jersey

[2]Department of Accounting, Drexel University, Pennsylvania

[3]Department of Management, Drexel University, Pennsylvania

Abstract. In this chapter, we provide a broad overview of accounting history commencing from 8000 BC, when simple tokens recorded evidence on transactions, through the ancient civilizations, where clay and papyrus were used, to the invention of the first printing press in the fifteenth century to modern times. We focus on how accounting philosophy developed to take into account legal, competitive, and especially technological changes in the environment. From the development of the Abacus in around 3000 BC to present day sophisticated accounting software, we discuss how accounting has changed and adapted to environmental needs.

1.1 Introduction

Accounting can be defined as a discipline, which at a particular point in time, encompasses a body of ideas, a number of conventions, a set of available tools/techniques, and a variety of actual practices (Boyns and Edwards, 1997). Since it communicates financial information, accounting is often called the *language of business*. Accounting has been in recorded existence since at least 2000 BC when the ancient Roman, Greek, Indian, and Egyptian civilizations began trading. In these highly sophisticated ancient civilizations, both traders and the ruling dynasties governing the country engaged in commercial transactions. John Alexander in *History of Accounting* noted that an accounting of the transaction was needed to protect all parties involved in the transaction. The earliest "intelligence techniques" in accounting were characterized by recorded transactions in clay and papyrus and systems of checks and balances to ensure that the records were accurate and could be verified. Early records indicate that the ancient Romans also developed their own elaborate system of checks and balances to account for receipt and payment of money.

In discussing the emergence of accounting, we characterize the different eras into ancient times, pre-renaissance, renaissance, industrial age, and information age. We discuss the environment in each of these eras, the technology prevalent in those times, and how a combination of environmental and technological changes impacted the development of accounting to adequately meet the information needs of both outsiders (investors, creditors, and suppliers) and insiders within the company (managers or owner managers).

1.2 A Brief Historical Overview of Accounting

1.2.1 Ancient Era (Commencing 8000 BC)

Accounting may have been in existence since the very birth of civilization. If we trace our roots back into the mists of history, ancient Jericho founded around 8000 BC could be considered to be the first "city." The first accounting records can be traced back to this time. Trading in the form of barter took place in this Dead sea site. The first records amounted to simple tokens (see Fig. 1.1).

Fig. 1.1. Clayball and its content of tokens representing 7 units of oil, from Uruk, present day Iraq, ca. 3300 B.C. (Source: Schmandt-Besserat, 2002)

These included clayballs of various shapes (oval, circular, etc) that represented specific goods, such as cattle and other livestock and agricultural items, such as wheat. This system was the first recording and representation of inventory and the beginning of the concept of numbers. Giroux (2001) notes that over the next 5,000 years, accounting records subsequently advanced from simple to complex tokens, to clay tablets, and then to the development of abstract symbols. The development of accounting occurred in conjunction with advances in agriculture, pottery, textiles, buildings, war and nation states. While simple tokens were sufficient initially, with the formation of the nation states, a more advanced form of recording was necessary resulting in the cuneiform writing in Sumeria around 3200 BC. However, calculations still remained in the form of making and counting tokens to represent transactions. The first real technological innovation that influenced accounting occurred around 3000 BC. At this time, bronze was "discovered" and used to make tools in the Middle East. This era officially became the start of the Bronze age. During this time, the abacus was first invented in China and later made its way to the western civilizations where it became an invaluable tool for accounting calculations. At this time, a parallel invention occurred in Egypt that also revolutionized recording of accounting transactions. This invention was the development of the papyrus scroll.

Fig. 1.2. Clay tablets dating back to about ca. 2900 BC   **Fig. 1.3.** Papyrus writing medium most common to the ancient Egyptians

It is interesting to note that, while Egyptians used papyrus scrolls, similar transactions were being recorded in Mesopotamia on clay tablets. The Mesopotamian equivalent of today's accountant was the scribe. In addition to writing up transactions, the scribe ensured that the agreements complied with the detailed code requirements for commercial transactions. Hence, the work of the scribe could be considered to be far more extensive than that of the modern day accountant. Apparently, the temples, palaces, and private firms employed hundreds of scribes. This profession was held in high esteem since it required knowledge of both writing and the law.

While the scribe was the "accountant" in Mesopotamia, the storehouse bookkeepers were the early "accountants" in ancient Egypt. The storehouse bookkeepers in Ancient Egypt had a much easier task recording transactions since they used papyrus scrolls that could hold more records. These bookkeepers had meticulous records backed by elaborate internal verification systems. The Royal houses also had auditors to check the work of the bookkeepers; if irregularities were discovered, it was punishable by fine, body mutilation, or death depending on the seriousness of irregularity. However, accounting in the ancient world, be it Mesopotamia or Egypt, never went beyond meticulous "list making." Further, accounts were not recorded in terms of money; gold and silver were not considered currency but items of exchange. However, this consideration changed around 2200 BC. The Code of Hammurabi, one of the earliest law codes, enforced standardized weights. Commercial transactions were now recorded in these standardized measures. The code, in fact, required commercial transactions to be recorded using these weights and measures and imposed penalties for violators. Payments were now based on fixed amounts of silver and grain. If we trace our way through the meandering paths of history, accounting records have also been discovered dating to the Chao dynasty (1122 to 256 BC). This form, though single entry was said to be the most advanced form of accounting till the emergence of the double entry system in the thirteenth century.

Fig. 1.4. Code of Hammurabi consisted of a collection of the laws and edicts of the Babylonian King Hammurabi, and the earliest legal code known in its entirety. ca. 1792 BC

Another major technological innovation that impacted accounting was the invention of coins in Lydia around 700 BC. It started with crude slugs of a gold and silver alloy of a standard weight. Later coins were stamped, first with simple lines and then with more complicated designs showing the Gods and Emperors of these ancient times. The most important contribution to accounting at this juncture is attributed to the Greeks. They introduced banking and started to mint money around 575 BC. This contribution was a major development since accounting transactions now started to be recorded in ancient money rather than standardized weights and measures. Bankers in ancient Greece are said to have kept record books, changed and loaned money, and even arranged for money transfers (just as Western Union today) for citizens with affiliate banks in distant cities. The ancient single entry bookkeeping records were not merely lists of items bought, kept and exchanged, or sold; they were also denominated in money, which was a fundamental difference to prior ancient systems.

We cannot continue the discussion of the history of accounting without discussing Ancient Rome. Rome was a nation state that successfully conquered its neighbors and many of the countries around the Mediterranean and large parts of Europe. Rome's contribution to the development of accounting was the convergence of the adoption of the coinage concept from Lydia, the abacus concept from China, the alphabet from the Greeks, the use of papyrus from the Egyptians, and the concept of banks and credit again from the Greeks. Rome's original contribution was the development of numbers (Roman numerals) and the establishment of the "corporation" concept by setting up entities that could own property, make contracts, and engage in many activities. In ancient Rome, accounting evolved from records kept by heads of families. The daily house receipts and expenses were kept in daybooks (the early precursor to modern day ledgers). Another contribution of ancient Rome was the development of the primitive income statement (profit and loss statement) and balance sheet. The authorities required to see not only excess money from business but also the first balance sheet in the form of assets and liabilities of the households. These, in turn, were used to determine taxes payable. This system also extended to governmental receipts and payments for those who maintained the treasury. Yet another contribution of Rome to accounting was the annual budget. Treasurers determined amounts that could be spent and investigated variances from budget at the end of the year. They also incorporated responsibility accounting since these variances were reported to the emperor (Julius Caesar personally supervised the treasury) who decided what actions to take against person or persons over budget.

1.2.2 Medieval Age (1000 – 1200 AD)

While the medieval times were generally considered to be a sterile period in the development of accounting, historian Michael Chatfield observed that medieval accounting "laid the foundations for the doctrines of stewardship and conservatism; and the medieval era created the conditions for the rapid advance in accounting technology that occurred during the renaissance." The major development occurred after the Battle of Hastings in 1066 when William of Normandy conquered England. From the accounting view point, the significant event was the writing of the Domesday Book in 1086 that surveyed the wealth of the kingdom to determine taxes and England's fiscal system. England's legal system and government and the basic methods of accounting (albeit single entry at this time) developed as a result of the need to record transactions and property ownership meticulously for the purpose of determining taxes. Another significant consequence to accounting as a result of the Norman invasion was the development of tally sticks. This measurement equates to the modern day "transactions of account" and displaying accounts receivable (debtors) and accounts payable (creditors) in modern financial statements. Tally sticks were primitive instruments of credit. They were wooden sticks that were notched to represent specific sums of money. The sticks would be split into two to serve as a receipt.

Another momentous event that impacted accounting was the Crusades that began in 1095. The objective of Western armies at this period was to conquer the Holy Land. Vast sums of money were needed to finance the armies. This necessity stimulated banking in Europe, and Italian city states began to prosper. As they prospered and engaged in more commercial activities, the need for better accounting systems became apparent. The next stage in the history of accounting moves to Italy. From the year 1000 AD, Italian merchants extended their trading initially to England then eventually to the Far East while improving single entry bookkeeping.

1.2.3 Pre-renaissance Age (Approximately 1200 to 1400 AD)

The Piscan document, an early document found by archaeologists, showed systematic (but primitive) bookkeeping by Italian merchants around the year 1100 AD. A century later, modern accounting, in the form of double entry book keeping, emerged, simultaneously and apparently independently, in several Italian cities at the high point of what Bryer (1993) refers to as the "commercial revolution" between 1250 to 1350. Initial double entry, he suggests, was initially formulated here and hence he refers to this as the "Italian method." In fact, accounting records of a company called Giovanni and Farolfi and Co documented a complete double entry bookkeeping in the year 1300.

The key feature of the commercial revolution in Italy was the rise of merchant capitalism, generating a new system of social relations. This evolution started in the large cities in northern Italy. As businesses grew and expanded, the owners needed more investors whom they brought in as partners. Thus, they gradually lost their power and individual decision-making became decision making by consensus among the partners.

Initially, these partnerships were small; and the partners divided profits in accordance with customary formulas. At this juncture, the role of accounting was merely the computation of profit at the end of a business period. Today's concern with "net worth" of a business and computation of return on investment as a performance measure was irrelevant and was not a tool of accountants during this period. However, as the commercial revolution continued, these partnerships became involved in large scale trading. Eventually, these partnerships transformed themselves into what is now referred to as joint stock companies. At this juncture in the pre-Renaissance period, the focus of accounting became not only the computation of profit but also computing partners' equity and change in equity. The rate of return on capital (still used in our modern age) became the cornerstone of accounting at this juncture since it became the basis of profit distribution. Bryer, in his paper, provides us with insight by discussing the earliest known business records dating back to a business that existed between two partners in Genoa, Italy. The partnership spanned the period 1156 to 1164 and the records comprise three sheets of figures discussing the business and computing profits based on capital contribution at the termination of the partnership. This example summarizes the role of accounting in the pre-Renaissance period, namely, that of recorder of business transactions for the purpose of profit distribution. The technology of this time only comprised copious notes in books referred to as ledgers.

Another important change occurred in the pre-Renaissance era. For the first time in history, capital was pooled for investment in commerce. Earlier investors traded with their own capital. But, as firms expanded and more merchants joined, individuals could no longer trace their capital as it became pooled with the capital of many others. Thus they, as individuals lost their identity in the large corporate enterprise. Further, many families provided capital but chose not to engage in the actual business itself. They hired people to manage their money in the firm. These people came to be referred to as managers, and owners who participated actively in the business became known as owner managers.

Karl Marx attempted to explain the emergence of double entry bookkeeping at this time by stating that capital became "socialized" mainly due to demand from investors for the frequent calculation of the rate of return on capital as the basis for sharing profits. Since this era produced the most "intelligent" business tool known to man, namely, the rise of the double entry form of bookkeeping, we need to spend time discussing its emergence and role and how the environment influenced its development. Littleton, one of the most famous accounting historians, stated that double entry bookkeeping arose to help management in decision-making. In

Littleton's view, the purpose of double entry bookkeeping was to aid the owner or owner manager not merely to measure and record transactions but also to explain the results to others so they, as a group, could make appropriate decisions for the benefit of the enterprise. Double entry bookkeeping was basically an intelligence tool of the times. The owners, if they did not participate in the business, wanted to be able to quantify transactions and to ensure a system of checks and balances. Chatfield, another prominent writer of this time, states that to divide profits fairly they needed an accounting system in which all transactions were recorded. The double entry system met this need.

Fig. 1.5. Painting of Fra Luca Pacioli and pupil, by Jacopo de Barbari (1440/50–1516), perhaps the most famous Renaissance painting with a geometric theme

The origins of modern day accounting are to a large extent uncertain. Even though we know it existed, the person to whom it is now attributed is an Italian mathematician by the name of Luca Pacioli. Pacioli was born in 1445 in Tuscany, Italy. He was a "Renaissance" man in that he had knowledge of diverse subjects including medicine, art, music, and mathematics. Pacioli, though accredited as being the father of modern day accounting, never claimed to have invented double entry bookkeeping. Thirty-six years before his treatise, Benedetto Cotrugli published a book titled 'Of Trading and the Perfect Trader', which included many of the features of modern day double entry accounting. Pacioli claimed familiarity with the manuscript and credited Cotrugli with originating the double entry method. Pacioli, though largely unknown and uncelebrated outside the field of accounting even today, had the distinct honor of mentoring Leonardo da Vinci. He was also a contemporary of the famous explorer, Christopher Columbus. In 1494, he wrote his famous treatise, *Summa de Arithmetica, Geometrica, Proportione et Priportinalite* (Arithmetica, Geometria, Proportioni et Proportionalita). Written as a guide to mathematical knowledge of the times, bookkeeping was one of five topics covered. The Summa's 36 short chapters on bookkeeping, entitled *De Computis et Scripturis* (Of Reckonings and Writings), were added he said so that the subjects of the Duke of Urbino could have complete instructions in the conduct of business. In this treatise, Pacioli devised and elaborated on a system designed to ensure that financial information was recorded both efficiently and accurately. The major technological innovation that truly contributed to the rapid spread of the accounting concepts was the invention of the printing press by Gutenberg in the year 1440. Printing presses spread through Europe in the coming decades, and the works of Cotrugli and Pacioli were read throughout Europe.

1.2.4 Renaissance Age (Late 1400s to 1700s)

The system set up by Pacioli gradually spread from Italy through the rest of Europe during the renaissance age in the fifteen and sixteenth centuries. Technology, at this time, was marked by what can be referred to as "successful voyages," namely, the ability of ships to circumnavigate the globe. In 1490, the first cargoes of pepper and spices reached Lisbon directly from India. The western route to the "Indies" was discovered in 1492. In 1493, an executive order from the Pope gave exclusive rights to Spain and Portugal to keep the "spoils" of their discoveries from foreign lands. This edict encouraged greater ventures. In England, merchants with the backing of their sovereign began to search for a northeast or northwest passage to China (Cathay as it was known then) to avoid conflict and find a shorter route (Bryer, 2000). For Spain, Portugal, and England, the costs of these voyages were now exorbitant and could not be funded by a single merchant. Long ocean voyages demanded expensive fleets of large, heavily armed vessels, and there were long delays and great risks. These costs resulted in the formation of joint stock companies comprising capital from a multitude of investors. In London in 1551, London merchants promoted a company to finance the Chancellor-Willoughby expedition that also sought a northeast passage free from Portuguese interference. This venture was the first of the "great English joint-stock companies" for foreign trade with an initial membership of over 200. However, the predominant English joint stock company was the East India Company founded in 1600. The company had monopoly trading rights for much of Asia with Thomas Stevens being appointed as the first "modern day" accountant.

The formation of a joint stock company had many advantages. Financially, it enabled the investor to distribute, and so minimize, the risk of hazardous enterprise. Scott (1951) explains this concept succinctly. "Suppose for instance, a capitalist was prepared to venture, he may be only fit out a small ship. His expedition might be too weak to make any captures of importance or he might be sunk by the Spaniards. If, on the other hand, he participated in a large joint stock company that had several expeditions, even if one were a total failure, he had every prospect of obtaining profits from his shares in the others." This context assists in understanding the history of accounting during this Renaissance period.

Karl Marx points out that these merchants, the owners of the joint stock companies, were "feudal" in their mentality. This terminology means they were only interested in the bottom line profit popularly referred to as consumer surplus. Bryer notes that few used any from of double entry bookkeeping. Accounting merely comprised computing the value of the merchandise brought back less the costs that financed it.[1]

During the late sixteenth century, however, there came into being a number of joint stock companies in which the assets of several individuals were placed either under the control and management of one body of administrators or under one partner or manager. These organizations needed a system of accounting that could provide relevant, organized, and impartial information in situations where ownership and management were separated. The attraction of the Pacioli double entry bookkeeping now was its supposedly greater comprehensiveness and its automatic check on accuracy. It also made possible the development of summary statements of profit and loss and of proprietary interest and assets should any one of the owners requested it.

However, it was during the *industrial age* that the system devised by Pacioli gained rapid importance on a global scale. The industrial age could be attributed to Abraham Darby. In 1709, he set up his own iron works engaging in the smelting of iron at the Ironbridge site in England. In 1733, John Kay invented a "flying shuttle" that basically replaced hand made textiles with the factory system. Their respective successes attracted many businesses, and the industrial age began in earnest.

---

[1] In Drake's strategic voyage to raid the West Indies in 1585 for example, Queen Elizabeth supplied two ships and 10,000 pounds, giving her a total investment of 20,000 pounds. At the end of the voyage, the joint stock was sold; the Lord Admiral claiming a tenth, the Queen 5 percent; the remainder, one-third to the owners, one third to the crew, and one third to the victuallers who gave the provisions for the voyage. As can be seen, there was no need for double entry to record each and every transaction since the "transaction" comprised, in many cases, raiding of the natives and other ships.

1.2.5 Industrial Age (1700s to early 1900s)

During this era, significant changes occurred in financial accounting; and a new field of accounting, management accounting, was born. The developments in these two fields will be considered separately.

1.2.5.1 Financial Accounting

During the industrial age, and subsequently the advent of large corporations, the concept of *economic entity* or separation of owners from the managers of business took place. As Weygandt, Kieso and Kimmel (2000) noted, the need to report the financial status of the enterprise became more important especially to ensure that managers acted in accordance with owners' wishes. Until the mid-to late nineteenth century, many companies were tightly managed by their owners who were, in effect, managers of their respective businesses. Since the owners acted as their own managers, disclosure of records showing profits was not seen as important. This perception was because the owners were intimately involved and knew the financial status of their businesses. Further, the financial capital input into the business was by the owners themselves. After the industrial revolution, businesses began to seek outside capital. They obtained money from investors and creditors. The investors, though considered to be part owners, were not responsible for running the business. Further, owners now delegated the running of their businesses to managers. Hence, they became interested in business profits to satisfy themselves that the business was run properly. Similarly, creditors too were interested in business profits to satisfy themselves that their loans would be repaid with interest. Thus, disclosure of financial information by managers of companies became more important and was considered to be an integral part of conducting business. This need resulted in most corporations adopting the rules set down by Pacioli. The accounting system developed by Pacioli was refined and modified. During that era, it became not only the language of business but also the language of *global* business since all countries have identical rules with respect to the use of accounting entries.

1.2.5.2 Management Accounting

Cooper and Taylor (2000) note that, while bookkeeping increased in importance during this period, another field of accounting was born due to different needs that arose because of the technological innovations which took place in this era. Josiah Wedgwood is credited as becoming the first cost accountant. The famous potter set up his plant in 1754. To avoid bankruptcy during a recession, Wedgwood examined the firm's manufacturing cost structure, overhead, and market structure. He thus became an accounting pioneer.

Why did cost accounting achieve pride of place as a special branch of accounting? Braverman (1974) noted that the battle to realize values and to turn them into cash, called for a special accounting of its own. Stacey (1954) links the development of management accounting (also called cost accounting) directly with the rising costs of production caused by the introduction of the Factory Act of 1862, which limited the exploitation of children and adults. He notes that the costs of production grew because children could not be exploited. While the profits could absorb the additional expenses incurred by the increased wages, entrepreneurs had to exercise stricter control over these additional costs to affect all possible savings in the processes of manufacturing. These efficiencies could not be put into practice without some rudimentary information culled from the accounts. The larger the undertaking, the greater were the opportunities for saving and the importance of keeping better records focusing on different types of costs grew.

Another important technological innovation that changed the environment of the mid-nineteenth century and impacted fundamentally on the new concept of management accounting was the emergence of the railroads and more effective forms of transport. In 1769, the first steam engine became operational due to the pioneering work of James Watt. Steam engines were used by textile factories, iron and steel manufacturers, and other businesses.

Boyns and Edwards (1997) and Chandler (1977 and 1990) point out that business activity in America in the early nineteenth century required little in the way of accounting information for decision-making. Chandler noted that the key to subsequent developments is to be found in changes introduced by the railroads where, during the 1850s and 1860s, nearly all the basic techniques of modern management accounting were invented. It was another 30 or 40 years before similar developments occurred in United States manufacturing and marketing businesses, due to their different requirements as compared with the railroads.

The developments, which began to occur after the middle of the nineteenth century, are seen by Chandler as part of a growing concern in the U.S. with changes in organizational structure as a means of achieving increased profitability; whereas previously attention had been focused upon technological developments. Certain U.S textile concerns, most notably Lyman Mills, began to pay more attention to costing matters in the depression of the 1850s; and steel manufacturers, such as Carnegie, began to carry out cost accounting and control practices after 1870. Boyns and Edwards (1997) observe that by the 1880s the Carnegie Steel Works' cost sheets (which they used as their example) were sophisticated and used to evaluate overall performance and performance of their departmental managers and foremen. The cost sheets were also used to check quality and mix of raw materials, to evaluate improvements in processes and products, and for pricing non-standardized items.

Thereafter, developments in cost accounting were closely related to the development of scientific management. Management accounting at this time was predominantly concerned with trying to identify and understand costs for the purpose of control. In the early years of the twentieth century, many factories began to be organized along the lines set by Emerson, Taylor, and Towne, and other active members of the American Society of Mechanical Engineers with the results being that the contract system was eliminated; gain-sharing and incentive plans were adopted; cost accounting based on shop orders or a voucher system of account was introduced; time studies were carried out; route, time, cost and inspection clerks were employed; and the manager's staff was enlarged.

In the late 1880s of the industrial age, the office was virtually untouched by technology. Cooper and Taylor note that the expansion of organizations in the late nineteenth century made operating the business using people extremely costly and interest turned to the possibility of some sort of mechanical writing machine. Technology during this period comprised various forms of office mechanization (i.e., Remington's typewriters).

However, Cooper and Taylor (C and T) note that the new technology in the form of mechanization had both positive and negative effects. The positive effects were that typewriters and other machines speeded up work processes and reduced labor costs by allowing the more expensive male clerks to pursue the more analytical side of clerical work. The negative effect was what is referred to as the process of *deskilling* accounting labor. To illustrate in the mid-nineteenth century, the entire process cycle from obtaining orders to sending the final goods to the customer would be fulfilled by the accountant who was conversant with the steps in the whole cycle. This cycle included, but was not limited to, recording the customer's order, checking the customer's credit status based on prior transactions with the business, sending documents to the delivery department to ensure goods were delivered, and checking if the customer was entitled to discounts. However, after the mechanization that characterized this era, the work processes of most organizations resulted in what C and T described as a *continuous flow process*. The work process was subdivided into minute operations each becoming the task of a worker or group of workers. One necessary division was the introduction of various ledgers (sales, purchases, nominal). The essential feature of this "parcelling" of individual processes was that the workers involved lost comprehension of the process as a whole and the policies which underlie it. With sufficient customers, one worker (or group of workers) would be left to post, for example, customer orders. This worker might see nothing of the credit worthiness of a customer or their sales history and, therefore, would be unable to assess whether there was anything unusual about a particular order.

C and T's conclusions are that the indefinable element of judgment and intuition based upon skill, experience, and a comprehension of several stages in the process had been removed. Moreover, clerical processes could now be controlled at various points by mathematical checks with, for example, the measurement of the number of invoices posted per day per worker or the quantification of mistakes made by an individual clerical worker. The net result was that cost accounting, though important, started off as a mundane field. Further, unlike in the pre-industrial age, clerical staff was not in a position to understand the whole cycle, thus reducing the value of the individuals in the accounting function.

While it is acknowledged that cost accounting initially developed as a mundane field, the tenets underlying modern cost accounting can be traced to 1923. Under controller Donaldson Brown and Chairman Alfred Sloan, General Motors developed the major cost accounting techniques that are now used by big businesses. These techniques involve the concepts of return on investment, return on equity, and the use of flexible budgeting.

1.2.6 Information Age

1.2.6.1 The Early 1950s to the Late 1960s

The information age can be traced to the development of the computer. In 1943, the first computer with electronic circuits was developed by Eckert and Mauchly at the University of Pennsylvania. In 1950, IBM began to develop electronic computers to add to their line of business equipment. From the accounting view point, the IBM 702 became available for accounting use in 1953. This year could be considered the beginning of the accounting computer age. When Arthur Andersen computerized the payroll of a General Electric plant using a UNIVAC I, it began the information age for business.

The invention of the computer revolutionized the accounting function because organizations could now record their business activity in an electronic format. Computers had the distinct advantage of being able to process large amounts of data without the tendency of being prone to error as human beings are wont to do. Computers also enabled the presentation of information at a level of detail previously unknown to the manual generation.

Fig. 1.6. The first UNIVAC computer

The environment of the 1960s was conducive to rapid technological change. Initially, computers were used for routine tasks that were mainly voluminous and repetitive. Examples of these tasks were payroll processing, processing of debtors (accounts receivable) transactions and balances and subsequent billing, keeping track of creditors (accounts payable) and inventory tracking and control, among others. Information systems, which carried such routine activities, came to be known as transaction processing systems. These systems were mainly for the management accounting function and included tasks such as recording and keeping track of sales for the purpose of analyzing sales reports and trends in revenues.

The fundamental change in information processing was that, once computerization had been achieved around the late sixties to the mid seventies, office information was reduced to "pieces" of data, and most work was automated. The advantage was that computerized information could be used to enhance control. The computer could, for example, help in identifying waste and areas where costs could be considered excessive. To illustrate, budgeted cost information could be fed into a computer that could compute actual costs, figure out variances, identify the significant variances, and report to management. Another feature was that, even if the variance was not significant, the computer could identify trends and report variances where the trend was not normal indicating a possibility of fraud. This improvement resulted in what accounting popularly refers to as "management by exception." Managers need not waste time on routine investigation but only those variances reported by the computerized system. Thus, this new technology accentuated the role of accounting to not merely reporting financial numbers but also as a tool for performance evaluation and efficient management.

The most important aspect for accounting was that computers greatly enhanced the ability of accountants to process data at rapid speed efficiently and effectively. This increased output due to computerization had two implications for management. They would be able to get by with less labor. The development of the first personal computer in 1976 by Steve Wozniak and Steve Jobs, who built the first Apple computer, also increased productivity of accountants but at a cost to labor. The labor that they needed could be less skilled and therefore cheaper. Cooper and Taylor cite an article where they noted that with each reduction in work force, the remaining workers were told to increase their output. Automation had reduced the staff in that office by more than one-third, and more mechanization was in prospect. The union spokesman in their respective case study said that the categories of jobs that had disappeared were those which required skill and judgment. Those remaining were the tabulating and key punching operations, which became even simpler, less varied, and more routine as work was geared to the computer.

What was the impact of the introduction of information technology in the form of computerized accounting to the work place? There was an increase in speed and volume; the tasks became subdivided and managers were able to adopt sophisticated methods for monitoring performance and setting targets for their workers. However, during the transition period from manual or machine-based accounting to computerized accounting, a degree of "skill enhancement" did occur. Accountants now needed knowledge of both computerized systems and manual systems; the environment was such that accountants with knowledge of both forms of systems could demand higher salaries. However, once the new computerized systems passed through what Cooper and Taylor refer to as the trial period, the necessity for highly skilled accountants and bookkeepers diminished. Accounting was most severely affected at the junior level. These junior staff now found their jobs degraded and transformed into data processing jobs with no prospects. Sadly, as Cooper and Taylor note, the position of more skilled bookkeepers and accountants was also weakened by the advent of computerization. Braverman (1974) cites the example of an U.S. multi-branch bank that reported that within 18 months of installing electronic bookkeeping machines, the bookkeeping staff of 600 had been reduced to 150, and the data processing staff had grown to 122. This change was in line with the experience of most banks with labor reductions of between 40 and 50 percent. Many bookkeeping staff was replaced by machine operators, punch card operators, and similar grades of workers.

One important result of the implementation of technology in the form of computers was the adoption of the behavioral concept of what is popularly referred to as "Taylorism." Taylor had espoused ways to increase efficiency in the work place. The introduction of computers enabled the concepts of Taylor to be applied to the accounting function. Braverman and Cooper and Taylor note that the removal of the "conception" part of the clerk's work is one of the key elements of Taylorism in an office. Taylorism basically believed in division of labor in the work place and every person being conversant or specializing in one task. Braverman noted that after computerization, the ability of the office worker to cope with deviations from the routine, errors, special cases, etc., all of which require information and training, virtually disappeared. He concludes that the number of people who can operate the system, instead of being operated by it, has declined significantly. These words though stated three decades ago hold true today.

It has been noted that, despite the rhetoric by politicians of all persuasions surrounding the need for a "skilled work force," the dehumanizing long run impact of Tayloristic "deskilling" is impacting the majority of the clerical staff involved in basic accounting work. It may in the near future begin impacting professional accountants. For the individual bookkeeper, the future is grim. The next stage in computer technology is likely to be cheap voice data entry systems. This has been described succinctly. The progressive elimination of thought from the work of the office worker takes the form, at first, of reducing mental labor to a repetitive performance of the same small set of functions. The work is still performed in the brain, but the brain is used as the equivalent of the hand of the detail worker in production, grasping and releasing a single piece of data over and over again. The next step is the elimination of the thought process completely.

1.2.6.2 1980s to the Present

In this period, most changes in the environment affected management rather than financial accounting. Initially, management accounting systems were designed and operated to provide information useful for cost identification and control by managers. In the 1980s and 1990s, the decision-making environment changed considerably. This change arose due to increased challenges from overseas' competitors, especially Japan, Taiwan, and South Korea and rapid advances in technological development.

The realization that foreign competitors were gaining a significant foothold led many innovative firms to adopt new techniques to improve productivity and competitive strength. These improvements included, but are not limited to, new technological innovations such as Just in time manufacturing, Total quality control management (TQM), and flexible manufacturing systems. These technological changes fundamentally changed the demands made on accountants and the type of information that the accounting function had to provide. Previously, information could be provided on a weekly or quarterly basis. However, information relating to inventory levels, production forecasts, and changes in sales forecasts due to unexpected changes in the environments had to be made on a real time basis. Even information on a daily basis was not considered sufficient in this new environment.

As the business environment grew in complexity in the late 1960s and 70s, accounting managers began to realize that summarized transaction data had a huge potential decision-making value. By the early 1970s, systems called Decision Support systems (DSS) began to come to force.

A DSS is defined as *'a system that can assist or replace the decision maker by combining current and historical facts, numerical data, and statistics from both inside and outside the organization and by converting these data into information useful in decision-making'*. While TPS typically improved the efficiency of existing processes, DSS made organizations more effective and gave them a competitive advantage. DSS have the capacity to perform "what if" analyses using data that it models and simulates. This simulation is done through the use of spreadsheets and statistical analysis. A DSS, in addition to having interactive capabilities, has the capacity to work on "loosely defined" tasks involving high degrees of uncertainty. From an accounting perspective, the DSS can aid in preparing variances and comparing those to variances in a prior period. The information might help the manager to determine if the budget has been attained for this period and to investigate reasons for adverse performance. These systems empowered managers to make decisions on their own. The early tool used to represent balance sheets and income statements was spreadsheets.

In the 1990s, as data capture technology improved and the amount of data stored grew, the need to prepare, organize, and present data to managers became essential. This requirement saw emergence of the Data warehouse. Inmon, who pioneered the concept and popularized the definition, defines a data warehouse as basically a "warehouse" containing detailed financial information relevant to a company. From an accounting viewpoint, data warehouses are helpful because financial information is obtained from sources both internal and external to the firm. The financial information is equivalent to an "on-line" general ledger system that contains detailed data for both current and past years. The data can relate to the company and financial information about its suppliers and competitors.

While the data warehouse provides the organization with memory, it is vital that managers utilize this data to make better business decisions. In 1996 the Gartner Group reported that:

By 2000, Information Democracy will emerge in forward-thinking enterprises, with Business Intelligence information and applications available broadly to employees, consultants, customers, suppliers, and the pub-

lic. The key to thriving in a competitive marketplace is staying ahead of the competition. Making sound business decisions based on accurate and current information takes more than intuition. Data analysis, reporting, and query tools can help business users wade through a sea of data to synthesize valuable information from it - today these tools collectively fall into a category called "Business Intelligence."

1.3 What is the Impact of Information Technology on Accounting?

Business intelligence (BI) constitutes is a broad category of applications and technologies for gathering, storing, analyzing, and providing access to data to help managers make better business decisions. BI applications include the activities of decision support systems, query and reporting, online analytical processing (OLAP), statistical analysis, text mining, data mining and visualization.

As O'Donnell and David (2000) note that while such information technologies have availed many new information alternatives, i.e., presentation lectures that could change the way decisions are made. Access to a database of basic transaction information makes it possible to acquire detailed accounting data and analyze it differently for each decision situation. Real time financial reporting could provide up-to-the-minute rather than weekly information for decision making. Systems can now provide flexible, interactive user interfaces that immediately respond to a myriad of information.

We cannot conclude this chapter without mentioning the turmoil that the accounting profession is faced with at the present. The Sarbenes-Oxley act has had a major impact on financial accounting. It seeks to increase the quality of financial reporting and also provides more stringent requirements on auditors who check financial statements. Accountants may be required to use the BI techniques to enhance the quality of the information they provide. These techniques are discussed at greater detail in the following chapters.

2 Importance of Data in Decision-Making

Patrick W. Devine[1], C.A. Srinivasan[2], Maliha S. Zaman[1]

[1]Department of Management, Drexel University, Pennsylvania

[2]Department of Accounting, Drexel University, Pennsylvania

Abstract. The ability to make effective decisions is crucial to an organization's survival in today's tumultuous business environment. In order for firms to evaluate alternatives and make informed choices they must have reliable and timely data upon which to make their decisions. Consequently, the development of effective data management techniques is of central importance to an organization. Yet, many firms are learning that this is no easy task as they find themselves inundated with nearly overwhelming amounts of data. Assessing the specific data management issues firms face and the development of an effective methodology to address these issues is a central focus of this chapter. Specifically, this chapter explores data management from a cybernetic approach and focuses on methods of transforming various forms of structured and semi-structured data into structured, useful data that an organization can utilize to make effective, informed decisions.

2.1 Introduction

Organizations have faced a complex and tumultuous environment over the last decade. Consumer confidence has been significantly eroded as scions of industry have crumbled under the weight of unethical and often illegal business practices. The age of electronic commerce, ushered in by the advent of the World Wide Web, enjoyed a brief reign, which ended when stakeholders began to demand outdated "old economy" standards such as corporate profitability and returns on investments. The resulting volatility of the current landscape was reflected in the Dow Jones Industrial Average that hit heights above, 11,000 and reached lows below 8,000. The end of the 1990s witnessed billions spent to defend against the impending Y2K disaster, which left unresolved the issue of whether the catastrophe would have happened in the first place. The times saw government taking on big business in the form of a federal antitrust suit with neither side emerging as the clear winner. Many organizations intrinsically assumed to be going concerns are now struggling just to survive.

The accounting profession has not escaped being significantly affected by these turbulent times. Indeed, the destruction of Enron and implosion of Arthur Anderson are the largest, but by no means the only, contributors to the current chaotic marketplace. Global Crossing, WorldCom, and a host of other organizations stand accused of fraud, deception, and corporate mismanagement. WorldCom, accused of committing fraud totaling in the billions, has filed for bankruptcy and even changed its name in an effort to separate itself from its checkered past. There has been a public opinion backlash against business in general, and the accounting professions specifically, which has had and continues to have significant repercussions (Resnick, 2002). The Federal government has responded with investigations, official inquiries, and the formation of the *Sarbanes-Oxley Act of 2002*, which has been referred to as "the most significant legislation affecting the accounting profession since the Securities Act of 1933" (Latshaw, 2003). Many organizations are reemphasizing their dedication to ethical practices and attempting to assure the public that this dedication is embraced across the enterprise (Blank et al., 2003). There is an increased scrutiny by all interested stakeholders into the accounting and management practices of organizations (Blackhouse, 2002). More attention then ever before is being given to the decisions made by these organizations and the factors that led up to these decisions.

At the core of every business transaction, every contract negotiation, every exchange of goods or services, exist a myriad of decisions made to achieve that result. "Should we lower prices to stay competitive or raise them to increase profits? Should we continue to outsource or learn to develop in-house? LIFO, FIFO, or weighted average?" The engine of business runs on timely and effective decisions, yet the reality is that half the decisions organizations make fail (Nutt, 1999). Businesses may avoid making these poor choices and make better decisions through basing these decisions on the foundations of accurate, timely, and relevant information. Inaccurate information is an expense that few businesses can afford, since the "garbage in, garbage out" problem has costly ramifications (Dubois, 2002). More often than not, the accuracy of the information is largely dependent on the timeliness of the information. In an environment where it is crucial to maintain a competitive advantage, the speed at which information can be disseminated is often the difference between corporate success and financial ruin.

While timeliness and accuracy of information are indisputably important, perhaps the greatest challenge that many organizations face is to find the "relevant" information. Recent studies have indicated that we are well on our way to producing more information over the next few years than has been produced in all of recorded history (Roth et al., 2002). Information technology improvements, such as the availability of improved bandwidth and advancements made in storage capabilities, coupled with the declining cost of such technologies have given organizations the ability to capture incredible amounts of these data. Finding the data to acquire has also never been easier. The interactivity of the World Wide Web, the numerous implementations of point of sale machines and "smart" terminals, and the advancements made in ERP systems have all combined to give companies access to almost limitless founts of data (Davenport et al., 2001).

The challenge facing many organizations is to sift through this nearly overwhelming mountain of data and find what they need in a timely fashion. This challenge is exacerbated by the fact that only about 15 percent of these data are in a usable format (Blumberg and Atre, 2003). As advanced as technology has become, information technology still needs structured data such as a tabular format in spreadsheets or databases, to effectively process it. Yet roughly 85 percent of an organization's data do not exist in this format, rather the data are in the form of e-mails, PowerPoint presentations, voice mails, and even meetings and conversations. Most organizations are unable to use or often even locate these "unstructured" data, and thus the potential of an invaluable resource lays unrealized. One study estimates that excluding opportunity costs, the inability to find the right information at the right time costs an average organization with one thousand employees $6 million annually (Document Manager Magazine, 2003). In addition to the costs associated with not finding the correct data, the under-utilization of all the data captured by the organization is also a growing problem. A typical company harnesses only 2 to 4 percent of the data that reside in its systems, notes IBM Corp. The remainder sits in databases and is never touched. In the 1990s, companies sat on gold mines of data silos and distributed data marts filled with inaccessible information. (Fitzgerald, 2003).

Thus, fully managing all data resources has become critical to organizations' continued viability. This chapter highlights issues that must be taken into consideration if companies hope to achieve this challenging task. It will begin with a focus on gaining an understanding of the role of data within the organization and assess the applicability of taking a "cybernetic" approach to data management. Specific data classifications and the utility of such classifications will be discussed. The analysis will conclude with a proposed methodology for realizing the full potential of the organization's data.

2.2 The Role of Data in an Organization

The dynamics of today's turbulent marketplace make it imperative for organizations to utilize their data resources effectively. The business landscape is still in a significant state of flux. Ten to fifteen years ago organizations were concerned about the growth of their information systems, the development of their local area networks, and facilitating informational access within the organization. Five to seven years ago organizations were hurriedly defining and implementing their organization's "presence" on the World Wide Web. Within the last three years, companies have been attempting to recover from and manage their way through the tumultuous landscape of e-commerce. Though clichéd, it is no less true, the only constant is change. Organizations need to evaluate on a continuing basis their business models, assessing organizational structure, management processes, strategic planning and information systems. The organization must learn and adapt to the environmental changes. Data, information, and business intelligence are critical to this process. Information has become vital for the organization's continuity and growth. Where the data originate, how the data are collected and cleaned, how the data are transformed into information and then knowledge, and how business can effectively utilize all of these intangible resources are key questions that the organization must be able to answer.

In addition to focusing on the technological dimension of data management, which concentrates on managing "explicit" knowledge, broader aspects, such as the people dimension, the organizational dimension, the process dimension, and in some cases even the cultural dimension (for multinationals), must be considered. Many organizations are just starting to realize the importance of the people or "social" dimension of information. Recent developments in "social mapping" software illustrate this concern. Through analyzing an organization's electronic mail, the software focuses on how information flows in the organization (Johnson, 2003). The study found definitive information sharing patterns that often had no bearing on the formal "organizational hierarchy" upon which the company was officially segmented. Attempting to "know what they know" is difficult for organizations. Much of the internal data are "tacit," and therefore, the social, organizational, and procedural aspects are essential for success.

One approach, which may help in the data management process for all forms of data, is for organizations to view themselves "cybernetically."

Before defining the cybernetic approach, it may be useful to view a specific problem it hopes to resolve. One of the main issues surrounding many companies' use of information is that they utilize information in a linear fashion. Thus, data get summarized into information and, with the aid of business intelligence and knowledge management tools, get transformed into knowledge utilized to make decisions. The problem for many organizations is that they view these decisions as the end of the process. Cybernetics challenges organizations to move away from this erroneous perspective and view the entire input-process-out framework as a cycle rather than a line. The missing dimension that "closes the loop" on this line is feedback.

Cybernetics is an interdisciplinary theory of systems that is concerned with the type of system called *organisms*. However, the focus of the business world is on the type of system called *organizations*. Cybernetics posits that both types of systems have much in common, and thus the study of organism may provide useful information for the study of organizations. The relevance of using cybernetics to study business may be viewed from two aspects: (i) simple growth laws apply to organisms as well as social entities such as manufacturing companies, etc., and (ii) both display overall integrated purposeful behavior. Therefore, research in the area of goal-directed biological systems has provided meaningful insights to approaches to problems in organizational behavior.

Though many disciplines have absorbed cybernetic principles, the union of cybernetics and business seems especially useful as "cybernetics has focused more on how systems function, that is to say how they control their actions, how they communicate with other systems or with their own" (Heylighen et al., 1999). If we look at an organization from a cybernetic viewpoint, we see it as an organism that is initially in a state of equilibrium with its environment. When fluctuations occur within the environment, the equilibrium is disturbed and action must be taken. In order to survive, either the fluctuation must be minimized or the organism must adjust. In a business context, the first option is generally not a possibility for many organizations. Even if an organization attempts to change the business "environment" (i.e., minimize the fluctuation) through advertising, lobbying, endorsing specific politicians, etc., this change is often slow and success far from certain. Thus, the option that is left to most organizations is to adapt. A brief look at the Coca Cola company illustrates this point.

Combining the terminology of cybernetics with the data management process, Fig.2.1 illustrates the process that Coca Cola employed. Over a decade ago, in the height of the cola wars, Coca Cola collected significant data on people's cola preferences. They processed these results utilizing various data management systems, which indicated Pepsi was more favored and used this information as a basis to make the decision to change their formula. Yet, this move, listed as one of the "100 dumbest ideas of the century" (Time, 2000), proved disastrous; and the feedback Coca Cola received caused them to reevaluate their decision and change back to the old formula a mere 79 days later (Sellers, 1995).

In cybernetics, the feedback process begins when a sensing mechanism provides feedback to the "comparator." In this case, the Coca Cola "comparator" received thousands of irate phone calls and letters and extremely negative coverage in the media. The second step involves the comparator evaluating the feedback against some form of benchmark or established objective. Coca Cola's objective was to improve product sales, and the comparator (the organization in general) established that they were not meeting this objective. The last step is for the Activator to take any corrective measures necessary to meet the established objective. Coke realized they made a mistake and took the corrective action of changing back to the original formula. If Coca Cola had not been able to process this feedback in a timely fashion, it could have been even more disastrous. In the recent past, many e-commerce firms were based on business models, which turned out to be incorrect. When the environment changed and investors became concerned with profits, some organizations adapted; many more did not and now cease to exist.

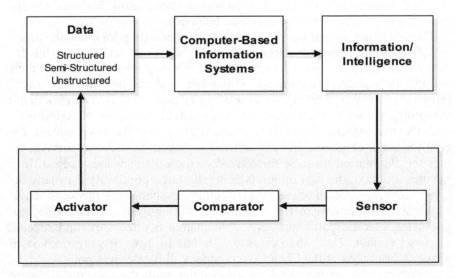

Fig. 2.1. Cybernetic Feedback Process

The cybernetic view of business hinges on one important notion – data. High quality data can result in quality information. The information must be accurate. One only has to look at Enron and Arthur Anderson to see the repercussions of when information fails to meet this criterion. Accurate information demands accurate data. Sources of data must be continually evaluated and tested for accuracy. Often times, this testing may involve a combination of both technical and manual evaluations; since "a sophisticated business intelligence system can tell in detail what data says, it cannot tell if data is lying" (Dubois, 2002). Companies must continually be on the lookout for new sources of data to supplement their traditional data sources. Just as the business environment is constantly changing, so too must information collection and processing be an ongoing, dynamic process that captures all forms of data.

What are data? In essence, data are facts. Items such as statistics, sports scores, and temperatures are all included under the umbrella of "data." From a business perspective, the initial thought may be text-based materials such as reports, spreadsheets, inventories, account payables, sales, etc. Until recently, this rumination would be an accurate perception; since traditionally, much business data came from point of sale machines such as cash registers, Enterprise Resource Planning systems, or other transaction processing systems. Most customer data were captured either through purchase transactions, forms such as registration and warranty cards that the customer filled out, or transcribed phone interaction between client and customer service representative. With the widespread acceptance and use of the Internet coupled with the evolution of technology, companies have started to expand their perception of what data sources are available. As noted earlier, new sources of data can be discovered in familiar venues such as emails, voicemail, websites, images, videos, PowerPoint presentations, etc. Electronic mail typifies one of these newly recognized data sources. An average person receives close to 3000Mb. of email a day. These electronic messages may contain contract data, customer interaction, and innovative ideas. Yet the majority of organizations fail to recognize this data source; and thus often times valuable data goes unnoticed, undocumented, and its existence is only known to the owner of the data. Such data are considered unstructured, making retrieval difficult. Companies are recognizing that these new sources of data are assets to their business and able to provide competitive edge if maintained and structured properly.

Regardless of source, data contain little value unless it undergoes processing. One thousand transactions recorded by a transaction processing system tell us little more than the fact that one thousand transactions have been recorded. Once data have been processed, summarized, or manipulated, the data now become information. As opposed to data, information allows the organization to gain an understanding its past and present business environment. The technology known as the data warehouse is key to this summarization process (Silverston and Graziano, 1998). Through a procedure of collection, cleaning, and processing, the data warehouse becomes a central repository for data and allows for summarization and querying (Williams and Sawyer, 2003). Now that those one thousand transactions have been processed, information such as purchasing trends, inventory levels, and revenue growth may be ascertained. As noted above, the right information can be critical to business success. Information can be the order from chaos. An accountant may look at the ledger of accounts receivable and see nothing but line after line of data. Yet when information such as an accounts receivable summary is presented, that same accountant can immediately learn what the financial outlook of the company is: what customers owe the most and for how long? which customers pay promptly and which are overdue?

While the importance of reliable information cannot be overstated, many organizations are learning that in today's competitive marketplace it is not enough. While the data warehouse is a necessary first step, companies can no longer be satisfied with the reliable summaries of past events and accurate synopses of their current financial situation which information provides. Organizations need to look forward, to anticipate future needs, requirements, surpluses and advantages, and plan effective strategies, which capitalize on this information. Companies need to rethink how they define "information" and acknowledge it as a corporate asset of equal if not more importance than "real assets" such as property, plant and equipment (Reick, 2001). Uncontrolled information generation is of no use to an organization (Raj, 1996). Rather, these corporate assets must be effectively focused, managed, and utilized to generate knowledge that will assist in the decision making process and help the organization adapt to the ever-changing marketplace. This information must assist the organization in evolving with, and responding to, the changes within its business environment. The technology that will facilitate this "cybernetic" process and assist in the development of competitive advantages is known as "business intelligence" (Cody et al., 2002).

Business Intelligence (BI) tools are now increasingly being leveraged by organizations to respond to their customers more effectively. In this context, business intelligence (BI) refers broadly to a set of software tools and applications that permit the organization to collect, organize, distribute, and act on critical business information. It encourages the use of its results as feedback that can improve the data collection process and help the organization better respond to changes in the environment. This technology will strengthen customer relationships by enhancing communication with customers and improving corporate customer intelligence. There is often confusion between the terms business intelligence systems and "knowledge management systems," or KMS. In many respects they are quite similar as knowledge management (KM) is the process of systematically and actively managing and leveraging an organization's store of knowledge and information. KMS and BI tools can both include technological aspects such as groupware, DSS, AI, virtual reality, genetic algorithms, etc. The value of BI may be viewed in a past-present-future context. Data are facts about past events. Summarized data, in the form of information, help tell a company about their past and somewhat indicates their present status. Business intelligence, or the knowledge generated from such systems, helps organizations make decisions for the future. It is of minor importance whether certain tools are labeled "business intelligence" and others are "knowledge management systems;" what is important is that information they provide and the knowledge that results from it is sound.

Table 2.1. Taxonomy of Data

Taxonomy	Classification	Examples
Environment	Internal	Accounts receivable, general ledger, payroll
	External	SEC rule, market news, interest rates
Format	Text	Memos, faxes, e-mail
	Image	Photographs, graphs, flowcharts
	Video	Depositions, video conferences, TV reports
	Audio	Voicemail, conversations, dictation
Structure	Structured	Spreadsheets, databases, web forms
	Semistructured	Web pictures, documented video, flowcharts
	Unstructured	E-mail, conversations, news reports

2.3 Taxonomy of Data

Before data can be transformed into meaningful information, it must first be collected and classified. These two steps are inexorably linked. Where the data come from plays a predominate role in determining the classification given to the data. For example, company generated data, such as a list of check disbursements, may be classified as internally produced, text based, structured data, while an analyst's advice to the CEO may be classified as externally produced, audio unstructured data. This classification process is the first step in assessing what procedures are needed to transform the data into one unified, coherent format in order to be effectively utilized by the data warehouse and business intelligence systems. Whether the data are produced internally or externally, are in the format of text, image, video or audio, and exist in a structured, semi-structured, or unstructured form must all be considered and will be discussed below.

2.3.1 External vs. Internal Data

Data may be classified as either internally generated or externally generated. Preference or utilization of one form of data over the other is largely dependent on the nature of the industry. Financial analysis services may rely heavily on externally generated data such as market indices and financial records of potential investments. Manufacturing firms tend toward generating internal data, such as inventory, work in progress, and project status reports. This tendency should not be considered an "either or" proposition, since the majority of businesses contain at least some internal and external data. Reliability of one form over the other also varies significantly and may be determined by subjective as well as objective standards. Many organizations feel more comfortable with internally generated data since they are the ones who created it; while others prefer externally generated data since the data may be perceived to be more objective then internally created data. Thus, while the board of directors may like the profitability estimates generated in the budget for next year, they would give more weight to independent analysts' financial forecasts. These forecasts, as well as market data, competitor developments, changes in tax laws, and SEC regulations are all examples of external data, which may impact an organization.

2.3.2 Data Format

The format the data exist in is also key to classifying it. Text has traditionally been the key focus of data management systems due to the processing limitations inherent in the systems. The advancements made in technology, coupled with the popularity of the World Wide Web, have brought a focus on non-text forms of data, such as images, video, and audio. Each of these formats brings their own intrinsic classification challenges, which today's data management systems must confront.

2.3.2.1 Text

Data in the form of text are generally the most common. Existing in a wide variety of forms, the clarity of textual data may vary depending on its specific format. Text in the form of financial data, such as dollar amounts or number of stocks sold, is very clear while text in narrative form requires a summation as well as interpretation of the relevant data. This summation, performed by human operators, may be biased by the subjectivity of the operator.

2.3.2.2 Images

Though less prevalent, data in the form of images are not uncommon. Images are usually created to support other forms of data and are rarely "stand alone" pieces of data. Examples may be pictures of employees, which accompany each employee record, or images of products, inventories, or assets, which the company wishes to include in its information systems. Images may also be non photographic in nature, such as graphs, charts, and flowcharts, and may be vital to business analysis. In addition to the common practice of supporting other data, images may also require additional data associated with them to help in the classification process (Martini, 1998), such as the image date, method of identification, photographer name for future reference. Additionally, the two dimensional nature of images (Zu, 2002) and image resolution must also be considered in the classification as well as storage process.

Video, becoming more common, shares many similar qualities with images and thus requires the same considerations. Additionally, since video is more storage intensive, decisions about how this form of data will be stored must be made. While many organizations will simply store the video "as is," the inherent limitations (i.e., the only way to extract information is to actually watch the video) have caused some organizations to take further action. Accompanying data in text form, utilizing metadata, or allowing frame-by-frame access are methods to gain access (Lienhart, 1996, 2002).

2.3.2.3 Audio

Data in the form audio employ differing classification techniques. Features inherent to audio such as silence ratio, spectral centroid, harmonicity and pitch (Lu, 1988) are all utilized to categorized audio data. The process of speech recognition has achieved limited success but is improving. Though not utilized frequently in data warehousing, speech recognition offers true potential for capturing audio data, such as voice mail and dictation, and storing it in more accessible formats. Manual transcription is also an option employed as a means of utilizing audio data. Accountants are faced with the challenge of gathering data in a world where business is becoming increasingly decentralized; and thus clients, other business units, and relevant data sources may be half a world away rather than just "right down the hall." As important data may increasingly come in the form of phone conversations and voice mail, it is incumbent that systems be developed which assist in the capture of these valuable data resources.

2.3.3 Data Structure

Just as data may exist in a number of different formats, it may also exist in differing levels of structure. Current information technology has become quite adept at dealing with data that conform to the technological limitations and guidelines proscribed by the system. This structured data has become a valuable asset upon which a growing number of organizational decisions are based. Yet, as noted earlier, a preponderance of the data that an organization collects does not conform to any set of proscribed system standards and thus is rarely used as an aid in decision making. Only by gaining an understanding of the structural differences in their data, may organizations arrive at solutions to take advantage of their data resources in all structures.

2.3.3.1 Structured Data

As name implies, structured data are data that have some form of inherent order or logical arrangement. Arguably, all data follow some framework and could be considered structured; (Hicks, et al., 2002) from a business perspective, structured data generally refers to tabular data found in relational databases having defined attributes for each entity (Miller et al., 1997). Structured data may also be data that are indexed or have been categorized in some way prior to collection. Currently, structured data are not restricted to any particular data format; but text is the most common due to its inherent order (alphabetical, numerical, etc.). The main benefit of structured data is the ease with which it may be processed. Already containing some prescribed set of standards, processing this form of data involves gaining an understanding of the specific ordering system employed or converting that ordering methodology to the set of standards used by the organization's data warehouse and business intelligence tools. This type of data is easily searched; and patterns and relationships, which may exist between the data, are easily identified. While the utility of structured data is by no means startling, what is surprising is that this form of data, as noted earlier, represents only an estimated fifteen percent of all data captured by an organization (Blumberg and Atre, 2003). The remaining 85 percent of the data an organization possesses is commonly referred to as *unstructured* data.

2.3.3.2 Unstructured Data

The polar opposite of structured data, unstructured data appear to lack any order or categorization. Specifically, unstructured data are any documents, files, images, reports, or forms that have no defined, standard structure to enable convenient storage in unit record or similar automated processing devices. Unstructured data cannot be defined in terms of rows and columns or records, and the data cannot be examined with standard unit record access.

Practically speaking, unstructured data may take the form of "internal" items such as interoffice memos, electronic mail, instant messages, phone conversations, voice mail, graphical files, or charts. Traditionally, this form of data has been distributed across a varied array of technologies, platforms, and formats and has only been utilized by small minority of individuals, (such as the recipients) within the organization (Cowen, 2002). Typical auditor-client e-mail correspondence may yield invaluable information about the audit engagement, yet there may be no procedures in place for these data to be disseminated to all who may benefit from it or recorded for future audits. Electronic mail is a great example of "data collection" technology evolving beyond an organization's ability to utilize it. This problem is endemic to the business world at large. There is no way to estimate the invaluable data in the roughly 31 billion e-mail messages estimated to be sent *per day* (IDC, 2003). Thus, organizations may be in possession of an incalculable wealth of data, yet they lack the means to access it, or more often than not, lack the perception to even be aware of it. This *information in jail* problem (Ramaprasad and Rai, 1996) is not just limited to internally created data, as large amounts of unstructured data are also generated externally and fed into organizations. Market data, governmental regulations, and legislative policy changes may all contain invaluable data for certain organizations. In a similar fashion, images, such as photographs, charts, and graphs, and audio data, such as voicemail and phone conversations, are rarely disseminated to any but a few individuals or business units; and thus the vast potential of this data is never realized.

2.3.3.3 Semi-Structured Data

Mid-way between structured and unstructured data is the category of semi-structured. This type of data, while possessing some standard attributes, does not conform to any rigid structure and thus is of varying utility to an organization. Semi-structured data may have some structure that can help identify it such as Author name or time of creation. Many forms of images, audio, and video exemplify this category of data. This embodiment is due to the fact that while the image or sound itself may be unstructured, it is generally stored with some identifier or structure, which defines the content of the file. While this definition does not necessarily bring out the true meaning of the data, it does serve as a useful tool to give some indication of the data content. A film taken by a security camera and stored by date and location gives the data somewhat of a structure because it can now be searched; yet it does not provide the wealth of information that is contained within the video. Websites are increasingly becoming a source of semi-structured data, as they contain a host of images that are categorized by file names and formats, which may or may not give an indication as to the "data" contained within the image. While this form of data does have many advantages over unstructured data, it would still be useful to somehow transform it to truly structured data.

Thus, data may exist in a wide variety of forms. Once only concerned with text, today's systems must now face a dizzying array of data that must be properly collected, stored, and processed. The exponential growth of the World Wide Web has only exacerbated this issue, as the Internet increasingly becomes a source of data in image, audio, and video format. What is needed is a way to realize the potential of all of these differing forms of data. What is needed is sound data management.

2.4 Need for Data Management

Data management is still in a significant state of flux as the tools and technologies continue to evolve; however, at the core, data management systems all are focused on generating and managing needed information and getting it where it needs to go (Boiko, 2002). Having focused on document management and various forms of digital data extraction in the past, the Internet is now becoming a key source of information due to the fact that "web-based portals are becoming commonplace as a single personalized point of access for key business information" (Robinson, 2002). Regardless of the specific data management systems employed, the key element organizations must focus on is the structure of the data. As noted earlier, most organizations only have the capabilities of utilizing structured data, leaving the volumes of unstructured data largely ignored. In order for the potential of this unstructured data to be realized, the data must be converted into a more usable, structured form. Thus, the challenge facing individual organizations, and the business world in general, is to develop effective and efficient methodologies for transforming the myriad forms of data into structured data. What follows is a general framework that is proposed in order to assist in this process.

2.4.1 Proposed Framework

As shown in the Fig.2.2, the proposed framework begins with the collection process. Data are collected from both internal and external sources. These data exist in a range of formats such as text, data, video, and audio. These forms all require different steps to be structured properly, and these steps are taken during the "scrubbing" process.

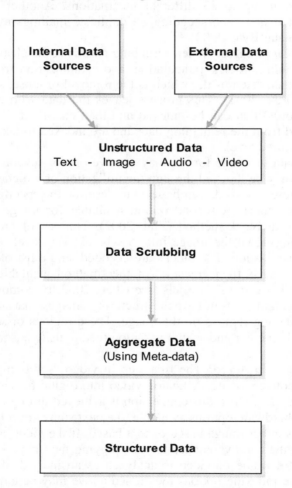

Fig. 2.2. Framework to transform unstructured data to structured data

2.4.4.1 The Need for Data Scrubbing

Once unstructured data have been collected from a variety of sources and exist in a variety of formats, it must then be "cleaned" or "scrubbed" before any further processing can be done. The process of scrubbing data involves checking for inconsistent formats, inaccuracies, and errors in the data and addressing these issues so that what remains is a consistent, accurate, and error-free repository of data. With data entering the system from a wide array of internal and external sources, the importance of this process cannot be understated. When assessing various databases within its system, one commercial bank found that in some instances customer names existed in up to 13 different incarnations. Another bank saved $170,000 that it had been spending on duplicate mailings as a result of scrubbing its data (Byte, 2003).

Clean Text and Images: When scrubbing text data, the cleaning process involves removing articles, punctuation, and capitalization from the data. The data are then "stemmed," which is the removal of tense, suffixes, etc. from words (Fox, 2001). This process leaves the data with only content words (keywords) that can be indexed and then classified. Key elements are then found from the remaining data and are indexed to take the data to the semi-structured level.

Cleaning data in image format may involve one of several methodologies. Images may be indexed through the utilization of a predefined list of keywords. These keywords can be used to describe the specific or generic objects in the image. A second option available for image cleaning is known as the keyblock method (Zhu, 2002). This set of procedures involves breaking down the image into "keyblocks" by level of resolution and vector quantization. The blocks are encoded, and a list of the various codes (codebook) is then created. Another method available is Unified Feature Matching using Fuzzy sets (see Chen, 2002 for complete description). This method is useful when structuring images that are to be retrieved by selecting regions on the image. These regions or segments are indexed based on color and spatial variation feature using a statistical clustering method.

Clean Video and Audio: The first step in video "scrubbing" generally involves the conversion of the analog video into digital format, if it is not already so encoded. Once this conversion is achieved through a variety of software and hardware options available, the next step currently involves a process that is either image based or text based. If the video is to be actually stored in the data warehouse then employing the image-based framework, each still frame of video is analyzed as an individual image; and then the image indexing options mentioned above may be employed. The text-based process categorizes the images using the text that accompanies a video. The text that accompanies the video and the resulting metadata (discussed shortly) may be encoded through a variety of methods such as the utilization of artificial intelligence (Wactlar, et al., 1999) or other automatic methods that are constantly evolving may be employed (Lienhart, 1996). The majority of audio files are converted to text using decoders, which turn the information into text. However, some research has been done on retrieving audio data using other key elements such as harmonicity.

Once indexed, it is beneficial to categorize similar terms together to make the retrieval process easier. The last step is the discovery of relationships that exists between key elements and the files in which they exist. This discovery can be done through a process of clustering. This process can be a useful to grouping text as well as data in other formats. Image data (Eakins, 1999) can be clustered or segmented based on color using color histograms, texture using second order statistics to calculate measures of contrast, coarseness, directionality, etc., shape using global features such as aspect ration and local features such as consecutive boundary segments.

2.4.4.2 Metadata

The data scrubbing process yields two significant results: clean data and metadata (Williams and Sawyer, 2003). The data are "clean," meaning consistent, free of errors, and in a format that may be utilized by the data warehouse and other data management systems. The creation of metadata is crucial to the data management process, (Lee, 2003) as it is a key step in transforming unstructured and semi-structured data into structured data. Metadata has been defined as "information documented in IT tools that improves both business and technical understanding of data and data-related processes" (Seiner 2003). Generally speaking, metadata is understood to be the "data about data." Accounting metadata may include items such as client name, data source, book vs. market value, and form of depreciation. Two specific characteristics that further explain the significance of metadata are the development of and adherence to a defined set to standards and an emphasis on sharing (Boiko, 2002). The development of a proscribed set of standards for metadata allows for uniformity in meaning across systems and facilitates the transformation of unstructured data into a structured framework. This consistency directly affects the second characteristic mentioned, because these standards allow for the sharing of data across applications and systems within an organization. This sharing permits the data to be aggregated and any patterns or relationships that may exist to be isolated and identified. In essence, the creation of metadata is the final step that allows data of various formats and structures to be transformed into a coherent set of data which may then be utilized to assist in the decision making process of organizations.

There are seemingly limitless technological options available to aid in the organizational decision making process. Data mining and data warehouses, business intelligence software, and content management systems have all made dramatic advances in the past several years. Yet for all this progress, one thing has remained constant since the day computers were first introduced in the business environment: the data must have structure. The source of these data may have changed and expanded, and the tools we use to process it may have grown significantly more powerful; but organizations are still faced with the decades old challenge of transforming these data into a structured format. The previous analysis offered guidelines for facilitating this process. While newer technological advancements may make this transformation easier over the coming years, the fact remains that each organization must address this challenge if they are to thrive and prosper.

2.5 Conclusions

The overwhelming amount of information and data in the new business marketplace has left organizations faced with the dual tasks of searching for the information they need in a timely fashion and also taking advantage of the wealth of data already contained within their systems. One perspective, which may be helpful to organizations, is to view the entire process from a cybernetic viewpoint. Despite the growing complexity of decisions an organization must make, it is still about the input-process-output-feedback cycle. Companies are faced with a wide array of technological solutions to handle this cybernetic approach to data management. Yet, the technology is only as good as the data it is processing. Effective means of structuring the wealth of unstructured data must be explored and implemented within the organization. Businesses are coming to the painful realization that effective management of their data, information, and knowledge is the only way to maintain competitive advantage (Hicks et al., 2002). Only through the utilization of all data resources, both structured and unstructured, may an organization hope to achieve this advantage.

The challenge of proper data management is only getting more difficult as the environment grows in complexity. All too often organizations emphasize the technological aspect of their data management solutions to the exclusion of all other relevant factors. Proper planning, analysis, and coordination of these systems are as important as the technology itself. All relevant stakeholders in this process must also be factored into the data management solution. There is a new emphasis on system responsiveness as today's end user, both inside and outside of the organization, has come to expect almost instantaneous results in this age of interactivity. These stakeholders, employees, and customers are perhaps the greatest untapped resource of unstructured data that an organization may possess. Learning to collect, structure, process, and *learn* from these individuals may well be the most significant data transformation challenge an organization faces and the true litmus test for its success or failure in this dynamic business environment.

3 Populating the Accounting Data Warehouse

Ken Jones

Claritee Group, LLC. Pennsylvania

Abstract. The value of an Accounting Data Warehouse to an enterprise is obvious to most business managers. A central place for decision support where the numbers tie to the books of the company is a great boon to the analysts in the enterprise. However, what are not obvious are the complexities and challenges that must be overcome to actually populate the Accounting Data Warehouse with useful information. This chapter reviews the common challenges that will be encountered in the creation of the so-called Extract Transform Load (ETL) process; the software plumbing that carries data from the source systems to the Accounting Data Warehouse. An overview of the basic components of an Accounting Data Warehouse is first presented to provide necessary background for the discussion. The common challenges encountered in extracting data, transforming it and then loading it into the final warehouse data structures are then described. All discussion is presented in conceptual terms without falling to low-level technical-speak. At the conclusion of the chapter, the reader will have a solid understanding of the relationship between the capability or usefulness of the Accounting Data Warehouse and the complexity and associated cost of the ETL process required to deliver that capability.

3.1 Introduction

The business manager stares across the table at his Information Technology (IT) counterpart. The timeline for the Accounting Data Warehouse project is slipping. The business manager wants to understand why. The IT project manager is patiently trying to explain the problems they have found during the early testing of the ETL process. The business manager's eyes begin to glaze over. In his mind, he asks these questions "Why is she telling me this? Why do I need to understand this stuff? Isn't this ETL stuff just for the IT guys?"

Although this scenario has been crafted to illustrate the disconnect that can sometimes occur between business and technology people in an organization, we believe this type of situation occurs frequently in the contemporary business environment. This situation occurs primarily because most people associated with the project believe that ETL is a technology challenge. This belief is incorrect. As we will see, this is a key misconception about ETL, a misconception that will manifest itself as a set of significant issues when business users begin to look at the information coming out of the Accounting Data Warehouse (ADW).

The purpose of this chapter is to explain ETL to a business manager audience. Our goal is to cover the topic in a manner that is useful to a business manager. Although the final ETL process is very technical in nature, our focus will be on management issues rather than engineering issues. The creation of an ADW is a non-trivial undertaking. There are a few key factors that will determine the success or failure of the undertaking. Our experience is that a business manager who understands the management issues related to the effort will stand a much greater chance of a successful outcome than one who does not.

This chapter is organized in the following way. We will first cover the basic elements of an ADW, describing each component at a high level. This background is essential for our discussion of the ETL process. We will then define the ETL process and explain the basic sub-processes. We will then delve into a collection of topics that demonstrate the relationship between the three C's of Capability, Complexity and Cost.

At the conclusion of this chapter, the business manager should be armed with a good understanding of the issues that will be faced in the construction of an ADW and the choices they will have to make with respect to the Capability/Complexity/Cost tradeoff.

3.2 Components of the Accounting Data Warehouse

As we have learned from prior chapters, the ADW is a repository of data collected from multiple operational systems in the enterprise. The repository is organized to support reporting and analysis that cannot be performed using any other single information system in the enterprise. The structure of the data in the ADW is designed to connect the transactions in the General Ledger (GL) with the underlying transactions in the Subsidiary Ledgers (sub-ledgers) that roll up to the GL.

The Extract/Transform/Load (ETL) process is the process that collects data from the operational systems and organizes that data for analytical purposes. Before we can discuss the ETL process in detail, we must first understand the basic components of an ADW. Consider the diagram presented in Fig. 3.1. There are four main vertical groupings of elements moving from left to right in the figure. These groupings are

1. Source Systems
2. Data Staging Area
3. Presentation Area
4. Data Access/Applications

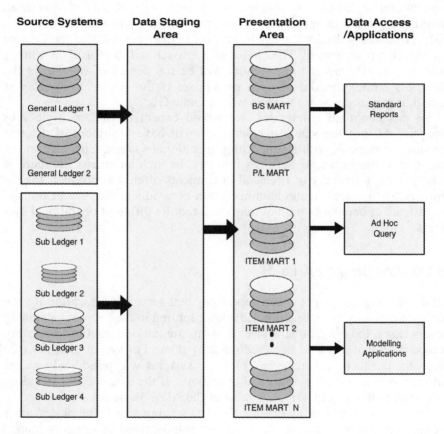

Fig. 3.1. Basic Components of an Accounting Data Warehouse

3.2.1 Source Systems

Source systems are operational systems that capture the transactions of the enterprise. The business of the business is recorded by these systems.

Source systems are designed to support rapid processing of many small transactions associated with specific business processes. Reporting capability in these systems will be focused on measuring those specific business processes. It is important to remember that operational (source) systems are naturally optimized for operations and not for analysis.

For the purposes of our discussion, we categorize all source systems as either a GL or a sub-ledger. In most enterprises, we would expect to find a single GL. In some enterprises, there will be multiple GLs. One reason for an enterprise having multiple GLs is growth through acquisition. When one enterprise acquires another enterprise, there will almost certainly be an overlap in terms of information systems. Both enterprises will posses a GL. A business decision must be made to either consolidate the GLs or operate them separately. The choice of approach will be based on a number of factors. One of these factors will be the degree of overlap in the business strategy/model of each enterprise. If the degree of overlap is small, it may make sense to keep two separate GLs.

In just about all enterprises, we would expect to find multiple subledgers. All but the smallest enterprises will have a number of discrete business processes with a supporting operational system. Consider an enterprise in the Financial Services industry. In such an enterprise, there is likely to be a diversity of financial instruments offered as products to customers. Differences in the administration of products like life insurance, certificate of deposit or mutual funds will require different operational systems.

3.2.2 Data Staging Area

The data staging area is a data repository that serves as a location for the complete history of transactions that are captured in the source systems. In many cases, the operational source systems are not designed to store every transaction that has ever been recorded by them. For system performance reasons, the technical managers of those systems will periodically purge information as a matter of normal operations. If the data staging area does not capture this lost history, the value of the ADW is greatly diminished.

In addition to capturing history, the data staging area is the place where source system data can be cleansed and standardized before it is loaded into the Presentation Area. Data cleansing refers to the process of improving data quality, where data quality is a measure of how accurately the data reflects reality. Data standardization refers to the process of enforcing consistency across disparate data sources. We will explore these topics in more detail in the next section.

A key point to note is that the data staging area is off-limits to business users. As we delve into the ETL process the reader will understand why this is so.

3.2.3 Presentation Area

The presentation area is the set of data marts that are available to consumers of the ADW. In one possible configuration, the presentation area would contain a Balance Sheet data mart ("B/S Mart"), a Profit and Loss data mart ("P/L Mart") and one or more Item data marts ("Item Mart"). We will consider each mart in turn.

The B/S Mart will contain a set of data structures sourced originally from the GL that support analysis of the journal postings to balance sheet related accounts in the Chart of Accounts (COA).

The P/L Mart will contain another set of data structures, again originally sourced from the GL that support analysis of the journal postings to income and expense related accounts in the COA.

The Item Mart(s) will contain a third set of data structures originally sourced from the sub-ledgers that contain the rich detail of business transactions that ultimately find their way into the GL. As we discussed earlier, there is often a summarization or roll-up of detail that occurs when sub-ledger information is posted to the GL. The Item Mart(s) will contain this detail that is so critical to understanding the activities of the enterprise.

3.2.4 Data Access/Applications

The final grouping in Fig. 3.1 is data access and applications. This grouping includes all tools that are used by customers of the ADW to get at the information in the Presentation Area. There are three basic categories of use of data in the ADW.

1. Standard Reporting
2. Ad hoc Query
3. Modeling Applications

Standard reporting refers to a series of defined static views of information (i.e. reports) based on data in the Presentation area. Such reports are often used to validate that "things are normal" or identify where "things are not normal". This type of data use is a typical entry point for business users and is at the leading edge of the continuum of sophistication in the use of data.

Ad hoc query refers to in-the-moment analysis of data in the Presentation Area. This type of analysis involves the execution of queries to answer a question that may not have been asked previously. An ad-hoc query may result because "things are not normal" and we need to get more insight into why they are not normal. This type of data use is also fairly common but does involve a significant step up in technical sophistication by the business user because it involves a much deeper understanding of the data.

Modeling applications are usually sophisticated analytical applications of the data in the Presentation Area. Such applications utilize the data to transform or derive new information that is used to guide decision-making. An example of this type of application is a forecasting model used to attempt to predict the future. Data mining applications are another example, where we may use complex algorithms to look for correlations between different variables in the data. Whatever the application, this use of data is very sophisticated and requires a deep understanding of the data.

3.3 The ETL Process

Having reviewed the basic components of an ADW, we can now explore the ETL process in more detail. The ETL process is a three-step process. The Extract step involves the extraction of data from the source systems and storing of this data in the data staging area. The transform step involves the data cleansing and data standardization processes mentioned earlier. The transform step is executed on the data in the data staging area. The load step involves the loading of the presentation area data structures from the data staging area.

Before we delve into the details of each step in ETL, we need to define the terms Capability, Complexity and Cost. We will be referring to these terms throughout the remainder of this document. Capability refers to capability of the ADW from a business perspective. Capability can be measured along a variety of dimensions. Some of these dimensions are the coverage of all possible enterprise data that is available in the warehouse, how much history is available, the degree of cleanliness and standardization of the data, the relative ease with which the design accommodates change in the business, and the perceived usability of the presentation area. The relative capability of the ADW is quite visible to the business user.

Complexity refers to the complexity of the ETL process. Ultimately, the ETL process is implemented as a collection of computer programs. The complexity of this collection of computer programs is determined largely by the required capability of the system. Capability drives complexity. We will see this as we review the ETL process in more detail. The other key driver of complexity is the capability of the technology team delivering the ETL process. There are many ways to solve the same problem with technology. There are wonderfully elegant and well engineered designs and there are those that are not. Complexity is not always obvious to the business user. This fact lies at the heart of the confrontation between the business manager and the IT project manager we saw in the opening of this chapter.

Cost refers to the cost of the creation of the ETL process. Cost is the sum of hardware, software and peopleware□ hardware being the computer infrastructure required to host the ETL process, software being the computer programs that perform the ETL process, and peopleware being the human resources required in the creation and maintenance of the ETL process. There is typically a direct relationship between complexity and cost.

With these definitions in hand, we can now examine each step in the ETL process in terms of required capability and the relationship with complexity and cost.

3.3.1 Extract

Data extraction is conceptually quite simple. However, it can be very challenging in practice. The effort involved in creating an automated extraction process involves two basic steps. Given the analytical need identified by the business user as a starting point, the first step is to study and understand how the data is organized and structured in the source system. The people performing this work must have a combination of business domain knowledge and specific source system application knowledge. Generally this does not come in a single person. It is common to find a small group of business and technology people performing this work. With this work complete, the second step is to create the data extraction programs to pull the information out of the source system. This is a technical task performed by software development people.

The capability requirements that influence complexity and cost in the extract step are

1. Number of source systems
2. Nature of source systems

The connection between the number of source systems that must be integrated in the ADW and the complexity/cost is fairly obvious. The effort to create and then maintain the extract process for each source system will be multiplied by the number of source systems. In general, the more source systems that must be integrated into the ADW, the greater the complexity and cost.

The nature of the source system can have a significant impact on the complexity of the data extraction effort. Information systems have been created to address just about every conceivable business function. We will consider only a small number of variables relating to the nature of the source system. The first variable to consider is the profile of use of the source system. Is the system used 24x7 or are 8x5? More specifically, is there a time when system use is minimal or non-existent so that a data extraction process can be executed without affecting the performance of the source system? In general, it will be easier to extract data from a source system when there is a window of time where nothing is going on in the source system.

The second variable to consider is where the data is hosted organizationally. The source system may be operated in-house within the enterprise or a third party may host it. In general, an in-house system will be easier to deal with. In this situation, there is a group of people within the enterprise that own and operate the source system. Getting access to these people and directing their work priorities will be easier than the equivalent group of people within a third party enterprise.

Case In Point: A client we worked with had outsourced the operation and support of their GL to a third party. Making changes to the data extraction process involved navigating a more complicated process defined by the third party than the equivalent internal process.

The third variable to consider is the geographical locations of the source system and ADW. If the source system and ADW are located in different countries, there may be technical constraints affecting the volume of data that can be moved from source to EDW in the window of time available for extraction. In addition, differences in time zones like those between the Americas, Europe and Asia add to the complexity of the overall ETL process. The window of time available for extraction will typically be during the nighttime hours of the source system. However, this point in time may occur during the business day at the location of the ADW. The decision of when and where to perform the subsequent transform and load steps with the extracted data must be considered carefully. When all of the source systems are operated in the same time zone, the complexity is reduced.

The forth variable to consider is the technical platform of the data repository underlying the source system. Although the spectrum is broad, we group systems into those built on a Relational Database Management System (RDBMS) and those that are not. In general, it will be a less complex task to extract information from an RDBMS than another non-RDBMS platform. The reasons for this are varied but stem from the fact that a RDBMS has become accepted as the best platform to host most applications. RDBMS technology is mainstream and the skill base within the IT industry is deep. It may be difficult and expensive to find the technical skills required to extract data from non-RDBMS outlier type technologies.

In general, it will be more difficult to get information out of a non-RDBMS based source system than a RDBMS based source system.

Case In Point: One of our clients had two non-RDBMS based systems of record. In one case the extraction process was deemed too complex to undertake. The second system required a third party consultant with profound knowledge of the underlying data structures to create the extract process.

The fifth variable to consider is the type of source system. Some systems capture and record an effective date for every transaction. Such systems are called journaling systems. Ledger systems are an example of a journaling system. A non-journaling system does not effective date every transaction. Non-journaling systems are much more common than journaling systems in the universe of all potential source systems. The effect of journaling versus non-journaling on the complexity of the extract process is significant. One of the fundamental tasks of the ETL process is to determine what has changed in the source system since the last time the source system was processed. This task is fundamental because in high volume systems, it may not be viable to process every transaction in the source system every time. More often, we can only afford to process the changes that have occurred since the last time we extracted from the source system. Journaling systems simply this task tremendously because the effective date of the transaction is stored with the transaction. The effective date can be used directly to see "what has happened" since some point in time. Conversely, figuring out what changes have occurred in a non-journaling system can be much more difficult.

Case In Point: In one case, the effort required to create the ETL process for a client sub-ledger system was five times that for the GL. The difference in effort was due primarily to the fact that the sub-ledger did not effective date many of the key data elements required for analysis. The ETL process had to account for this situation by detecting the changes that had occurred since the prior run.

3.3.2 Transform

Data transformation is not an obvious requirement in the creation of an ADW. While it is obvious to most business managers that data must be extracted for source systems to feed the warehouse, it is not obvious that this data cannot be used "as is". The reality is that a great deal of time will be invested in crafting data transformations in the ETL process.

The capability requirements that influence complexity and cost in the transformation step are:

1. Completeness and correctness of data
2. Standardization of the meaning of data from different source systems

Data completeness and correctness is a fundamental requirement of the ADW. There will be little or no value in creating an ADW if the data on which decisions will be made is missing or incorrect. Data will be missing from the ADW because it was not captured consistently in the source system. A specific data element will not be captured consistently in the source system because it was not mandatory for the processing of the source system. The complete population of data elements that can be captured in an operational system will naturally fall into those that must be captured to support the business process the operational system supports and those that are informational in nature. A business manager looking to analyze the information from an operational system can only depend on the mandatory data elements being available for analysis. The informational data elements may or may not be available. This sometimes comes as a surprise to business managers. If the informational data is required for analytical purposes, the data element must be made mandatory in the operational system. In addition, an effort must be performed to capture the missing data elements for historical transactions. This may be a significant undertaking and will probably have been unexpected by the project planners. This situation is one of the possible reasons for a slipping timeline for the ADW project.

The situation of missing data in operational system is easy to understand, but how can data be incorrect in the ADW? If the ADW is sourced by a single system, the possibility of the data being incorrect in the ADW is minimal. The extraction and transformation processes will be operating on a single logical set of data. However, this is not a typical situation. In most cases, the ADW will be integrating data from more than one operational system. There may be information about a product or customer that is captured in more than one source system. Connecting these different views of the same product or customer can involve complex logic in the transformation step because the source systems are not integrated well at the operational level. In general, the less integration between the source systems, the greater the complexity of the integration effort in the transform step and the greater the effort in ensuring that the data in the ADW is correct. We make this point only to communicate there can be significant challenges and effort in the transformation step to simply ensure the integrated data is correct. This is not always obvious to the business manager.

Data standardization refers to the process of enforcing consistency across disparate data sources. As we have already mentioned, different source systems often collect information about the same "things". Continuing our example, many source systems will capture transactions that reference customers and products. In an ideal world, there would be one source of reference information for customers and another for products. However, in practice this is not usually the case. Two source systems that reference the same customer may capture slightly different names for that customer. There is work that must be performed to standardize or conform the two different names for a customer into one name. When you multiply this piece of work by all of the data elements that are common to different source systems, the result can be a significant effort involving a large number of people through the enterprise. This effort turns out to be a consensus building exercise more than a technical exercise. This need for this effort will not surface until the data in the source systems is examined. For this reason it is often difficult to predict this effort before the project is well underway and the data in the source systems can be examined.

3.3.3 Load

The load step in the ETL process involves the loading of cleansed transformed data into the data structures that the customer of the ADW will use. The complexity of this step lies in the design of the presentation data structures. The capability requirements of these data structures are

1. Usability/Understandability
2. Performance of data access
3. Resilience to changes in the business

A common complaint from business users is that it is very difficult to understand how the data is represented in an operational system. A seemingly simple report may involve a join of many database tables. This complaint is valid, there is high complexity in this task; and this will always be case for any non-trivial application. The reason for the complexity is function of the fact that the operational system is a transaction processing type of information system. The details of why data is organized this way for transaction processing systems is not important for our discussion. However, it is clear that if we expect business users to be able to use the ADW, the data must be organized in a very understandable way.

Once constructed, the ADW will contain large amounts of data. Typical use of an ADW will involve navigation and summarization of potentially large subsets of the total data. The navigation and summarization process involves the execution of queries against the data structures in the ADW. The performance of such queries is critical. If it takes too long to get results from the ADW, it simply will not be used. The data structures must be organized to support fast query access.

Change is constant in business. The analytical needs of a business will change over time so the data collected in the ADW will also change over time. As more and more applications are created against the ADW, the impact of changing the data structures can be significant. The impact will be felt in the effort to understand how the change will affect existing applications coupled with the effort to actually change the applications. Given this situation, the data structures in the ADW must be organized to minimize this type of impact.

The three requirements we have outlined are best met by a data design approach called "Dimensional Modeling". This data design approach is mature and well documented in Kimball (2002). Dimensional Modeling is a complex topic that is well beyond the scope of this discussion. What is important for the business manager to understand is that Dimensional Modeling is a specialization in the area of database design. As such, it is unlikely that the in-house IT organization will have this skill set if there have been no prior data warehousing initiatives in the enterprise. In this case, there will be a need to go outside the in-house IT organization to find these skills through hiring or training of existing IT personnel.

3.3.4 Common

There are some capability requirements of the ADW that are not specific to any one step of the ETL process. These capability requirements are

1. Requirement for history
2. Volume of data
3. Real-time content versus historic content

The requirement for history in the ADW can have a significant impact on the complexity of the ETL process. It is very likely that an enterprise will have been in operation for some time before the need to create an ADW is recognized. Some percentage of this history will need to be loaded into the ADW as a starting point for analysis. In some enterprises, this percentage will be low. In others, this percentage may be very high. The more history is required, the greater the complexity of the ETL process.

From a data extraction perspective, the impact may be minimal if all of the history is still available in the source system. This is often not the case though. As mentioned previously, it is standard procedure to periodically archive historical data in an operational system. This procedure is usually performed to ensure system performance is not adversely affected. As the data in the system grows, it usually takes more time to search and update any given data item in the system. The archiving ensures that only relevant data is actually stored in the source system. If archiving has occurred and the history recorded in the archive is required for the ADW, an extra step of identifying the archives and restoration of the require archives must be performed. This extra step requires effort in planning and execution. Another distinct possibility is that the enterprise has been through a conversion from one operational system to another. Some of the history required in the ADW may be recorded in the backups of some long since forgotten system. If this is the case, we have just added another (surprise) source system requiring an extract process.

The impact of history on the transform step may be large. It is very likely that the business of the enterprise has changed during the window of time spanned by the required history. Products may have been come and gone. Market demographics may have changed. The legal entity structure of the enterprise may have been altered. In short, there are any number of possible major differences between the current state of the enterprise and any historical state. Someone will have to identify these changes and decide how to deal with them. The changes themselves will not be obvious until the data is examined. At this point, new data cleansing rules may need to be defined and implemented. There will be new standardizing efforts required if there is a need to extract data from long since forgotten historic source systems.

The volume of data is a factor in the overall complexity of the ETL process primarily because there is always a window of time that the ETL process must be completed within. As volume goes up, the processing time goes up. Even with very fast computers, the volume of data that must be processed in the ETL process may require specific approaches like parallel processing. An approach like this requires significantly more time in design, implementation and testing. Ongoing maintenance of such a solution is also more difficult.

The degree of timeliness or currency of the data in the ADW will have a significant impact on the complexity of the ETL process. Does the ADW need to contain data that was current at the last closed month end? Does it need to be as of yesterday close of business? How about as of a few seconds ago? This need will be driven by the nature of the analysis that must be performed. In the case of financial analysis, the most likely data currency need is as of yesterday close of business. It is possible that having access to real time information from sub-ledger systems in the ADW may be valuable. However, the complexity of delivering real-time information into the ADW is an order of magnitude higher than yesterday close of business. The increase in complexity comes in the form of a new approach for dealing with the transactions that have occurred since the last ETL process was executed. Although the data structures containing the real-time information are similar to those recording previously loaded history, new mechanisms for the ETL process will need to be designed, constructed and tested. Extraction is now replaced with a real-time replication mechanism where transaction activity is "pushed" by the source system into the data staging area. The data transformation processes that are typically design to process transactions in batch, must now process each transaction as it occurs. The load step will now load individual transactions into the real-time partition of the presentation area. The key point is that the move from a yesterday close of business to a real-time view of the enterprise in the ADW comes at great cost in terms of complexity. If the value of having real-time information justifies the cost of increased complexity and cost then so be it.

3.4 Some Final Thoughts

The potential benefits of an ADW to an enterprise are fairly easy to understand for most business managers. A central place where the activity posted in the general ledger can be connected to the rich detail of the business transactions that generated those postings has tremendous possibilities. The possibilities are limited only by the information that can be captured in the ADW and the imagination of how the data can be used to increase revenue, reduce expenses or better manage risk. What is far less obvious is the effort required to create an ADW.

As we have seen in our discussion, the creation of the ETL process can be a very complex effort. We have seen how the complexity of the effort will be driven by the required capability of the ADW and that the relationship between the capability and complexity is not always obvious. Things that seem simple to a business manager may involve significant organizational and technical challenges. Some of these challenges cannot be understood until the effort is well underway and the data from the source systems can be examined. The scope for surprises is great.

Our ultimate goal in this discussion has been to help business managers understand what is being undertaken in the creation of ADW. Although the complexity can be high and the challenges significant, the task is not impossible. It is our belief that a business manager who is armed with an understanding of the issues presented in this discussion stands a good chance of never having to sit across the table from their IT counterpart and risk having their eyes glaze over in confusion and disbelief.

4 The Accounting Centric Data Warehouse™

Daniel W. Hughes

Claritee Group, LLC, Pennsylvania

Abstract. At the heart of every organization, regardless of location or industry, is the accounting function. The accounting function is responsible for gathering, recording, and reporting on all of the financial transactions consummated by the enterprise. Using sophisticated transaction applications, accountants aggregate financial activity from disparate functions of the business and record a summary of the transactions in the general ledger (GL). Within the GL, data is organized in the chart of accounts, which represents the physical organization of the business. Business units, departments, products, and accounts are examples of chart of account segments. Accounting then produces the financial statements (i.e., balance sheet and income statement) from the data in the GL. The financial statements are distributed to internal and external stakeholders to evaluate the performance of the enterprise.

This method of capturing and organizing data works very well; however when it comes to reporting and analysis, limitations exist. Transaction systems are not designed to support dynamic analysis. Complicated data models make querying the database an arduous task. In addition, reporting from the GL is limited to the intelligence captured in the chart of accounts. Therefore, to improve financial reporting capabilities, a different approach is used. This approach is an Accounting Centric Data Warehouse™ (ACDW). To build an ACDW, the data in the GL is extracted and joined in a separate repository with supporting data captured in the operational subsidiary ledgers (sub-ledgers). The sub-ledgers are the applications used to capture the operational transactions of the business. Sales orders, loan servicing, accounts payable, accounts receivable, and inventory are all examples of sub-ledgers. By creating a platform that brings the GL and sub-ledger data together, a deeper level of financial analysis is possible. The ACDW contains summary level balances from the GL down to the supporting transaction detail from the sub-ledgers. With an ACDW, top down or bottom up analysis is possible. Over time sub-ledgers can be incrementally integrated into the ACDW to create a single enterprise decision support platform.

4.1 Introduction

Before we discuss data warehousing, it is important to understand the role of accounting in the organization and how it functions. The accounting function is responsible for gathering, organizing, and validating the financial transactions of the enterprise. Accounting must record each transaction in accordance with standards set forth by professional and government bodies (e.g., Internal Revenue Services, Securities and Exchange Commission, and Financial Accounting Standards Board). In addition, financial institutions and investors have requirements for assessing the financial performance of their interest. Financial institutions want to know how secure their debt is, while investors are interested in their return on investment. To meet these demands, accounting is aided by sophisticated computer systems designed to record financial transactions in accordance with accounting principles. In the subsequent sections of this chapter, we will discuss how the modern accounting function is organized, the limitations on reporting and analysis of the modern accounting system, and how progressive companies are improving delivery to stakeholders of financial performance information through the use of sophisticated data warehouses.

4.2 The Modern Accounting System

The principles and methods underlying the modern accounting system are not much different from the accounting systems of the past. Although software applications and computer servers have replaced paper ledger books, typewriters and filing systems, the double entry bookkeeping approach remains intact. A ledger is still the term for a repository of financial transactions, and a journal entry is still the method used to record financial activity into the ledger.

The accounting function is supported by sophisticated software applications designed to process large volumes of data. Global firms may process millions of transactions in a single month, while mid-size companies could easily see up to 100,000 transactions per month. Large retailers like Amazon or Dell can process thousands of sales orders in a single day. But with this complexity, come many challenges. Organizational changes, system upgrades, and technology advancements make for a dynamic environment.

Two types of applications support the accounting function of any organization: the General Ledger (GL) and Subsidiary Ledger (sub-ledger). The GL serves as the central repository for all financial activity, while the sub-ledger captures the detail transactions related to specific processes within the enterprise. Treasury, inventory management, accounts payable, order entry, and purchasing are all functions supported by separate sub-ledgers. The transactions captured in the sub-ledgers are periodically aggregated and recorded in the GL. Two types of reports are used to assess the financial performance of an enterprise: financial and managerial. Financial reporting comprises the balance sheet and income statement. These two reports represent all of the financial activity of the firm. The financial reports are presented to stakeholders, such as management, investors and creditors, to measure the enterprise. Financial reports are created from the GL or consolidation tool if there is more than one GL.

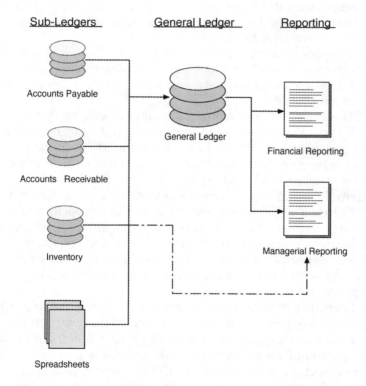

Fig. 4.1. Modern Accounting System

Managerial reporting is intended for internal consumption and is used in planning and operations by managers and employees of the enterprise.

Managerial reports help managers assess their area of responsibility. An example of a managerial report may include revenue by product or customer for a particular period. Managerial reports generally comprise data from the GL and sub-ledger applications. (See Fig. 4.1)

In the rest of this section, we will review the specific function of the GL and sub-ledgers. We will discuss the mechanics of these applications to understand how they are used to capture intelligence about the enterprise. We will review why the current model of collecting and reporting on financial performance is limited in its capability, and finally we will see how progressive companies are using data warehousing to improve performance analysis.

4.2.1 The Role of the General Ledger

In this section, we will review the role of the GL in the accounting system to understand why the GL is such an important application, as it establishes the framework for measuring the enterprise.

What is a general ledger? Investorwords.com defines it as a book of final entry summarizing all of a company's financial transactions, through offsetting debit and credit accounts. The accounting function is responsible for maintaining the GL.

The GL is classified as an online transaction processing system (OLTP). An OLTP system is defined as an operational system of record that captures the transactions of the business (Kimball, 2002). In the case of the GL, its main function is to record financial transactions in accordance with accounting standards and statutory requirements. Within the GL, all financial activity is recorded in a common structure known as the chart of accounts (COA). The COA is a data structure designed to represent the physical organization of the business. For example, COA segments may include business units, natural accounts, cost centers, products, and projects. These segments categorize each transaction in the database. Using the COA segments, reports and queries can be created to analyze the financial performance. (See Table 4.1)

Each financial transaction entered into the GL is referred to as a journal entry (JE). JEs contain a minimum of two records: a debit and credit. The debit and credit, referred to as double entry accounting, are required to keep the accounting entries in balance. JEs contain information about each transaction, such as the posted date, COA segment, accounting period, source, and description. The JE may be a summary of transactions from the sub-ledger applications or individual financial transactions recorded directly into the GL. The JE attributes (i.e., posted date, COA segment, accounting period, source and description) are a rich source of business intelligence. When aggregated, the JEs tell a story about how the organization is managing its financial resources. (See Table 4.2)

Financial and managerial reports are prepared and distributed to stakeholders based on the intelligence contained in each JE. Expense reports can be generated from the GL to show managers, based on their department and business unit, how much they have spent during a particular period and where they are in relationship to the budget. Or a sales report can be generated to show revenue by product for a specific region. The level of sophistication will depend on the intelligence captured in each JE.

As the repository for all financial transactions, GL establishes the framework for enterprise reporting through the COA. Therefore, great care must be taken when setting up the COA. Decisions made during the setup will limit or enhance future business intelligence capabilities. JEs should contain as much information about each transaction as the COA will support. Many of the GL applications allow for custom fields to be defined so additional information can be captured with each JE. The intelligence in the GL is only as good as the data entered. For companies with disparate GLs, the challenge becomes conforming the JE information during consolidation. The best practice model is to have one GL to enforce a standard across the enterprise, which is not always possible with business acquisitions and disparate operations.

Table 4.1. Chart of Accounts Segments

Business Unit	Natural Account	Cost Center	Product	Project
0100	41001233	ADM123	4563	MKT12

Table 4.2. Journal Entry Sample

Journal Date	Journal ID	Journal Source	Journal Line Description	BU#	Account	Cost Center	Dr	Cr
1/1/03	123	AP	Record Expense	1000	500000	ADM001	500	
1/1/03	123	AP	Record Liability	1000	200000	ADM001		500
1/15/03	456	AR	Record Revenue	3000	400000	ADM002	1000	
1/15/03	456	AR	Record Accounts Receivable	3000	100000	ADM002		1000

As discussed, the intelligence captured in the GL is based on the COA segments and other information captured in the JE. But what about the underlying transaction details, such as customer or vendor information. Since the GL only contains aggregations of data, how would a reader of financial or managerial reports get access to the data supporting the report line items? As we will see in the next section, the transaction details, supporting the balances in the GL, are contained in the sub-ledger applications. We will discuss the role of the sub-ledgers and why the data captured in those applications is so important to providing stakeholders with a complete view of the organization.

4.2.2 The Role of the Subsidiary Ledgers

In this section, we will discuss the role of the sub-ledger in the accounting system. We will define the term sub-ledger and review the different types of applications. We will also discuss how a well-designed sub-ledger application can be used to enhance business intelligence.

What is a sub-ledger? Dictionary.com defines it as details of an account supporting the amount stated in the general ledger.

Since the GL is the repository of all financial transactions, we refer to all supporting systems as sub-ledgers. Like the GL, the sub-ledgers are OLTP systems designed for capturing and processing transactions. Sub-ledgers contain details of business activity consummated by a specific function or process of the enterprise. Sub-ledgers range from very sophisticated applications (e.g., equity trading, point of sales order entry, inventory management, accounts payable) to simple spreadsheet systems. Data about customers and product orders, vendors and invoices, or product inventory are examples of sub-ledger functions. In addition to the transaction attributes, COA segment information such as business units, cost centers, and natural accounts is also captured in the sub-ledger for GL reference. Each transaction is assigned a COA segment. These segments are used to aggregate activity into JEs for posting to the GL. Sophisticated sub-ledgers may have COA business rules defined for each transaction type, while simple spreadsheet sub-ledgers have to be manually summarized and recorded in the GL. The number and sophistication of sub-ledger applications can vary depending on the nature of the enterprise and its organization.

Starting in the 1980s, many companies began implementing integrated OLTP applications known as Enterprise Resource Planning (ERP) systems. An ERP system is defined as any software system designed to support and automate the business processes of medium- and large-size organizations. These processes may include manufacturing, distribution, personnel, project management, payroll, and financials (Dictionary.com).

The ERP applications are divided into modules serving different functional needs. Supporting the accounting function, examples of modules are accounts payable, accounts receivable, purchasing, and inventory management. In an integrated application, entities such as customers, vendors or products are shared across modules to eliminate data redundancy. A vendor record viewed by purchasing would be identical when viewed by accounts payable. Therefore, data redundancies of entities like customers and vendors are eliminated in an integrated system. In addition, workflow techniques can be used to streamline processes among functions. Purchasing can monitor inventories for replenishment points, and accounts payable can forecast purchases that need to be paid. The integrated approach allows the organization to monitor cross-functional activity on a single application platform.

Many companies implement ERP applications to perform core business functions (i.e., general ledger, accounts payable, accounts receivable, purchasing, fixed asset tracking, and cash management). Because these functions are mature, best practice processes have been built into the applications. Therefore, a company can benefit from world-class practices by implementing the application. In the 1990s, ERP vendors made a strong push into manufacturing and supply chain processes; but for many companies, the ERP applications are implemented to perform common business functions where the processes are well defined. The benefits of ERP systems are shared entities, seamless interfaces into the GL, and best practices for recording intelligence about each transaction. The major ERP vendors are PeopleSoft, Oracle, and SAP.

But the ERP applications do not support all business functions. There are many industry or company specific functions supported by personal databases (i.e., MS Access), manual spreadsheets, and niche software products. For example, functions like credit card servicing or healthcare billing are generally too industry specific for an ERP vendor to include in their product offering. The ERP vendors address many of the common mature functions that have larger market share. To meet specific needs, companies must build their own applications or buy a niche software product. Remember, every organization will have a variety of disparate sub-ledger applications to service the transactional needs of the business.

Contained within every sub-ledger application is valuable information. Whether a spreadsheet or a sophisticated OLTP application, information about each transaction can help stakeholders throughout the organization understand financial performance. The sub-ledgers contain the data explaining balances in the GL. Why did sales change X% this year? Or why did inventory grow Y$ this period? To answer these questions, functional managers analyze data in the sub-ledgers. Custom reports, data extracts, and online database queries are common methods of accessing the transaction data in the sub-ledgers.

When designing a sub-ledger application, it is important to think from an enterprise perspective. What are the key questions to understand about this function? Are all of the COA values being for every transaction? Are controls in place to enforce users of the application to enter critical data? It is not uncommon to see sophisticated sub-ledger applications offer limited intelligence because the COA and transaction records are incomplete. The intelligence about each transaction recorded in the sub-ledger will only be as good as the source data. In the next section, we will discuss how accounting brings all of this information together to produce financial and managerial reports.

4.2.3 The Accounting Close Process

In this section, we will briefly talk about the accounting close process. Understanding the close process will help you see how the GL and sub-ledgers link to produce financial and managerial reports.

At the end of each period, usually a month, the accounting function performs a process called "closing the books." Closing the books simply means compiling all financial activity for a given period and recording it in the GL. On the surface, this process seems to be straight forward; but the process of reconciling the sub-ledger data to its source; and preparing it for posting to the GL is an arduous task. As mentioned in the sub-ledger section, the integrated applications perform this function very well. But remember, not all sub-ledgers are part of an integrated package; therefore, the number of disparate sub-ledgers will determine the difficulty of the close process. An example of a sub-ledger close procedure is sales commission accruals. Many companies have customized databases or spreadsheet models to calculate commissions. Each month sales are fed into the model and the commissions are generated. Accounting uses the information from the model to record commission accruals (an accumulated amount to be paid in the future) in the GL.

Another example is accounts payable. Once an expense invoice is received, the data is keyed into the accounts payable sub-ledger to record the vendor expense and liability to the firm. The accounts payable function is then responsible for disbursing cash to pay for expenses entered into the sub-ledger. During the accounting period, the sub-ledger transactions are aggregated and posted in the general ledger to record the expense, liability, and cash disbursements activity. As part of the close process, accounting personnel verify the postings from the sub-ledger are accurate and complete.

Once all sub-ledger transactions for a specific period are recorded in the GL, the accounting period is closed - meaning no more entries are permitted in the GL for that period. Financial and managerial reports are produced and distributed to stakeholders for review. The accuracy and efficiency of the sub-ledger plays an important role in closing the books. World-class finance functions perform the close process in fewer than 3 days, but most companies close the books in 5 to 15 days. In the next section, we review the reporting and analysis limitations of the modern accounting system.

4.3 Limitations of the Modern Accounting System

In this section, we review the limitations on reporting analysis of the modern accounting system. We will see how reports generated from the GL provide a limited view of the organization, and why the OLTP applications are strong in transaction processing but weak in analytical capabilities.

When accounting completes its month-end close process, the financial position of the organization is ready for presentation. Both internal and external stakeholders receive either a complete set of financial statements or a sub-set, depending on their reporting needs. Senior management may receive a complete package of financial statements (i.e., Income Statement, Balance Sheet, Cash Flow Statement) showing a consolidated view of the organization, while internal line managers may only receive a sub-set (managerial report) of information based on their specific business units or departments. As we have already learned, the intelligence captured in the JE determines the reporting capability of the GL. Now, what if senior management wanted to know why a particular financial statement line item changed, such as accounts receivables, or customer profitability for a particular period? In the current model, the GL does not contain enough information to answer questions about the underlying transactions. To understand why accounts receivable changed or the profitability of a customer, you must have access to the transaction detail recorded in the sub-ledgers. But if the organization has two disparate accounts receivable systems, access to data in both applications would be needed – a task that gets more complicated as the number of disparate systems increases. Understanding profitability might include a large number of disparate systems because there are so many components of profitability. The relevant point is that questions requiring underlying transaction data cannot be answered with ease in the current model. Separate analysis has to be performed on the source data to answer behavioral type questions.

But what about the integrated applications? Isn't this problem addressed since all the data are in a single platform? The integrated applications are designed to efficiently capture transactions but not to serve as analytical or reporting platforms. Many OLTP systems have complex data models to support the transaction function. Therefore, specialized skill sets are needed to develop custom reports and queries. In addition, querying an OLTP system can place a considerable amount of demand on an application thus affecting the performance of its main function – capturing transactions. Many companies have similar problem with reporting from their integrated systems as existed with their legacy systems.

Therefore, a new model must provide stakeholders with access to the financial transactions of the business. By integrating the GL with the sub-ledgers, progressive companies are creating a single repository for analytical reporting. Sub-ledger users can perform dynamic analysis of their data, while consumers of financial and managerial reports can have access to greater detail. In the next section, we will discuss a common approach for building a data warehouse to consolidate enterprise data.

4.4 The Accounting Centric Data Warehouse ™ (ACDW)

We have seen how the current accounting systems model is optimized for operational purposes, thus leaving analytical capabilities sub-optimal. In this section, we will describe an approach for improving financial analysis and discuss how progressive companies are using data warehousing techniques to improve their analytical capabilities. Before beginning, let us define some of the terms used in the data warehousing industry.

A goal in defining these terms is to provide a conceptual understanding of the domain without delving into specific technical approaches, technologies, or software products. As with any discipline, there is a lot of jargon used in the data warehousing industry. Two common terms that must first be defined: data warehouse and data mart.

What is a data warehouse? A data warehouse is defined as a copy of transaction data specifically structured for querying and reporting. (dwinfocenter.org) Think of a data warehouse as a repository to capture transactional data from one or more OLTP systems in the enterprise.

What is a data mart? A data mart is more specifically subject or department oriented, and is a subset of the data warehouse that looks at one particular view of the data (Shacklett, 2001). For example, a data mart may be designed to support accounts receivable analysis. Therefore, the accounts receivable sub-ledger would be the source system of the data mart. Users could query the data mart to answer questions about accounts receivable transactions. The emphasis of a data mart is on meeting the specific demands of a particular group of users in terms of analysis, content, presentation, and ease-of-use. Users of a data mart can expect to have data presented in terms that are familiar.

Some key points to remember about data warehouses and data marts are:

- A data warehouse contains information copied typically from more than one transactional system used in the enterprise.
- A data warehouse deals with large amounts of data because it involves the union of information from multiple transactional systems.
- The data in the data warehouse is organized to support reporting and analysis that cannot be performed using any other information system in the enterprise.
- A data mart is a piece or component of the data warehouse.
- A data mart is focused on addressing the needs of a specific process or function of the enterprise.

Then what is an accounting centric data warehouse™ (ACDW)? Is it a data mart focused on addressing the needs of accounting? If this definition is true, shouldn't it be called an accounting data mart? The answer to both of these questions is "No."

An ACDW is a warehouse that has been designed with a deliberate strategy for integrating data contained within the GL to data captured in the sub-ledgers. The basis for this strategy is the understanding that every financial transaction consummated by the enterprise ultimately rolls up to the balance sheet or income statement. It is a data warehouse where measurements of business processes in the enterprise can be connected to assets, liabilities and equity, or income and expense. In this model, the organization can be viewed from a cross-functional view starting with the financial statements. For example, accounts receivable could be viewed from an aggregated amount represented on the balance sheet down to individual customer transactions – all from a single reporting platform. If a senior manager wanted to see accounts receivable by customer, she could easily view that because all of the components would be available. Designing an ACDW takes careful thought. The idea behind this design is to join the data in the GL to the data in the sub-ledger to achieve an integrated view of the organization.

Building an ACDW is an incremental process. Over time, a collection of data marts, each supporting a different analytical need or business process, are developed to compose the ACDW. What makes the ACDW different from a data warehouse is the GL integration. With the GL data, a complete top to bottom view of the enterprise is available. Financial and managerial reports can be developed with greater detail.

As additional sub-ledgers are added to the ACDW, the repository becomes more valuable to the enterprise and eventually the single platform for all financial decision support. In the next section, we will discuss the application of the approach in more detail. (See Fig. 4.2)

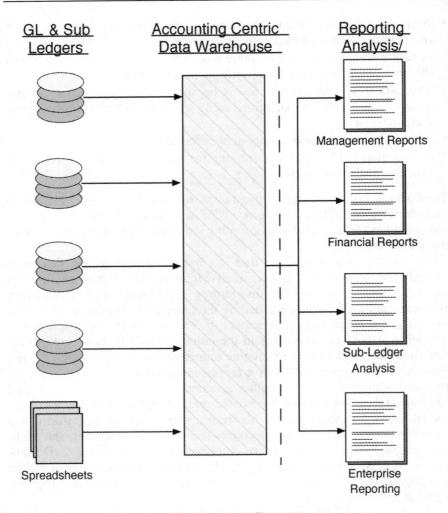

Fig. 4.2. Accounting Centric Data Warehouse™ Model

Understanding the interdependency of the GL and sub-ledger applications is the first step toward achieving sophisticated performance analysis. As we have already learned, the GL is the only repository in the enterprise that contains a complete view of financial activity. Therefore, the GL is the core application in an ACDW. In firms that have more than one GL, a consolidation tool is used to bring the activity in each GL into the ACDW. Since financial reporting, which is focused on external stakeholders, is generally performed from the GL or some consolidation tool, we will focus our discussion on managerial reporting. Managerial reporting, as discussed earlier in the chapter, provides internal management with information to assess and measure the operational performance of the enterprise. Depending on the level of sophistication, managerial reports contain information derived from the GL or a combination of data from the GL and sub-ledger(s).

Let us begin with an example. What if management wanted to analyze revenue by customer for a particular product? In most cases, customers are not included as a GL COA segment; therefore, answering this question would require customer information from the sub-ledgers. As mentioned earlier in the chapter, the COA segments are generally reserved for organizational categories like business units, products, departments, and accounts. Because a customer is an external entity and most companies have thousands of customers, it would not be feasible to maintain this information in the COA. Sub-ledger applications, such as accounts receivable (AR) and order entry (OE), are used to maintain the details of every revenue transaction. For many firms, it is common to have more than one AR or OE application to record revenues, each supporting a different business line or division. Without a repository that combines the GL revenue with the sub-ledger customer data, a manual compilation would have to be performed to analyze revenue by customer. This type of manual approach has obvious limitations: it's inefficient and time consuming to prepare, and there is no ability to perform ad-hoc querying of the data. In addition, customers who exist in more than one sub-ledger would have to be identified and combined to accurately measure their total activity. Using an ACDW approach, the data from the GL and sub-ledgers would be combined into a repository to create a single view of the revenue by customer. The data from the sub-ledgers would be replicated periodically (usually daily) and loaded into the ACDW. The data would be organized, using data warehousing methods, to combine the GL and sub-ledger for analysis. The sophistication of the analysis would be a function of the intelligence captured in the GL and sub-ledgers, which could continuously improve over time. Additional attributes could be added to the sub-ledger transactions to improve the analytical capabilities of the ACDW. Using the ACDW, a systems infrastructure would be established to analyze the sub-ledger transactions. (See Fig. 4.3)

Now that we have demonstrated how revenue analysis can be improved, let us take a look at how additional data sources could be added to improve the analysis value of the ACDW. Continuing with our example, what if management now wanted to understand customer profitability? Because there are two components to profitability - revenue and expenses – expenses would also have to be added to the ACDW to complete the analysis. Expenses would be matched up with revenue at the customer level to get profitability.

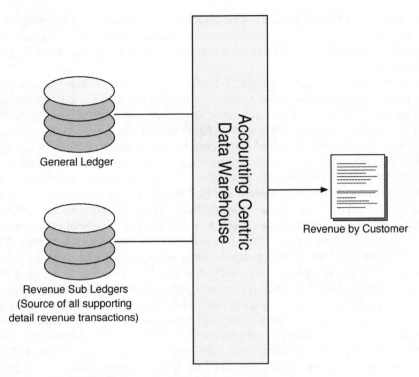

Fig. 4.3. Revenue by Customer Example

To begin, we divide expenses into two categories: direct and indirect. Direct expenses include all activity required to procure and sell the product or service. Indirect expenses would include all other costs required to support the enterprise. To integrate the expenses into the ACDW, the first step would be to identify the respective data sources for the indirect and direct expenses. Depending on the sophistication level of the sub-ledgers, an allocation of expenses may have to be assigned to each customer. More sophisticated sub-ledgers would have the ability to assign direct expenses at the customer level. For indirect expenses an allocation would be needed to assign costs to each customer. This function could be performed in the data source or ACDW. Once the revenue and expense data are joined in an ACDW, customer profitability would be possible. As additional data sources are added, the ACDW becomes more valuable. (See Fig. 4.4)

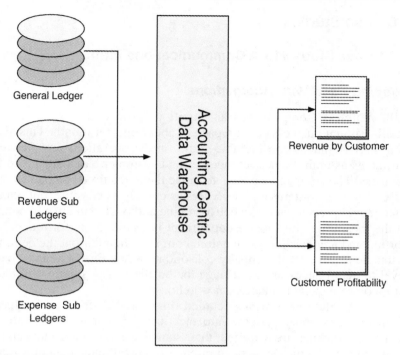

Note. Revenue and Expense Sub-Ledgers = Source of all supporting detail and revenue expense transactions.

Fig. 4.4. Profitability Example

Expense analysis could also be analyzed from the ACDW. This example we just went through was simplified to illustrate how an ACDW can improve over time as data sources are added. In practice, customer profitability is the most challenging analysis because there is no single repository of revenue and expenses. Complex OLTP systems, political territory, and lack of leadership make it challenging to build an ACDW. These challenges are why most companies are limited in their ability to perform enterprise analysis. However, progressive companies have demonstrated that it is possible to create an ACDW and have reaped many analytical fruits from their labor. A consolidation of the GL and sub-ledgers into a single repository provides management with an analysis tool to help answer questions about the business. Below are four case studies that provide additional examples of how an ACDW can be employed to solve performance analysis problems.

4.6 Case Studies[1]

4.6.1 Case Study #1 - A Communications Firm

Keeping Pace With Acquisitions

ABC Wireless Company has an ambitious growth strategy of acquiring small regional businesses - at a pace of about one per month. This acquisition activity places considerable strain on the operations and finance departments as both the new companies and customer bases are added to the business. The company's goal is to move these acquired companies over to ABC Wireless' systems and processes as quickly as possible, but often, the changeover process can take between nine and twelve months to complete. In the meantime, the finance department is unable to perform detailed reporting and analysis for the acquired company. In addition, the department is unable to get a total company consolidation in a timely manner with the level of detail necessary to manage the business. The solution: implementation of a financial management warehouse.

ABC Wireless now brings detailed financial data from all its disparate financial operational systems into the financial management warehouse. As new companies are acquired, their standard chart of accounts and other financial data is quickly mapped into the financial management warehouse structure. The Result: ABC Wireless can now pull in the acquired company's data in just 30 to 60 days. Now, the company the can perform financial reporting and analysis on whatever dimension necessary – geographic, divisional, product or corporate-wide. In addition, the acquired company's management staff has the ability to do reporting and analysis at a greatly improved level, a capability that offers immediate business insight into new opportunities that the parent company has by the acquisition. Best of all, this financial changeover occurs while the risk analysis group is leveraging the financial data in the warehouse for more informed and effective analysis and decision-making. Plus, ABC Wireless's marketing operations can also use much of this same data to do in-depth customer profitability analysis and create more focused and targeted campaigns.

4.6.2 Case Study #2 – A Retail Firm

Detailed View of Financial Activity Across Five Brands

Current Trends is a specialty retailer with five distinct brands represented in over 1,400 stores worldwide. The general brand managers for Current

---

[1] TeraData White Paper, Getting to The Bottom Line, September 2002.

Trends operate autonomously. Each organization has its own CFO who is responsible for analysis, financial systems management, and the consolidation and reporting of financial results. While this process was acceptable for each individual brand, Current Trends had other reporting issues, as it was unable to get a detailed enterprise view of the financial activity across the brands. In addition, auditing expenses were rapidly increasing due to the disparate nature of the underlying data and the rapid growth of this data. After its recent public offering, management at Current Trends felt that their financial processes needed to be streamlined; and the accuracy of the results needed to be more certain. As a major retailer, Current Trends had been operating a data warehouse for customer relationship management for several years. They made a decision to extend their warehouse for financial data to enable the finance operations across all brands to operate more efficiently. In making this move, the company was able to improve close process and overall analysis of data. However, the most measurable return has been in the area of audit. By using the warehouse, internal auditors are now able to perform ongoing trend analysis that will flag any deviations. After a deviation is identified, it is very easy for the auditor to quickly trace the transactions associated with the change and then return to the system of record to audit the actual transactions. This advancement has enabled auditing to perform more audits in less time. The data warehouse has allowed Current Trends to achieve significant savings in the audit process while still ensuring that the operations of the company are within standards.

4.6.3 Case Study #3 – A Transportation Firm

Detailed Accounts Receivable At Every Level

Ship-it-Fast is a transportation company that focuses on the consumer and small business market. The company ships millions of packages annually throughout the United States from small offices in more than 300 locations. With the high-volume transactional nature of its business, Ship-it-Fast saw a need for efficiency improvements in its accounts receivable. The company had multiple billing and shipment-tracking systems that collections clerks worked with to resolve outstanding invoices. Unfortunately, the accounts receivable operations were time-consuming and provided management with only a high-level view of accounts receivable status. Ship-it-Fast began a corporate-wide initiative to bring the detailed billing along with shipping data into a financial warehouse, including all of the detailed accounts receivable sub-ledger data. Armed with this information, Ship-it-Fast is now able to do detailed accounts receivable analysis at any level within the company and can easily identify areas where additional collection efforts need to be focused. In addition, the credit department can access all of the information about an account to become more effective in setting credit lines.

4.6.4 Case Study #4 - A Financial Services Firm

Adding Value to Analysis

Consumer First Bank has thrived for over 50 years by serving the needs of the consumer. One major challenge for the finance group was the amount of time they needed to produce the regulatory reports required by the FDIC and other governing agencies was growing significantly. Consumer First Bank had as many as five full-time analysts dedicated to meeting the special reporting requirements, making it a costly, time-consuming effort. But despite that investment of time and money, the reports the analysts generated were viewed as low value to the management team. Why? Because there was no easy way to understand the data the reports contained. Just as important, because of the complex and cumbersome reporting requirements, the financial analysts at Consumer First Bank would spend less than 20% of their time doing real value-added analysis. An initiative was started where Consumer First Bank decided to bring all of its financial data into one central data repository to better streamline the bank's financial reporting and analysis processes. As a result, the financial analysts create monthly, quarterly and annual standard and regulatory reports in 1/5 the time. Managers can now access the financial data from their desktops on a daily basis, giving them the ability to see potential problems and to take appropriate actions before the close of the month. Corporate management also has the ability to easily drill down to the details contained in the federal reports, which now bring real value. In addition, the bank's risk analysis group is leveraging the financial data in the warehouse for more informed and effective analysis and decision-making. Plus, Consumer First Bank's marketing operations can also use much of this same data to do in-depth customer profitability analysis and create more focused and targeted campaigns.

5 XBRL: A New Tool For Electronic Financial Reporting

Jia Wu and Miklos Vasarhelyi

Department of Accounting and Information Systems, Rutgers University, New Jersey

Abstract. eXtensible Business Reporting Language (XBRL) is a computer markup language for the purpose of corporate business reporting. XBRL is based on XML, which is the universal format for structuring documents and data on the web. In an XBRL compliant report, each financial and non-financial item is enclosed by a pair of XBRL tags, which describes the meaning of the item. These tags provide semantic information to the reports and make the financial reports not only human readable but also computer comprehensible. Leveraging the power of computers and the Internet, XBRL provides the financial community a standard to electronically and automatically prepare, publish, exchange, and extract financial statements. It is expected that XBRL will have widespread effects on financial reporting. First, preparing financial reports will be easier with XBRL. Financial information needs to be keyed into the computer only once. XBRL-ready accounting software can generate financial reports in different formats, such as for SEC filing, loan application, or corporate web reporting. It greatly reduces the manual input burden and entry errors. Second, the publication and exchange of financial reports can be facilitated. Because XBRL-compliant reports use standardized tags, the reports can be conveniently exchanged between different software and computers, independent of the software formats and computer platforms. The financial statement users can view an XBRL report as easily as browse a web page. Third, since XBRL-compliant reports are computer comprehensible, the financial information contained in these reports can be reliably and automatically extracted through XBRL-enabled applications for financial analyses. The cost of financial analyses can be largely reduced. Decision makers, investors, creditors and other financial statement users can be alleviated from the burden of manually analyzing the financial reports. Small- and mid-sized companies will have an equal opportunity to compete with industrial giants for the capital market. XBRL is undergoing fast development. Since its inception in 1998, over 170 companies and organizations including Big 4 accounting firms, FDIC, Microsoft, and SAP have joined the XBRL consortium. XBRL will become a key standard for electronic financial reporting in the near future.

5.1 Introduction

The objective of this chapter is to introduce a new accounting tool called XBRL that can help accountants, decision makers, analysts and regulators to prepare, exchange, extract and analyze financial reports. eXtensible Business Reporting Language, better known by its acronym XBRL, is an XML-based markup language for the purpose of electronic corporate financial reporting. XML is the universal format for structuring documents and data on the web. Basically speaking, in an XBRL-compliant report, each financial and non-financial line item is enclosed by a pair of XBRL tags, which describes the meaning of the enclosed item. These tags provide semantic information to the reports and make the financial reports not only human readable but also computer comprehensible. Leveraging the power of computers and the Internet, XBRL provides the financial community a standard to electronically and automatically prepare, publish, exchange, and extract financial statements.

It is expected that XBRL will have widespread effects on financial reporting. The beneficiaries of XBRL include but are not limited to accountants, company decision makers, creditors, financial analysts, and regulators. First, for accountants, preparing financial reports can be facilitated with XBRL. Financial information needs to be keyed into the computer system only once. XBRL-ready accounting software can generate financial reports in different formats, such as for SEC filing, loan application, or corporate web reporting. It greatly reduces the manual input burden and entry errors. Second, for financial statement users, the publication and exchange of financial reports can be simplified. Because XBRL-compliant reports use standardized tags, the reports can be conveniently exchanged between different software and computers, independent of the software formats and computer platforms. The financial statement users can view an XBRL report as easily as browse a web page. Third, since XBRL-compliant reports are computer comprehensible, the financial information contained in these reports can be reliably and automatically extracted through XBRL-enabled applications for financial analyses. The cost of financial analyses can be largely reduced. Investors, creditors and other financial statement users can be alleviated from the burden of manually analyzing the financial reports. Small- and mid-sized companies will have an equal opportunity to compete with industrial giants for the capital market.

XBRL is royalty-free and can be integrated with market-available software, which reduce the cost of using XBRL to a minimum. Users do not need to pay royalty fee to apply XBRL standards in their financial reports. Neither do the companies need to overhaul their existing information system to use XBRL. XBRL add-on modules can be imbedded in market-available software. Microsoft, together with PricewaterhouseCoopers and NASDAQ, has developed a pilot XBRL application called "Excel Investor's Assistant" that can be imbedded in Excel. It can switch financial reports between traditional, Excel and XBRL formats with only a few mouse clicks. Ratio analysis, which can be presented in charts and diagrams, can be completed in just a few seconds. SAP and PeopleSoft have also added XBRL functionality into their ERP (enterprise resource planning) packages. XBRL-compliant financial reports can be created automatically since all the required financial data are available within the ERP systems. Moreover, it is expected that an XBRL-compliant report can be generated as easily with a few mouse clicks in the near future.

In this chapter, we briefly discuss the history of XBRL development in section two. Then, in section three, we compare HTML, XML, and XBRL to give a clear picture of the differences and similarities between these three markup languages. In section four, the three components of XBRL are discussed. We discuss how XBRL can aid business intelligence in section five. We explain how XBRL works in this section as well. The benefits of using XBRL for financial reports preparers and users are explored. Section six primarily provides an XBRL vendor list. The last section concludes the chapter and points out some potential issues that need to be resolved for XBRL development.

5.2 A Brief History of XBRL Development

The start of XBRL can be traced back to April 1998, when a CPA named Charles Hoffman began to develop prototypes for financial reporting using XML. American Institute of Certified Public Accountants (AICPA) supported and funded Hoffman's initiative. In June 1999, Hoffman and several other people created a business plan for XML-based financial statements, called eXtensible Financial Reporting Markup Language (XFRML). Later in the year, they changed the name to XBRL since business reporting covers a broader range of reports than financial reporting.

XBRL is undergoing fast development. The number on the XBRL steering committee increased from 12 in 1998 to 220 in mid-2003, including many leading accounting, technology, and government organizations. The jurisdictions of XBRL have expanded from the U.S. into 12 European and Asian-Pacific countries. The first taxonomy---XBRL CI taxonomy, which serves commercial and industrial companies (representing 80% of publicly-traded companies in the U.S.), has been completed. XBRL specification for general ledger is currently available. It can tag the data at the general ledger level and facilitate data transmission between the transaction reporting and business reporting. XBRL specification has grown from 1.0 version to 2.1 version now.

Additionally, a few companies have begun to adopt XBRL in their financial reporting. In February 2001, Morgan Stanley became the first company that tags its financial statements in XBRL for SEC filing and web reporting. Microsoft became the first technology company that uses XBRL for financial reporting in March 2002. The fast development and adoption of XBRL indicate the great potential role for XBRL to play among the business reporting world in the near future. More and more software vendors have joined the development of XBRL-enabling software. Microsoft, PriceWaterhouseCoopers, and NASDAQ launched the first XBRL pilot project in July 2002. UBMatrix, CaseWare and many other companies offer products that can create XBRL-compliant reports as well as XBRL taxonomies.

To explain XBRL clearly, we need to discuss HTML and XML. HTML, XML and XBRL are all members of the markup language family. Markup language is different from other computer languages such as C and Java. It is not used for building computer applications. Instead, markup language is used for formatting and structuring data in a document and explaining the meaning of the data to the computer. Simply speaking, markup language adds tags to data items. These tags either tell how data should be formatted and presented to the user, such as HTML tags, or indicate the meaning and function of the data item, (in other words, it adds meta-data to the document) such as XML tags. Markup languages tend to be both platform-independent and language-independent. Markup language runs on various operation systems such as Windows, Unix, Linux, etc. It also adopts Unicode, which can represent hundreds of written languages in the world including Asian, Arabic and European languages. Generally speaking, markup language has more flexibility and interchangeability than other computer languages.

Table 5.1. Timeline for XBRL history and development

Time	Achievements
04/1998	Charles Hoffman began to investigate the possible use of XML for financial reporting.
06/1999	Business plan for XFRML was created with the support of AICPA. Later XFRML changed its name to XBRL.
10/1999	First XBRL was held and the development of CI taxonomy was launched. XBRL committee had 12 members.
07/2000	XBRL specification 1.0 and CI taxonomy was released
02/2001	Morgan Stanley became the 1st company to tag its financial information in XBRL
06/2001	XBRL for general ledger taxonomy was released
12/2001	XBRL specification 2.0 was released
03/2002	Microsoft became the 1st technology company that reports its financial data in XBRL
07/2002	Microsoft, PWC and NASDAQ launched the XBRL pilot project
04/2003	XBRL steering committee has 220 members

5.2.1 HTML

HTML is the most common form of markup language in use today. HTML is used for web page presentation purpose. All the web pages we can browse are built in compliance with the HTML standards. Compared with XML, HTML has a limited number of tags. These tags tell the web browser a wide spectrum of presentation parameters, including font type, font size, font color, paragraph break, and other format information of a web page. To illustrate, let us look at an HTML snippet.

```
<H1 ALIGN=center>What is HTML</H1>
<p>HTML is a <strong>Markup Language</strong>.</p>
<P> The book <em>HTML For Dummies</em> tells you in de-
tail about HTML.
```

Each line item in the above snippet is enclosed by a pair of tags, one beginning tag and one ending tag. The ending tag is indicated by an additional back slash. The tag <H1 ALIGN=center> tells the browser that the data enclosed should be presented in Header Font Number 1 and aligned to the center. The tags <p> and </p> represent the start and the end of a paragraph respectively. The tag <strong> tells the browser to display the enclosed text in Bold fonts. Similarly, <em> tag tells the browser the enclosed words are in Italic font type. As we can see, all the above tags are concerned with presentation format issues. A web browser such as Internet Explorer can process these tags and present the following web page to the user.

5.2.2 XML

XML, the acronym of eXtensible Markup Language, is a more powerful data-centric markup language than HTML. eXtensible denotes that XML is extensible to many derivative languages for specific industries or cross industries. For example, chemXML is designed specifically for chemical industry; ebXML is defined for e-business transactions. Unlike HTML, which uses predefined tags, XML allows users to do their own tag definitions. These tags describe the semantics and structure of data in a document, which can be understood and processed by computer applications. With the growth of e-business and integration of supply chain partners, there is a rising demand for a common computer language for companies to communicate with each other both vertically and horizontally. The emergence of XML can satisfy this demand. Industry-specific as well as cross-industry XML-based languages can facilitate data exchange and business transactions, allowing clients to manipulate data views and permitting intelligent systems to customize information.

When writing XML documents, the user needs to define tags following a standard called Document Type Definition (DTD) to ensure the client computer application can recognize and validate the XML document. DTD is currently fading out and will eventually be replaced by the more flexible, descriptive and intuitive XML schema. DTDs and schemas are usually stored in a central repository called namespace. All user-defined tag information can be found and retrieved from namespace. At the client side, an XML parser is required to recognize the tags.

To illustrate, let us look at an XML example:

```
<?xml version="1.0" standalone="yes"?>
<!DOCTYPE address_book SYSTEM "abml.dtd"
<address_book>
<entry>
<first_name>Jia</first_name>
<last_name>Wu</last_name>
<nickname>Jack</nickname>
```

```
<organization>Rutgers University</organization>
<address type="home">
      <street>180 University Avenue</street>
      <city>Newark</city>
      <state>New Jersey</state>
      <postal_code>07102</postal_code>
      <country>USA</country>
</address>
</entry>
</address_book>
```

The XML version and its DTD are specified at the beginning of the document. Each data element in the above example is bounded by tags, which tell the computer applications what are the meanings and uses of these data. If the tags are absent from the above example, computer applications will have great difficulty in understanding and processing these data though these data may still be intelligible to human users.

5.3 XBRL

XBRL is an XML-based markup language for the purpose of financial reporting. It inherits the attributes of XML and specializes in financial reporting. XBRL provides a standard method for the financial community to prepare, publish, extract and exchange financial information electronically. Through XBRL, users can prepare digital financial reports, which include the balance sheet, income statement, statement of owner's equity, and statement of cash flows. In addition, non-financial information, such as management notes and auditor's reports, can also be incorporated into XBRL-based financial reports.

XBRL is made up of three technical components-specification, taxonomy and instance documents. Specification and taxonomy are guidelines for XBRL tag definition. A detailed description of these three components is provided in the following section. XBRL tags provide semantic information for the enclosed data item. These tags tell the computer applications what the enclosed item is about. To illustrate, let us take a look at the following code snippet.

```
<?xbrl version="2.0" ?>
<group xmlns:ci=http://www.xbrl.org/us/gaap/ci/2002-07-
31> entity="NASDAQ:Microsoft" period="2002-12-31" sche-
maLocation="http://www.xbrl.org/us/gaap/ci/2002-07-31
scaleFactor="3" precision="9" type="statements"
unit="ISO4217:USD" decimalPattern="#.#" formatName="">
```

```
<group type="ci:Balance Sheet.Assets.CurrentAssets">
<Cash>3016</Cash>
<ShortTermInvestments>35636</ShortTermInvestments>
<AccountReceivable>5129</AccountReceivable>
<Inventories>673</Inventories>
```

<?xbrl version="2.0" ?> indicates the version of XBRL. The next line
<group xmlns:ci="http://www.xbrl.org/us/gaap/ci/2002-07-31" displays
the location of the namespace for XBRL and the document's taxonomy,
which is CI taxonomy under U.S. accounting principles (GAAP). An
XBRL-enabled application can retrieve taxonomy information from this
location and parse the data accordingly. The next several lines tell us that
the reporting company is Microsoft, and the reporting period ends at the
end of year 2002. The tags such as <Cash>, <ShortTermInvestments>, and
<Inventories> tell us what accounts the enclosed numbers represent. These
tags can be read straightforwardly not only by human beings but also by
XBRL-enabled computer applications. As we can see, XBRL is very similar to XML; but it is specifically concerned with financial reporting issues.

Table 5.2. A comparison of three markup languages

	HTML	XML	XBRL
Function	Web page presentation	Data processing	Financial data processing
Flexibility	Limited	Great	Great
Tags	Predefined	User defined	User defined
Components	Tags	Schema (DTD), tags	Specification, taxonomy, instance document, tags
Parser	Web Browser	XML-enabled applications	XBRL-enabled applications
Similarities	Plat-form independent, language independent, easy for document exchange		

5.3.1 XBRL Components

XBRL consists of three major components: the XBRL specification, XBRL schema, and XBRL instance documents.

5.3.2 XBRL Specification

XBRL specification aims at standardizing the creation of XBRL taxonomies and instance documents. XBRL allows each user to define his/her own set of meta-data tags. However, unless these tags are created following certain uniform standard, information exchange would be inhibited since the tags defined by one user may be incompatible with and incomprehensible to the other user's application. XBRL specification is such a uniform standard that provides guideline on how to design taxonomies and instance documents in XBRL. It defines XBRL elements and attributes that can be used to prepare, exchange, and analyze financial reports, ensuring that user-defined tags do not overlap or clash. These elements and attributes include syntax of instance documents, syntax of taxonomies, semantics of instance documents, and semantics of taxonomies.

Table 5.3. Example of XBRL specfication elements

	Elements	Examples	Meanings
Syntax of instance document	Company ID, reporting period, entity names	NASDAQ:MSFT	The company with NASDAQ ticker symbol MSFT
		CUSIP:41009876AB	The entity with CUSIP number 41009876AB
Syntax of taxonomies	Elements, Monetary and shares datatypes, rollup	<element name= "CurrentAsset.CashandCashEquivalents" type= "xbrl:monetary"/> <element name="significantAccountingPolicies-Note.stockBasedCompensationPolicy" type= "string"/>	Define the elements. Note that both the colloquial name and its immediate parent are included in the element

5.3.3 XBRL Taxonomies

XBRL.org defines taxonomies as a "standard description and classification system for the contents of accounting reports. XBRL taxonomies can be regarded as extensions of XML Schema. Information producers take their accounting information from their accounting system and code it in a standard fashion as described by the taxonomy." Taxonomies are used for different types of business reports. As we know, accounting can be divided into several subsets, including financial accounting, management accounting, SEC reporting, IRS reporting, etc. Each subset usually requires a special set of accounting terms, policies, and methods for reporting. Additionally, different accounting standards may require different taxonomies. For instance, U.S. General Accepted Accounting Principles (GAAP) are different from International Accounting Standards (IAS). Therefore, two taxonomies may be needed to prepare the business reports in accordance with these two different standards.

Consequently, XBRL communities have determined to create one taxonomy for each accounting subset. For example, there are taxonomies for general ledger, financial reporting, management reporting and SEC certification. Currently, two taxonomies are available to the market. One is U.S. GAAP CI taxonomy, which deals with financial reporting for commercial and industrial companies under GAAP. The other is GL taxonomy, which is concerned with reporting at the transaction level. A number of new XBRL taxonomies, including taxonomy for management notes and discussions, taxonomy for SEC certification, and taxonomy for IAS accounting, are either under development or under review.

5.3.4 XBRL Instance Document

An instance document is an XBRL-coded business report. It can be an XBRL-tagged balance sheet, an XBRL-tagged debt covenant report, or an XBRL-tagged SEC 10Q filing.

XBRL specification, XBRL taxonomies and XBRL instance documents constitute the XBRL world. An XBRL instance document includes the XBRL specification version ID as well as the name and location of XBRL taxonomies. Upon receiving an XBRL instance document, the XBRL-enabled application can process the instance document in accordance with the matching specification and taxonomies.

5.4 XBRL and Business Intelligence

XBRL has far-reaching implications for the entire business community. XBRL can dramatically facilitate business reporting. The processes of preparing, presenting, extracting, and analyzing financial reports can be largely automated using XBRL-enabled applications. Both financial report preparers and users can harvest the huge benefits from XBRL.

5.4.1 Benefits For Financial Report Preparers

Accounting computerization has already for a large measure alleviated accountants' workload. XBRL can further increase the efficiency and effectiveness of accountants' work. XBRL can facilitate the preparation of financial reports. Traditional financial reporting requires multiple inputs of financial data for different types of financial reports. Accountants need to input a company's entire set of financial and non-financial data for its annual report to be placed on the company web site. They may input the same set of data again to prepare an SEC 10K filing or a credit report filing for bank loan application because these reports have different data and format requirements. These multiple entries of data into the computer system not only waste time and labor but also result in many input errors. XBRL eliminates this redundant task. Since XBRL applies standard tags to the raw financial data, an XBRL-enabled application can understand and process the data. The same set of data can be used across applications. Accountants can enter data once into the computer system and use it multiple times. It would be time saving, effort saving, and paper saving for accountants to prepare different business reports for different purposes using different formats. It is comparable to having a word document file that can be converted effortlessly into txt, pdf, and rtf documents.

XBRL can be integrated with ERP systems, corporate data warehouses, and other corporate information systems. ERP systems and corporate data warehouse can capture data at the transaction level and feed the data into XBRL-ready applications. Then the information can be tagged in XBRL using XBRL GL (general ledger) taxonomy. Afterwards, the general ledger level XBRL-compliant report can be further processed, consolidated, and customized for different user needs. The entire process can be computer automated without human intervention. This practice will further reduce the costs for financial report preparation.

5.4.2 Benefits for Business Report Users

In addition to facilitating accountants' business reports preparation, XBRL can also streamline the extraction and analysis of business reports for a large variety of financial report users. These users can include company decision makers, auditors, creditors, financial analysts, stockholders, as well as regulators.

Different financial report users usually have different interests in the financial reports. Local managers may be interested in the sale volume and inventory turnover ratio. Top decision makers may be interested in the overall profit of the company. Auditors may be more interested in knowing if the company hidden financial problems. Creditors will be interested if the company will be able to pay back the loans. Stockholders and financial analysts are usually interested in the company's earnings, stock dividends and growth potential. Regulators usually pay more attention to if the company has complied with the laws and regulations. For example, IRS officials may pay attention to the company's taxable income and payments.

Currently, these users have to manually extract relevant data from business reports and then import these data into various computer applications for analyses. A bottleneck lies in this manual data extraction process. Computerized data extraction is hampered for four major reasons. First, not all the companies use the same set of accounting terms. For example, "cash" and "cash and equivalents" can mean the same accounting item (Kogan et. al, 2002). It would be easy for human users to identify but will cause confusion for computer programs. Second, what makes things worse, there is no consistency for the report layout and format. The length of an annual report can vary from 5-7 pages to 70-80 pages. An income statement can be found at the beginning, middle, or end of an annual report. A line item, such as inventory, can be located at the 3rd, 4th, or even 5th line under the current assets account. The inconsistency in accounting terms and report formats prohibits the automation of data extraction and analyses from business reports.

However, with the adoption of XBRL, these problems can be easily solved. If financial reports are encoded in XBRL tags, XBRL-enabled computer applications can quickly scan the tags in the report, locate the desired line items, and extract the data for analyses. Since these XBRL tags are clearly-defined standard tags, the computer application will not have any confusion in identifying the needed data. The financial report users only need to inform the application what type of information they are interested in, and the application can extract the relevant information for them automatically. Thus, the time for data extraction can be greatly reduced by using XBRL.

XBRL can also facilitate the information exchange of financial reports. Traditional financial reports have limitation in information exchange. First, financial reports are usually prepared in different file formats by different computer applications. For example, a study of online financial reporting found that the formats of online financial reports include pdf, word document, txt, excel, and html. These files have limited compatibility. Smooth information exchange is rendered impossible by these incompatible file formats. Moreover, different platforms, such as Windows 98, Windows 2000, Windows XP, Unix and Linux, have created more barriers for financial report exchange between different platform-dependent applications. Second, financial reports can be prepared in different languages, including but not limited to English, German, French, Chinese, Japanese, and Korean. Current financial analysis software suites are language dependent. Most of these applications can only process financial reports in one language, mostly in English. A huge portion of non-U.S.-based capital markets is excluded from the financial community due to language barrier. Last, but not least, different accounting standards, regulations and policies have prohibited seamless comparison between financial reports prepared under different accounting standards. U.S. GAAP, International Accounting Standards (IAS), and other proprietary national standards such as Japan's accounting principle prevent expedited exchange and analysis of the financial reports because the information contained in these financial reports is not comparable if the user is not familiar with these different standards.

XBRL can nicely resolve the above-mentioned problems. First, if a financial report is coded in XBRL tags, the conversion of this report into other formats can be as easy as several mouse clicks, using the XBRL-ready application. Microsoft has already added an XML module into its Office XP software package. It is expected that an XBRL module for Office applications will soon be available. On the other hand, the conversion of financial report in various formats into XBRL-compliant document is also effortless. University of Kansas has developed a prototype of an XBRL conversion tool, which can convert a text-format financial report into an XBRL-encoded one. UBMatrix and CaseWare are among the increasing number of software vendors who are developing XBRL-enabled applications to create XBRL-encode financial reports.

Second, in order to overcome the language barrier, XBRL uses Unicode as its default font. Unicode can support over 120 languages, which makes XBRL language independent. Hence, even if a human user does not understand the language in the financial report, an XBRL-ready computer application can automatically translate and analyze the financial reports for the user.

Third, the barrier caused by the different accounting standards can also be removed by XBRL. Each XBRL-compliant financial report contains taxonomy information, which indicates the type and location of the taxonomy. Financial reports based on different accounting standards use different XBRL taxonomies. An XBRL-ready computer application can retrieve the matching taxonomy from the designated location and process data contained in the financial reports accordingly.

In summary, XBRL is a language independent, platform-independent, accounting-policy independent standard. Its adoption can facilitate financial report preparation, extraction, exchange and analysis. Accountants can prepare financial reports with ease. More frequent financial reporting is made possible by XBRL. Using XBRL-enabled software, Managers can have both very detailed and highly consolidated view of a company's financial data. More effective decisions can be made. Auditors can integrate their auditing software with XBRL business reports. Financial data can be electronically fed into the auditing software as opposed to manual input. Thus, auditing sample size can be dramatically increased, and the audit risk can be lowered. Frauds and errors can be detected more promptly. With XBRL, investors and creditors can follow more companies, including domestic and international, large and small ones. The capital and loan market will become more rational and efficient. Similarly, regulators can monitor more companies' financial performance.

5.5 XBRL Software Vendors

Although XBRL is a recent innovation, several software companies have already developed XBRL-enabled applications. A well-known application is a jointly-developed project called "Excel Investor's Assistant" by Microsoft, PricewaterhouseCoopers, and NASDAQ. This application can pull financial data from the Internet, build XBRL instance documents, and conduct financial analyses of 21 selected companies. The beauty of this application is that it is a macro which runs on the widely-used Excel. Therefore, no new software is required. It can prepare XBRL instance documents, perform ratio analysis, compare up to five companies' financial measures, and analyze financial and nonfinancial information. Every process and task can be completed in seconds.

A number of business software vendors have developed XBRL-enabled applications. Generally speaking, current market available applications can be categorized into two major groups: XBRL instance document builder and XBRL taxonomy builder.

Fig. 5.1 shows the initial startup screen of the application. It allows the user to input the fiscal period and company names for analysis. In this case, Microsoft and Intel are added for analysis. The fiscal period is from 1st quarter in 1997 to 4th quarter in 2002. The application retrieved the XBRL documents for these two companies from the Internet immediately after the "Build Analyses" button was pressed.

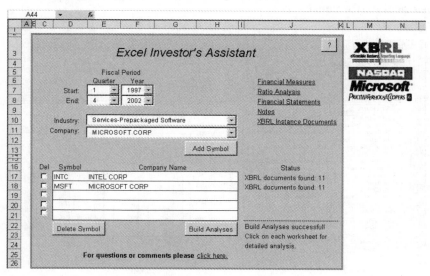

Fig. 5.1. Excel Investor's Assistant initial screen

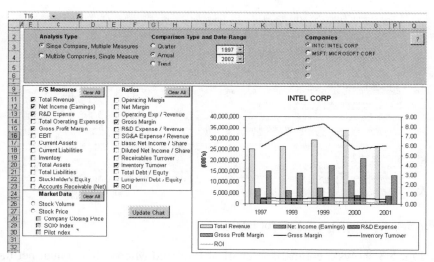

Fig. 5.2. Time series comparison

Fig. 5.2 displays the screenshot a time series comparison chart of Intel Corp's annual financial measures and ratios, such as total revenue, gross profit margin, inventory turnover, and ROI. Through the charts, financial statement users can instantly compare the current financial performance to historical performance.

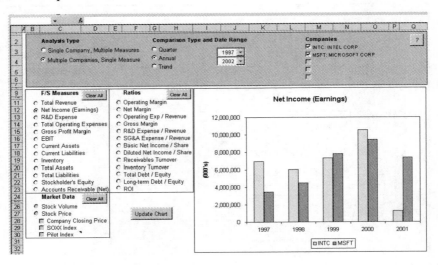

Fig. 5.3. Comparison chart

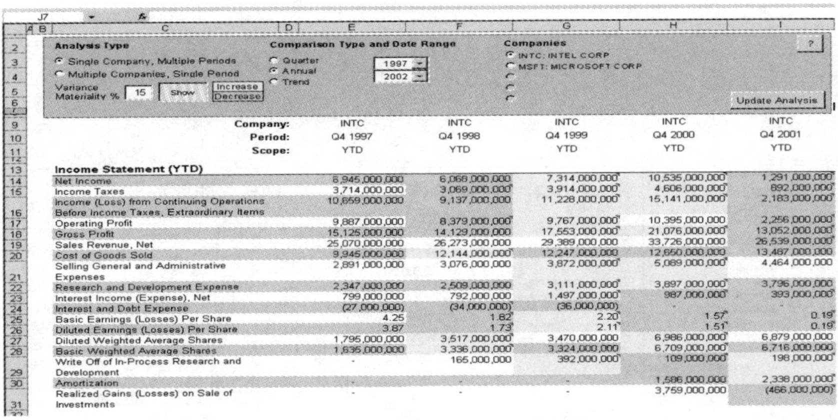

Fig. 5.4. Accounting numbers for Intel

Fig. 5.3 shows a comparison chart of Intel and Microsoft's annual net incomes from 1997 to 2002. The financial measure comparison between these two companies is clearly visualized through the charts. Fig. 5.4 presents the accounting numbers for Intel. The increase and decrease of accounting numbers can be indicated by different colors. The variance percentage will pop up if the mouse is moved over the appropriate numbers.

XBRL instance document builders focus on making XBRL-compliant business reports. These applications either generate XBRL-compliant business reports directly from the corporate data warehouse such as PeopleSoft and SAP's financial modules and CaseWare's **Working Papers**; or the applications convert traditional business reports into XBRL-compliant reports such as Hyperion Solutions' **Hyperion Reports** and PricewaterhouseCoopers' **EdgarScan**.

XBRL taxonomy builders allow users to create their own taxonomy. As we know, variations exist in different business reporting requirements for different business entities. Standard taxonomy is not all inclusive, which may not always satisfy business reporting needs. Sometimes an organization needs to create its own taxonomy. XBRL taxonomy building applications can help to create new taxonomies, ensuring that the taxonomies created conform to XBRL specifications and can be mapped into the company's database. This type of application includes UBMatrix's **Taxonomy Builder**, DecisionSoft's **X-Meta**, and Fujitsu Ltd's **Taxonomy Editor**.

In addition, another group of XBRL vendors provides a repository for XBRL instance documents. These vendors include **EdgarOnline** and **OneSource Information Services**.

5.6 Conclusion

XBRL can facilitate financial report preparation, exchange, extraction and analysis. Business report preparation and analysis will be much faster and less costly than ever. The adoption of XBRL technology has far-reaching benefits for accountants, decision makers, creditors and regulators. Financial data only needs to be entered into the computer system once and can be used multiple times. The workload for accountants can be reduced. Financial reports in XBRL can be easily exchanged through the Internet. Data extraction and analysis from XBRL-coded financial reports can be largely automated by computer applications. Financial report users can analyze more efficiently and effectively.

XBRL will invoke great changes and create new opportunities in the financial reporting community. For accountants, since financial reports can be prepared more efficiently with XBRL, it is possible that more frequent and detailed financial reporting will be made. As a result, financial reports will be more transparent and informative. For company management, they can know more accurately how their unit performs as compared with other units and previous periods. Better decisions can be made based on the information contained in XBRL reports. For auditors, XBRL reduces the opportunities for management fraud and manipulation of accounting numbers. Additionally, audit sampling and testing are facilitated with XBRL. These improvements will dramatically reduce auditor risks and cut the auditor's workload. It is also expected that XBRL will enable continuous auditing. Auditors can use XBRL to perform audits on a high frequency or even real time basis. With XBRL, creditors can closely monitor a large group of clients' debt covenant compliances at the same time. They can make better and faster credit decisions and increase the customer base. For investors, XBRL can help them to follow more companies than before and improve their investment decisions. Mid- and small-sized companies can compete with large companies for the capital market, since the cost of investment analysis will be reduced by using XBRL. Regulators will also have better control of their subjects since XBRL can provide improved monitoring functionality.

In order for XBRL to be widely employed in financial reporting, a few issues need to be solved. First, good taxonomies need to be created. Only two taxonomies, CI and GL, are available. We need more taxonomies to satisfy various reporting requirements. Second, regulators need to encourage the use of XBRL in financial reports. Only with the regulators' help can XBRL be quickly adopted. Third, more user-friendly XBRL-enabled software must be developed. Many financial statement preparers and users are not very technically inclined. The promotion of XBRL in the financial reporting community relies heavily on user-friendly and affordable XBRL applications. If these issues are resolved, we are sure to see that XBRL will be widely used in the near future.

Table 5.4. XBRL vendor list (Adapted from "XBRL Progress Report---April 2003")

Vendor Name	Application	Function	Web Site
CaseWare International	CaseWare Working Papers; CaseWare IDEA	Supporting XBRL GL compliant files, Working papers can create XBRL tagged instance documents	www.caseware-idea.com
Creative Solutions	Write-up Solutions; Trial Balance Solutions	Creating XBRL-tagged financial documents	www.CreativeSolutions.com

Table 5.4. (cont.)

Vendor Name	Application	Function	Web Site
DecisionSoft	X-Meta; XBRL Took Kit	X-Meta can create taxonomies; Took Kit can validate taxonomy and instance documents	http://xbrl.decisionsoft.com
EDGAR Online	XBRL Repository	A central repository for companies to submit their XBRL business reports, or promote XBRL applications	www.xbrl-express.com
Fijitsu Limited	Interstage XWander, Taxonomy Editor, XBRL Converter, XBRL Validator	Creating XBRL taxonomies, convert reports into XBRL- compliant documents, and validate XBRL documents regarding syntax, schema, and XBRL semantics	http://xml.fujitsu.com/en/tech/xbrl/index.html
Hyperion Solutions	Hyperion Reports	Creating XBRL instance documents under existing reporting paradigm	www.hyperion.com
iLumen	iMonitor	Its financial monitoring and benchmarking network supports XBRL and can convert multiple-format reports into XBRL	www.iLumen.com
FRx	FRx Fianncial Reporter 6.5	It can create XBRL instance document and supports XML; providing financial reporting and analysis function for leading accounting and general ledger applications	www.frxsoftware.com
Navision	Navision	It can import taxonomies and generate XBRL reports	www.navision.com
OneSource Information Services	Applink	It offers XBRL reports for 25,000 global public companies with 5 years annual and quarterly data	www.onesource.com
Oracle	Financial Statement Generator	It can import XBRL taxonomy and use it to create XBRL-compliant reports	www.oracle.com

Table 5.4. (cont.)

Vendor Name	Application	Function	Web Site
PeopleSoft	Financial Management Solutions	It has XBRL functionality which can create XBRL instance documents for SEC filing and investors' business reporting.	www.peoplesoft.com
PPA GmbH, Germany	PPA Benchbase	It provides 7000 German companies' financial reports in XBRL format	www.ppaworld.com/xbrl
Pricewater-houseCoppers	EdgarScan	It can extract filings from SEC server and convert them into XBRL-compliant reports	http://edgarscan.pwcglobal.com/XBRL/XBRLatPwC.html
SAP AG	Strategic Enterprise Management	It can import taxonomy, pull data from data warehouse, and create XBRL business reports.	www.sap.com/financials
Semansys Technologies B.V.	Semansys XBRL Composer	It integrates XBRL with business intelligence. It supports taxonomies management, XBRL report creation, reception and interpretation.	www.semansys.com
Universal Business Matrix, LLC	UBmatrix Taxonomy Builder, UBmatrix Studio	It is a comprehensive suite that can support XBRL taxonomy building, instance document creation, editing and validating	www.ubmatrix.com
XBI Software Inc	Convenant Monitor	It can use XBRL to monitor clients' banking covenants.	www.xbisoftware.com

6 Online Analytical Processing in Accounting

Darpan S. Jhaveri

General Accounting Department, Bristol Myers Squibb Co., New Jersey

Abstract. In this chapter we ascertain the significance of OLAP (On-line Analytical Processing) and its various tools useful for Accounting. We start with a brief history of OLAP. Then we define OLAP. We move on to analyze various types of OLAP- the Relational OLAP (ROLAP), the Multi-dimensional OLAP (MOLAP), the Hybrid OLAP (HOLAP) and the Desktop OLAP (DOLAP). We discuss some applications of OLAP tools in various areas of accounting. Finally, through a series of comparisons, we evaluate the different types of OLAP and select the type that could suit your needs.

An accountant commonly faces questions such as, "What is the profitability for fourth quarter across the X region for main products A and B?" This type of question requires multiple dimensions or perspectives on the data, such as time, region, and products. Multidimensional analysis is the process of analyzing data across multiple dimensions, such as sales per month for each product in each region, product performance by city by store, etc. Compared to the spreadsheet, which allows analysis of only two dimensions at a time, multidimensional analysis allows users to analyze data from an infinite number of viewpoints. An OLAP system would allow multidimensional analysis enabling you to gain insight into data through fast, consistent, interactive access to a wide variety of possible views of information. It allows you to view your data in the same way you think of your business and to see what is ultimately driving your business.

6.1 Introduction

Today's business world is faced with tremendous competition and information overload. Most of the enterprises have loads of data and statistical information; but they are not able to use it to the full potential for their business purpose. They have already reached a stage where they possess organized and ready-to-use information. In the past, enterprises used query and reporting tools based on SQL for simple access to business information. What they now need is a system that would enable them to use available information in an intelligent manner and provide results, which could give them a competitive edge over other industry players. Today, enterprises require tools for business performance management and business optimization as they strive to become more competitive in the global economy. The current business environment is characterized by break-through technologies, intense competition, frequent innovations and strict regulatory compliance. Business intelligence tools have tremendous potential to utilize available information in order to help enterprises remain competitive and reap good profits. These requirements are driving the demand for the On-Line Analytical Processing (OLAP) tools that are better suited to meet these requirements as they enable decision support, trend analysis, monitoring strategic business decisions and what-if analysis. OLAP is becoming the Business Intelligence technology of choice in various areas of business whether it is Operations, Finance and Accounting, Marketing, Planning, etc.

6.2 Evolution of OLAP

OLAP's history can be traced back 40 years (see Table 6.1). OLAP is based on multidimensional analysis, the history of which goes back to 1962, with the publication of Ken Iverson's book, *A Programming Language* (APL). However, APL was too complicated for anybody other than the professional programmers. By 1970, a more application-oriented multidimensional product – EXPRESS - had made its first appearance. More multidimensional products appeared in the 1980s, which aimed at functional applications. These brought forth many modern day concepts, like full screen multidimensional viewing, data editing, automatic recalculation, integration with relational data and client/server computing. By mid-1980s, the term EIS (Executive Information System) had been born. However, the EIS did not support ad-hoc decisions and what-if analysis. By late 1980s, spreadsheets were becoming dominant in end-user analysis. Using Windows, Excel became a big threat to spreadsheet players. Excel includes sophisticated version of PivotTables capable of acting as a desktop OLAP.

In August 1993, the late Dr. E.F. Codd, published a white paper, entitled *"Providing OLAP (On-line Analytical Processing) to User-Analysts: An IT Mandate"*. This paper coined the term 'OLAP' and brought multidimensional analysis to the attention of more people than ever before (Codd,

1993). Since 1993, there has been significant growth in the OLAP market and major advancement of this technology. Many tools have been introduced, and the past decade and current industry trends show the biggest-ever growth of multidimensional applications.

Table 6.1. OLAP History (Pendse, 2003)

Period	Event	Remarks
1962	Publication of A Programming Language by Ken Iverson	First multidimensional language.
1970	EXPRESS - made its first appearance.	First application-oriented multidimensional product - One of the major OLAP technologies
1982	Comshare System W available	First OLAP tool aimed at financial applications.
1984	Metaphor launched	First ROLAP aimed at marketing applications.
1985	Pilot Command Center launched	First explicit EIS product; introduced many concepts that are recognizable in today's OLAP products.
Late 1980s	Multidimensional spreadsheet world	This approach of bringing multidimensionality to spreadsheet users became popular
1991	IBM acquired Metaphor	The first of many OLAP products to change hands.
1993	Codd white paper coined the OLAP term	This white paper brought multidimensional analysis to the attention of more people than ever before.
Post 1993	Significant growth in the OLAP market	The past decade and current industry trends show the biggest-ever growth of multidimensional applications.

The development of OLAP tools has been influenced by at least two aspects of corporate information stores that have changed dramatically over the past decade. First, the substantial growth in the amount of data collected and stored by organizations; and second, the expansion in requirements for access to corporate data. Increasing numbers of non-technical users have resulted in new requirements for cleaner data, better analysis tools, and faster response time. In next section, we understand what OLAP means and how it works.

6.3 What is OLAP?

OLAP designates a category of applications and technologies that allow the collection, storage, manipulation and reproduction of multidimensional data, with the goal of multidimensional analysis. To make sense of change in an ever-changing world, you need to understand and even anticipate change. You need the flexibility to look at the information from all sides and in different dimensions. You need to ask "What if?" instead of "What happened?" OLAP gives you the power to retrieve answers to such business questions quickly and easily. The OLAP system extracts data from the data warehouse and manipulates it to give the results quickly depending upon the query submitted by the user.

OLAP can be defined in just five key words: *Fast Analysis of Shared Multidimensional Information - (FASMI)* (Pendse, 2003). This definition has now been widely adopted.

- *FAST* means that the system is targeted to deliver most responses to users within about five seconds, with the simplest analyses taking no more than one second and few taking more than 20 seconds.
- *ANALYSIS* means that the system can cope with any business logic and statistical analysis that is relevant for the application and the user and keep it easy enough for the target user. It allows the user to define new *ad hoc* calculations as part of the analysis and to report on the data in any desired way, without having to program.
- *SHARED* means that the system implements all the security requirements for confidentiality, and if multiple write access is needed, the system handles multiple updates in a timely and secure manner.
- *MULTIDIMENSIONAL* is the key element. The system provides a multidimensional conceptual view of the data, including full support for hierarchies and multiple hierarchies, as this view is certainly the most logical way to analyze businesses and organizations.
- *INFORMATION* is all of the data and derived information needed, wherever it is and however much is relevant for the application. The largest OLAP products can hold at least a thousand times as much data as the smallest.

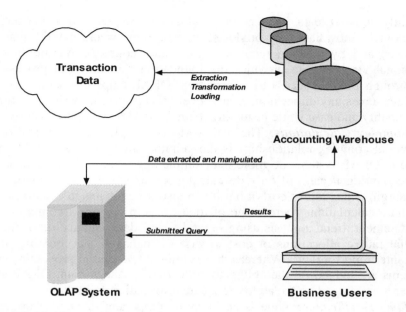

Fig. 6.1. OLAP system and dataflow

OLAP involves the dynamic and extensive manipulation of unlimited variables of data and complements On-Line Transaction Processing (OLTP).
OLAP transforms raw transactional data to reflect the real dimensionality
of the enterprise as understood by the user. The flexibility of OLAP systems allows business users to become more self-sufficient. Managers are
no longer dependent on IT to make changes. OLAP enables managers to
model problems that would be impossible using less flexible systems with
lengthy and inconsistent response times (see Fig. 6.1).

While OLAP systems have the ability to answer "who" and "what"
questions, it is the ability to answer "what if" and "why" that sets those
systems apart from Data Warehouses. OLAP and Data Warehouses are
complementary. While a data warehouse stores and manages data, OLAP
transforms Data Warehouse data into strategic information. OLAP ranges
from basic navigation and browsing (often known as "slice and dice"), to
calculations, to more serious analyses such as time series and complex
modeling. As decision-makers exercise more advanced OLAP capabilities,
they move from data access to information to knowledge (Forsman, 1997).

Most OLAP applications possess the following three key features
(Forsman, 1997):

1. *Multidimensional Views:* Multidimensional views are inherently representative of an actual business model. Rarely is a business model limited
   to fewer than three dimensions. For example, accounting managers typi-

cally look at data by scenario (actual vs. budget), by organization (branch, subsidiary), by products, by time (day, week, month, quarter, year) and by location (county, region, city, country). A multidimensional view of data provides the foundation for analytical processing through flexible access to information. OLAP helps managers analyze data across any dimension, at any level of aggregation, with equal functionality and ease while insulating them from complex query syntax.

2. *Complex Calculations:* The real world is complicated - the ability to model complex relationships is the genuine strength of an OLAP system. OLAP systems do more than simple aggregation. For example, in accounting it can not only do calculations as simple as calculation of margin (sales minus costs); but it can also do complex calculations like share calculations (percentage of total) to help prepare a common size statement; trend analysis using several years' data; calculation of financial ratios; allocations of cost in case of managerial accounting (cost center reporting) etc. Whereas the traditional transaction processing systems are judged on the ability to collect and manage data, OLAP systems are judged on the ability to create information from data.

3. *Time Intelligence:* Time is an integral component of almost any analytical application. OLAP systems understand the sequential nature of time (December always comes after November). Accountants almost always measure performance over time, for example, this quarter versus last quarter, this quarter versus the same quarter last year. In another example, a Cost accountant would want to identify expenses incurred year-to-date, expenses incurred in a particular month, what was budgeted for a quarter last year as compared to this year, etc. OLAP systems allow slicing and dicing data by time periods.

In addition to these features, there are a number of options for storing and processing OLAP data. Based upon each option, there are different architectures. In the following section, we will try to understand different types of OLAP architectures.

6.4 OLAP Architectures

Much confusion exists about OLAP architectures, with various terms and architectures like ROLAP, HOLAP, MOLAP and DOLAP proliferating. In principle, there are primarily two aspects in formulating OLAP architecture, namely, where to store OLAP data and where to process OLAP data.

6.4.1 Storing OLAP Data

Most data in OLAP applications originate in separate systems. In some applications, however, the data might be captured directly by OLAP application. When the data come from other applications, it is usually necessary for the active data to be stored in a separate, duplicated form for OLAP application. This separate and duplicated storage may be referred to as a data warehouse or a data mart. There are essentially three options for storing OLAP data – relational database, multidimensional database and client machines. Many products use more than one of these, sometimes simultaneously (Pendse, 2003).

- **Relational database (RDDB):** The foundation of RDDB is that OLAP capabilities are best provided directly against the relational database, i.e., the data warehouse. Data from transaction-processing systems are loaded into the database. Database routines are run to aggregate the data. Indices are then created to optimize query access times.
- **Multidimensional database (MDDB):** In this case, the active data are stored in a multidimensional database on a server. The foundation of this architecture is that data must be stored multidimensionally to be viewed multidimensionally. Information from a variety of operational systems is loaded into a MDDB through a series of batch routines (series of non-interactive jobs done all at one time). Once these data have been loaded into the MDDB, the general approach implemented in this architecture is to use the corporate data store to build a series of multidimensional cubes of pre-computed data specifically designed to address a specific or a narrow range of inquiries. Once this compilation process has been completed, the MDDB is ready for use.
- **Client-based files:** In this case, relatively small extracts of data are held on client machines. They may be distributed in advance or created on demand (possibly via the Web). As with multidimensional databases on the server, active data may be held on disk or in RAM; and some products allow only read-access.

These three locations have different performance characteristics, with relational databases being a great deal slower than the other two options. They also have different capacities, with relational databases having the highest and the client-based files, the lowest.

6.4.2 Processing OLAP Data

Parallel to three possible locations for storing OLAP data are three options available for processing the data - Multi-Pass SQL, Multidimensional server engine and Client multidimensional engine. It should be noted that multidimensional calculations need not occur in the place where the data are stored. (See "The OLAP Report" Pendse and Creeth, (2002) for further explanation on OLAP processing.)

6.4.3 OLAP Architecture Grid

Theoretically, based upon three storage locations and three locations for processing data, nine possible storage/processing options can be formulated (see Table 6.2). But of these nine, some do not make much sense and are not practical. For example Multi-pass SQL queries run against relational data warehouse and hence cannot be used with MDDB or the client-based files. Consequently, in practice there are only six architectures possible as is explained in the grid below. The six options are grouped under three major classifications:

Table 6.2. OLAP Architectural Grid (Pendse, 2003)

Multidimensional data storage options	Multidimensional processing options		
	Multi-Pass SQL	Multidimensional server engine	Client multidi-mensional engine
Relational database	1	2	3
Multidimensional database	-	4	5
Client-based files	-	-	6

- **Relational OLAP ('ROLAP'):** Architectures in cells 1, 2 and 3 represent ROLAP architecture. As shown in Fig. 6.2, end users submit multidimensional queries to the RDDB engine, which then dynamically transforms the requests into SQL execution plans. The SQL is submitted to the relational database for processing; the relational query results are tabulated; and a multidimensional result is returned to the end user. ROLAP is a fully dynamic client/server architecture, which accesses data directly from data warehouse. It performs the analysis on the fly, i.e., it is capable of utilizing pre-calculated results when they are available or dynamically generating results from atomic information when necessary. It does not require placing data on a separate server. The accounting manager can submit a query to display the sales of a particular product during a month in a particular region. The ROLAP would extract a pre-stored result or would perform the calculation dynamically and return the result instantly to the user.

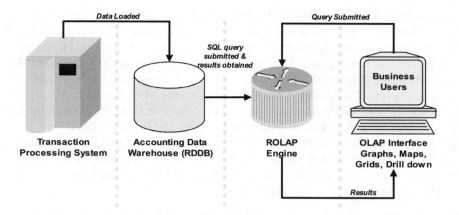

Fig. 6.2. ROLAP Architecture

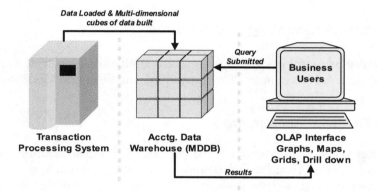

Fig. 6.3. MOLAP Architecture

- **Multidimensional OLAP ('MOLAP'):** Architectures in cells 4 and 5 represent MOLAP architecture. As shown in Fig.6.3, users request reports through the interface, and the application logic layer of the MDDB retrieves the stored data. This architecture is a compilation-intensive architecture. It is a static architecture, which principally reads the precompiled data. MOLAP has limited capabilities to dynamically create aggregations or to calculate results that have not been pre-calculated and stored. For example, an accounting manager can run a report showing the corporate Profit/Loss account or Profit/Loss account for a particular subsidiary. The MDDB would retrieve precompiled Profit & Loss figures and return the result to the user.

- **Desktop OLAP ('DOLAP'):** Architecture in cell 6 represents DOLAP architecture. In DOLAP, a multidimensional data cube is created and delivered to an individual user's computer. Data are requested from a relational or multidimensional database, and the data set is returned to the requesting client. A SQL query executes against the database and returns a result set to the desktop, which can then be pivoted and manipulated locally. They normally have good database links, often to both relational as well as multidimensional servers and local PC files.
- **Hybrid OLAP ('HOLAP'):** Apart from the above three, another classification that is widely used currently is known as Hybrid OLAP, which uses benefits of both ROLAP and MOLAP tools. It uses the combination of architectures in cells 2 and 4.

Let us now discuss how some OLAP tools could be used in various accounting areas and the benefits available to an accounting manager in particular and to the organization as a whole.

6.5 Some Accounting Applications

OLAP can be useful in various areas of accounting like Financial Accounting, Managerial Accounting, Tax Accounting and Financial Modeling.

6.5.1 Financial Accounting

This area could be considered as the nucleus of all the accounting areas. It provides relevant financial information to investors, creditors, government and other external parties through the income statement, balance sheet, cash flow statement and statement of shareholder's equity. Let us see how OLAP tools could be valuable in areas of financial accounting.

6.5.1.1 Consolidation

Financial Consolidation is a reporting mechanism whereby the financial statements of more than one company are combined in order to prepare meaningful financial statements of the combined operations. Even the simplest financial consolidation consists of at least three dimensions - an account, one organizational structure and time. With increased analysis and comparison, the number of dimensions could easily increase. There are numerous reasons that make consolidation complex. A few are noted below (Pendse, 2003):

- Currency translation must occur with reporting on international operations, depending upon the nature of the transaction, i.e., whether it is a Balance Sheet item or an Income statement item. Also, a decision must be made as to what exchange rates to use, etc.
- Elimination of inter-company transactions must occur to give a true and fair view of the combined operations. For example, Purchases for Parent Company A would not necessarily be the combined purchases of subsidiaries B and C together. There may be some purchases by Company B from Company C or vice versa. These inter-company purchases need to be eliminated before consolidation.
- Proper controls must be in place to check that the consolidation of particular accounts is done only once. An error here could render the consolidation meaningless.
- Systematic updating is also necessary to ensure that after the consolidation updates should be allowed only by authorized people.

OLAP tools can help by pre-defining various dimensions to take care of the complexities. Not only would the user be spared the trouble of knowing what dimensions to set up, but also certain complex operations, such as currency translation and inter-company eliminations, could be completely automated. The system could also be 'informed' of which items are debits and which are credits; so that in case of 'imbalance', the system could automatically prompt the variance. Further, through the drill down facilities, it would also be possible to find out which of the accounts or journal entry created the error. This feature could relieve the user from the tedious and monotonous arithmetical accuracy and at the same time enable him to use the analytical power of the tools. He could use the tool to analyze the results by querying to check consolidation of only two or three companies, for two or three years, for two or three regions, etc.

6.5.1.2 Reporting

Every organization, whether small, medium or large, has a responsibility for producing financial reports for management (to meet management's business defined needs) and additionally in case of public limited companies for producing other reports for the regulatory authorities (to meet statutory requirements). Today's financial and accounting managers are responsible to support senior management with critical data and also maintain compliance with changing accounting requirements. These include reporting requirements outlined by the FASB (Financial Accounting Standard Board), IASC (International Accounting Standards Committee), US GAAP (Generally Accepted Accounting Principles), Canadian GAAP, UK GAAP, and others.

An OLAP tool can accommodate the detailed line-of-business information required by these standards-setting bodies. Flexible reporting tools help users quickly determine whether there is compliance with the requirements. In addition to statutory reporting, OLAP tools are also useful for management reporting. Management reporting is different from formal financial reporting. It usually has less emphasis on the balance sheet and more on the income statement and cash flows. It may be done more often - usually monthly, rather than annually and quarterly. There will be less detail but more analysis. The emphasis is on faster rather than more accurate reporting, and there may be regular changes to the reporting requirements. OLAP-based systems enable faster and more flexible reporting and better analysis than alternative solutions. Further, in case of different business structures (legal structure, management structure, product structure), the same reporting tool will be expected to produce reports for various structures. Through OLAP, it may be economically possible to deploy good solutions to many users for general-purpose management reporting applications.

OLAP tools shorten the consolidation and reporting process through automation, integrated communications, a powerful processing engine, and an integrated data model that eliminates reconciliation problems. Some products automate the entire consolidation process and adapt to changing reporting standards and greater disclosure requirements.

6.5.1.3 Comparative Analysis

To succeed, businesses need to accurately monitor financial operations and effectively measure the success of critical corporate initiatives. Comparative analysis enables business users at all levels to obtain and analyze the important information necessary to know the performance of their business as well as manage customer and vendor activities. Comparative analysis usually involves the calculation of numerous business ratios and comparing performance against history and budget. There is also an advantage to be gained from comparing product groups or channels or markets against each other.

OLAP tools provide an intelligent way to track and manage the financial performance. Once the financial information has been input, the system automatically produces some standard reports to help analyze and track financial performance. The reports developed by some tools include ratio analysis, common sizing, cash flow analysis, sales and profitability analysis. Custom report and custom ratio features allow the system to be used with a variety of industry and business types. Taking the analysis process one step further, some tools automatically create projections based on existing company data. They allow modifying each balance sheet and income statement account to create unlimited "what-if" scenarios. Each projection then can be viewed monthly, quarterly, or annually. The program may also contain a powerful graphics program, which enables illustration of any trend or change in financial performance.

**British Telecommunications Uses OLAP For Financial Consolidation, Reporting And Analysis - ** *Hyperion, Customer success*

British Telecommunications (BT), one of the world's leading providers of telecommunications services, has operations in more than 30 countries worldwide. Before using an OLAP tool, employees used spreadsheets to consolidate and report financial data, which resulted in delays; the quality of data suffered, and there was lack of time to analyze data. By using the OLAP tool in the strategic markets area, BT reduced the amount of time spent on data collection and financial consolidation by two person-days. This savings provided the users an opportunity to spend less time producing the numbers and more time analyzing the number. BT also uses this OLAP tool for complex currency conversions; monthly financial reporting, such as balance sheets and P&Ls; and product profitability analysis.

"We are getting much better data so we can manage our business," said a systems development accountant at BT. "Our business is always changing, which means our decision-makers need more and more information in shorter time scales." BT's largest OLAP application includes 185,000 accounts and 300 entities.

6.5.2 Managerial Accounting

Managerial Accounting involves preparation, reporting, and interpretation of accounting information for the use of decision making by internal parties within the organization. OLAP tools can help design reports that provide the necessary information in an effective format, efficiently prepared in a timely manner and customized per user requirements. Following are some of the areas where OLAP could be useful.

6.5.2.1 Budgeting and Forecasting

Every organization needs to prepare a budget at least once a year. Some companies try the top-down approach; others try the bottom-up alternative; while still others combine the discipline of a top-down budget with the commitment of a bottom-up process. However, traditional budgeting assumes a static business environment, a fantasy in today's volatile global economy. You can lose a few months while preparing a budget based on numbers that are already out of date and still lack the ability to respond to marketplace changes. To have real value, a budget must be a living plan that helps management to be flexible and responsive. Some of the OLAP tools have the ability to revise budgets quickly based on performance, to prepare rolling forecasts, and to streamline the entire budgeting cycle. They also have control facilities that indicate out-of-range data and exceptions and track which budget holders have or have not entered their numbers. Unlike fragmented spreadsheets, these budgeting software solutions manage the entire budgeting process.

But before the management can budget, it must forecast. Only by knowing today what the future is likely to be can reliable plans and budgets be created and implemented in time to maximize revenues and minimize risk. It is difficult to predict what lies ahead with any degree of confidence. Some OLAP tools enable users to quickly and easily select a subset of data on which to base a prediction. It prepares forecasts at any level - by product or product line, by month or quarter, by region or office. The system then analyzes the data, automatically selects the appropriate forecasting technique, and then generates hundreds of impartial, statistically accurate forecasts in a very short time. Predicted results are then compared to the budget, and management is prompted about potential problem areas or unrealistic budgets and forecasts. It also enables 'what-if' analysis to analyze that if a particular criteria or state of nature changes then what would be the forecast and budget.

Budgeting And Forecasting At Jewson - *Applix Customer success*

In 1997 when Jewson, one of the UK's largest builder's merchants, acquired Harcros, it effectively doubled its branch network. Prior to the merger, spreadsheets were the finance department's primary tool for budgeting and forecasting. These spreadsheets managed adequately before the merger but could not cope with the organization's expanded network and increased data volumes requiring analysis. Jewson acknowledged the need to invest in a new business intelligence application.

After evaluating a broad range of software from high-end business intelligence packages to basic accounting packages, Jewson used an OLAP tool for the first time in spring 1999 for its yearly budgets. The OLAP tool incorporated five to six levels of hierarchy from the head office to the branch, handled a high level of calculation and reduced massive data entry. Users could view multiple dimensions of data and also 'slice and dice' these data to quickly and easily create an unlimited number of custom reports. A planning accountant at Jewson said," ... makes our life a lot easier. It is a powerful and easy-to-use system that provides us with continual month-to-month management accounts which greatly facilitate our budgeting activities and give us comprehensive control over costs that matter to us in our running of the business."

6.5.2.2 Variance Analysis

Once the forecast has been made and operations budgeted, the next step is to observe whether the actual results are occurring as per the budget or is there any variance. Comparing actual with budget is an integral part of how companies run their businesses. It is difficult to have the actual results match the budget exactly. There are always some variances, which may be favorable or adverse. In order to decide future strategies, management must understand why the actual results were different from the budget. Analysis that helps the management understand the differences is known as Variance analysis. For example Price/Volume/Mix is where a variance is broken down into those components that depend on price variance, volume variance and product mix variance. The management needs to know whether the revenues are increasing because of more sales or because of maintaining the costs better than expected.

There are some flexible OLAP tools that enable comparison of not only *actual versus budget* figures but also allow easy comparison of current *year actual* versus *last year*, *current year actual* versus *mid-year forecast* or *mid-year forecast* versus *budget*. Some products offer features for 'what-if' analysis. Real-time budget variance analysis can be possible with just a click of a button. For example, a calculation based on anticipated unit sales can be updated any time to show actual sales, and managers can analyze both price and unit variance for more informed decision-making. One-time calculations allow analysis of different scenarios within a single plan sheet, and multiple revisions enable analyzing of changes that impact the whole plan. In addition, with the ease of drag-and-drop, the overall plan can be recast to analyze the anticipated effects of reorganization or expansion.

6.5.2.3 Activity-Based Management

This management methodology for planning, controlling, and improving labor and overhead costs is based on the principle that activities consume costs and therefore focuses on work rather than workers. Resources are assigned to activities, then activities are assigned to cost objects based on their use. This methodology allows managers to determine capacities of critical resources, price products, conduct inventory valuation, identify physical and operational constraints, and analyze cost and return on investment (ROI) or increased cash flow requirements.

With powerful 'what-if' capability, an OLAP tool can enable decision-makers to develop and test multiple scenarios and strategies within their business model. They can compare potential performance-improving alternatives and evaluate operational and financial impacts of various production and management strategies—all at no risk to the organization—by plugging in such variables as outputs (e.g., products, services, and/or internal deliverables), capacities, costs, and revenues. Using such tools, production managers can determine the operational impact of introducing new product lines, changing procedures, and sharing equipment. Operations managers can accurately ascertain capacities of critical resources, such as equipment and personnel, thereby giving business planners the information needed to manage growth in the most cost-effective manner. Results can be explored with a click of a mouse and in virtually any format imaginable. Analysis of any number of performance measures, such as direct and indirect activity costs and product and client profitability, is possible with ease by utilizing the powerful multidimensional data analysis cubes generated by some OLAP tools.

Barclays' Activity Based Management - *Hyperion, Customer success*

Barclays Bank PLC, a United Kingdom-based financial services group, has almost 2,000 U.K. branches and 80,000 employees in more than 60 countries worldwide. To survive competition and satisfy the corporate customers (who are price and service conscious), Barclays had to look into managing its costs. It needed to accurately model future business activities as well as calculate capacity and capacity utilization - two of the biggest influences on unit costs. Barclays found one OLAP tool an excellent choice. The software's modeling features have moved Barclays' business forward, providing the capability to use "what-if" analysis for activity-based costing and management. Managers can now make strategic decisions by looking at which categories of activities they can minimize or streamline without impacting customer service. They can now model the implications of a particular course of action and then go back and validate what happens if they take that action.

Barclays' manager of the Costing Department, Corporate Banking Finance, says, "… gives our managers access to practical, usable information that provides guidance and real decision support, which moves the business forward."

6.5.3 Tax Accounting

Tax accounting is a specialized field within the Accounting profession. It involves both the preparation of income tax returns and the planning of business activities and structuring those activities to minimize the income tax burden. To a large extent, tax returns are based upon financial accounting information; however, the information is often adjusted or reorganized to comply with income tax regulations. For example, a deduction claimed while preparing the income statement for statutory reporting may not be allowed as a deduction for income tax purpose; the depreciation method used for financial reporting maybe different from that used for tax reporting. An OLAP system for financial reporting (as explained above) would typically include a module, which facilitates tax accounting.

6.5.4 Financial Modeling

Financial modeling is a tool traditionally used in businesses to define and compare the impact of specific business initiatives and alternative scenarios on a company's financial position. Complex, real world phenomena are simulated in order to obtain greater understanding of the dynamics that drive them. Physical activities of an enterprise are identified and linked with costs and revenues. Revenues and expenses often follow consistent patterns that are captured by the model. The model enables users to predict the profitability and assess the impact of future similar ventures. Financial modeling is a cost effective, practical way to test risks and assess financial implications before committing to corporate change. For example, before making an important capital investment, a company can, by using a capital budgeting model, find out which of the investment alternatives would provide the highest NPV. The model, in such a case, would simulate the expected cash outflows and inflows as would occur in a real world and then rank the various alternatives using the NPV criteria. A financial model can be simple (e.g., computation of NPV) or very complex (e.g., Efficient Portfolio Modeling). A financial model is a mathematical representation of a company's business. It may relate to the company in its entirety or just a subset. It may be used to:

- Test scenarios - what happens if interest rates fall by 1%?
- Make major decisions – what value should be paid to acquire a particular company?
- Enforce a common analytical structure on routine decisions – e.g., loan approval for banks.
- Compute financial measures such as IRR, NPV, Depreciation, Loan Amortization, or Tax Table lookup.

An OLAP application could enable corporate financial planners to build complex models quickly without the need to perform any programming. Models can be developed and debugged more quickly; maintenance is easier, and calculations could be faster than standard spreadsheets. Mathematical, statistical and financial functions can be built-in. With functions like Internal Rate of Return (IRR) and Net Present Value (NPV), tables for depreciation and tax payments, forecasting techniques like regression analysis and Winter's methodology, models can be built quickly.

Now understanding the potential of OLAP tools, we evaluate the different OLAP architectures discussed earlier to find what could be feasible for an organization. ROLAP, MOLAP, DOLAP and HOLAP each has its own strengths and weaknesses; and there is no single optimum choice. The choice of architecture does affect the performance, capacity, functionality and particularly the scalability of an OLAP system such that, for different purpose, different OLAP architectures could be beneficial. We discuss these choices in the next section.

6.6 Selecting OLAP Architecture

Business environment demands that an OLAP application maintain high performance despite large user counts, massive data volumes, and complex reports and queries. Before choosing an OLAP application, it is important to check that it fulfills certain criteria (Microstrategy Inc., 1995).

6.6.1 Characteristics of a good Accounting OLAP

To enable full-functioned analysis, a good accounting OLAP application should have the following characteristics:

- **Support Sophisticated Analysis:** The decision makers use key performance metrics to evaluate various operations. These metrics need to be presented in a customized manner to facilitate such evaluation. Such results can be obtained from transactional databases and can be pre-calculated and stored or can be generated on demand by using the query process. For example an Accounting manager would want a query to show the profit margins by product by store in North American stores between June 24 and June 30. Other tasks in accounting could include calculating metrics of key financial ratios, creating abbreviated income statement by quarter for last six quarters, etc. An efficient accounting OLAP application should support such detailed and sophisticated analysis.
- **Dimensionally Scalable:** Decision makers need to analyze data from a number of different perspectives or dimensions. They need to evaluate various operations, of various products, in various regions, and for various periods. Accounting analysis involves extracting high quality result sets or reports from large volumes of transactional data. For example, a manager would want to find out the increase in sales of Product A, in store B, of region C, during a week, as a result of X amount spent on advertisement. These are just a few of the dimensions; in reality, organi-

zations have large numbers of dimensions in their data models. The accounting OLAP application should be scalable to handle the dimensional richness.

- **Handle Data Volatility:** Volatility describes the degree to which data and data structures change over time. Data with a low level of volatility remain relatively constant as opposed to highly volatile data. Accounting data are mostly operational data and hence highly volatile. Accordingly, an effective accounting OLAP application should be able to handle highly volatile data.

- **Scalable to Atomic Data:** Atomic data refers to the lowest level of data granularity required for effective decision-making. In the case of Accounting, an organization might have thousands of Accounts receivables, thousands of Accounts payables, hundreds of expense and revenue accounts, hundreds of branches and multiple products or services. Thousands of transaction combinations occur, and a manager may need to know minutest details. For example, before calculating bad debts, the accountant would need to know when the sale took place, what were the terms, how often the customer deals with the organization, how is the credit record, etc. Thus it is quite common for an accounting system to have many gigabytes of atomic level information. An accounting OLAP application should be able to scale to thousands of gigabytes of atomic information to be effective.

An OLAP application with the above attributes could be very effective. DOLAP's performance typically lies in between the performance of MOLAP and ROLAP. HOLAP is a combination of MOLAP and ROLAP technologies. Thus, we can restrict our discussion to comparison between MOLAP and ROLAP and try to discover which could be used under what circumstances. We will, in the following section, develop the framework that can be used to compare the two architectures. Of the four important functional characteristics of OLAP cited above, both ROLAP and MOLAP are capable of similar level of analysis. Thus our basis of comparison can be reduced to the remaining three attributes, namely, Dimensions, Volatility and Atomicity.

6.6.2 Framework for Analysis

- **Data Compilation:** When data need to be consolidated, OLAP applications can either calculate these values dynamically or retrieve them from a pre-calculated data store. To provide the required performance, OLAP applications typically pre-calculate some (or all) of these values. This function is known as data compilation. The degree of data compilation affects two aspects (Microstrategy Inc., 1995):

1. <u>Batch requirements</u>: Because of the magnitude of the raw data and the complexity of data cubes, it is necessary to build the cubes with a batch processing method. A higher degree of compilation requires more batch processing requirements because highly compiled data need longer time and more space to process.

2. <u>Query requirements:</u> This aspect is the time required for query response. Higher the compilation, lower the query requirements. By compiling every possible aggregate and every possible index, the application ensures that the query response will be fast.

Both aspects inversely impact each other i.e., higher the data compilation, greater the batch requirements, but lower the query time and vice versa.

- **Resource Requirements:** By combining the Batch requirements and the Query requirements, we can derive the total processing requirements. We then compare the total processing requirement with the maximum available level of processing resources. An increase or decrease in the power of the server hardware will have the effect of increasing or decreasing the maximum available processing resources. Based upon the maximum available resources, the system designer will have to decide upon the compilation level; and whether it is required to minimize the batch requirements or to achieve highest query performance or to achieve some balance.

6.6.3 Comparison of the Two Architectures

Having established the framework for analysis, let us now evaluate the two architectures based upon the three attributes short-listed above. ROLAP applications tend to be neutral to the degree of data compilation, giving the system designer the ability to decide where to balance query requirements and batch requirements. However, the performance may suffer in the case of lower compilation; and the response may take a longer time. In contrast, MOLAP requires high compilation and therefore provides less flexibility to the systems designer. MOLAP is feasible only at a high degree of compilation. At the same time, as a result of higher compilation, MOLAP provides higher performance and analytical power. Let us now analyze each of the three attributes.

- **Dimensions:** Lesser the number of dimensions, greater is the possibility to have high data compilation with less use of resources. Thus, either of the architectures would give good results. A MOLAP system could be preferred for higher performance and analytical power. As the number of dimensions increases, it becomes difficult to have high degree of compilation. However, a ROLAP application with some compilation (say 40-50%) would still be able to provide good results. After a certain point, the number of dimensions would be beyond MOLAP's scope and a ROLAP with much less compilation (say 10-15%) could be able to provide better results.

- **Data Volatility:** If the data are less volatile, there is no need to recalculate and process the already pre-calculated and summarized data. A highly compiled system can be developed that can provide fast response time. Both ROLAP and MOLAP are viable options. MOLAP should be chosen for higher performance. However, when the data volatility increases, summarized data need to be recalculated frequently. MOLAP, which favors high compilation, would not be a viable solution. ROLAP, which is neutral to degree of compilation, would be a better option to implement at a lower degree of compilation.
- **Data Atomicity:** For a given amount of atomic data, the degree of compilation is the main determinant of database size. The more the atomic data are compiled into higher aggregation levels, the larger the size of the database becomes. A highly compiled data model becomes unfeasible as the amount of atomic data increase. MOLAP is not feasible because of its bias towards high compilation. By not requiring fully compiled data models, ROLAP architecture is better equipped to handle large data volumes.

6.6.4 Selection of Architecture

Each of the architectures has its advantages and drawbacks. An organization has to accept that its choice of one over the other will ultimately result in a trade off depending upon the performance requirement and resource constraints. Table 6.3 below provides some guidance for selecting one architecture over the other.

As for DOLAP architecture, the primary advantage is to collect, aggregate, and calculate data in advance of the analytic act, so that a prebuilt cube is ready to give good query performance to analytic users. Although some implementations of DOLAP systems require downloading a cube to a PC, the PC-based cube yields snappy responses to queries and enables off-line analysis. However, the ability to drill-through into detailed data is limited in some DOLAP architectures and may require integration with a separate query tool. The compilation process tends to be relatively simple in a DOLAP architecture, which can enable quick deployment of analytic solutions. DOLAP is useful but not very scalable. It could be used by people who need to run business queries using relatively small data sets extracted from production systems, e.g., a small proprietorship firm. DOLAP systems are popular and typically require relatively little IT investment to implement. They also provide highly mobile OLAP operations for users who may work remotely or travel extensively. However, most are limited to a single user and lack the ability to manage large data sets (Russom, 2000).

Table 6.3. MOLAP or ROLAP

ATTRIBUTES (Dimensions, volatility, atomicity)	Performance Requirement	Resource Constraints	
		Yes	No
HIGH	HIGH	ROLAP*	MOLAP
	LOW	ROLAP	ROLAP/MOLAP**
LOW	HIGH	MOLAP	MOLAP
	LOW	ROLAP	ROLAP/MOLAP**

*   Performance would not be as high as expected but better than that provided by MOLAP under this scenario.
** Depending upon factors such as cost, maintenance requirements, database restructuring etc.

The HOLAP solution purports to combine ROLAP's dynamic access to relational data with MOLAP's more sophisticated analytical capabilities and instantaneous access to high-level aggregates and stable—or less volatile—data. However, the new hybrid products vary greatly. While they are all in some way a combination of MOLAP and ROLAP technologies, they do not necessarily deliver a best-of-both-worlds solution (Alalouf, 1997). Depending upon the organizational needs, a particular Hybrid product might be selected.

The latest development in OLAP architecture is the evolution of OLAP servers as a major component of the data warehouse. OLAP servers have server-defined rules for handling complex calculations. Such calculations can be defined once and used many times. This technology is evolving and is not a competitor to the relational data warehouse but rather is an extension (Mundy, 2002).

Different organizations have varied data characteristics. A proprietorship organization would have less accounting data as compared to a corporation. The various dimensions that need to be considered for decision-making by an accounting manager of a multinational company would not be required by the accounting manager of a not-for-profit-organization. Similarly, the accounting data of a conglomerate are highly volatile and huge compared to that of a corporation with few products. There is not 'one best' OLAP architecture for a particular type of organization. Depending upon the type of business and the nature of decision-making, the Accounting managers can, by using the explanation provided above, decide upon an OLAP architecture, which fits their budget and meets their performance requirements.

6.7 Conclusion

Every company's accounting software holds invaluable information that can help executives make better decisions. Summarizing transactions to meet information-analysis needs and presenting that information in an easy-to-understand format has always been a challenge for systems administrators. OLAP applications can help satisfy companies' information needs (McKie, 1999). OLAP can be used to analyze data from any accounting module and not just the financials. Over the past few years, the visibility of OLAP vendors and the sophistication of OLAP tools have increased, making OLAP yet another tool that accounting software vendors are using to differentiate their software from the competitions. Extracting greater value from your accounting system by providing more flexibility in the ways that you can manipulate and view your financial data is the goal of OLAP. The accounting vendors have embraced OLAP in a number of ways as they integrated certain OLAP functionalities into their core product as standard features.

7 Bankruptcy Prediction Using Neural Networks

Murugan Anandarajan[1], Picheng Lee[2], Asokan Anandarajan[3]

[1]Department of Management, Drexel University, Pennsylvania

[2]Department of Accounting, Pace University, New York

[3]School of Management, New Jersey Institute of Technology, New Jersey

Abstract. This study is an extension of prior studies that have used artificial neural networks to predict bankruptcy. The incremental contribution of this study is threefold. First, we use only financially stressed firms in our control sample. This sampling enables the models to more closely approximate the actual decision processes of auditors and other interested parties. Second, we develop a more parsimonious model using qualitative "bad news" variables that prior research indicates measure financial distress. Past research has focused on the "usefulness" of accounting numbers and therefore often ignored non-accounting variables that may contribute to the classification accuracy of the distress prediction models. In addition, rather than use multiple financial ratios, we include a single variable of financial distress using the Zmijewski distress score that incorporates ratios measuring profitability, liquidity, and solvency. Finally, we develop and test a genetic algorithm neural network model. We compare its predictive ability to that of a backpropagation neural network and a model using multiple discriminant analysis.

7.1 Introduction

The ability to predict bankruptcy is important for many user groups including creditors, investors, regulators, and auditors. Auditors, in particular, are currently facing a litigious environment where failure to predict bankruptcy can result in substantial litigation costs[1]. Misclassification as healthy of a potential future bankruptcy candidate is referred to by Taylor and Glezen (1994) as an audit failure. Audit failure, in their opinion, includes audit opinion misclassification due to improper assessment of the client firm continuing as a going concern. Increased litigation against auditors makes audit failures more costly and necessitates that audit firms find ways of improving the accuracy of their bankruptcy prediction techniques. Even though this topic has been extensively explored in the literature, the growing number of litigations against auditors calls for a reexamination of financial distress prediction models.

Predictive modeling, which is perhaps the most-used sub field of data mining (others being clustering and frequent pattern extraction), draws from statistics, machine learning, database techniques, pattern recognition, and optimization techniques (Hong and Weiss, 2001). Data mining is the exploration and analysis, by automatic or semiautomatic means, of large quantities of data in order to discover meaningful patterns and rules (Berry and Linoff, 1997).

In this chapter, we propose a data-mining approach to building a financial predictive model using artificial neural networks (ANNs) to help auditors to decide whether to classify a financially distressed firm is a potential candidate for bankruptcy. We compare the predictive performance of two types of neural network learning methodologies, namely, back propagation and genetic algorithm. In addition, the networks' predictive results are then contrasted with the prediction accuracy rate obtained from a discriminant analysis model.

The rest of this chapter is organized as follows. The next section provides a description of artificial neural network models and is followed by the predictive model development methodology. The results are then discussed, and the paper concludes with implications of the study for managers and directions for future research.

---

[1] Some examples of very large settlements include Ernst and Young compelled to pay $400 million (Baliga 1993) and KPMG Peat Marwick paying $186.5 million (Baliga 1994).

7.2 Artificial Neural Networks

7.2.1 Description of Artificial Neural Networks

An Artificial Neural Network (ANN) is a parallel, dynamic system of highly interconnected interacting parts based on neurobiological models. The underlying principles of an ANN are based on that found in the biological sciences. Here the nervous system consists of individual but highly interconnected nerve cells called neurons. These neurons typically receive information or stimuli from the external environment. For instance, the neurons in the human eye register the brightness of light in a room. These stimuli pass through the network by neurons releasing neuro transmitters to the neighboring neurons. The connections between the neurons are called synapses. The stimuli can either excite the neuron or inhibit it. If the receiving neuron is excited by the information it receives, it will "fire" when it gets the input and pass the information on to other neighboring neurons. If the neuron is inhibited, the input of the information is dampened and not passed on. In other words, the neurons process the information and pass it on only if it is considered important, thus eventually producing a response.

Similar to the biological counterpart, ANNs are designed to emulate the human pattern recognition function through parallel processing of multiple inputs i.e., ANNs have the ability to scan data for patterns and can be used to construct nonlinear models. An ANN consists of a number of neurons, which are distributed in a number of hierarchical layers. One of the most widely implemented neural network architecture is the Multilayer Perceptrons (MLP) model. This network has a multilayered, feed forward, hierarchical structure. This multilayered structure consists of input and output layers as well as one or more hidden layers. The total number of neurons, number of neurons on each layer, as well as number of layers determine the accuracy of the network model. A typical MLP is shown in Fig. 7.1. The neurons in the input layer represent the attributes or stimuli in a dataset. These inputs $(x_1, x_2, \ldots x_n)$ initiate the activations into the network.

As illustrated in Fig. 7.1, these inputs are combined in the lower portion of the neuron. The upper portion of the neuron takes this sum and calculates the degree to which the sum is important using a transfer function to produce an individual output.

The transfer function serves as a dimmer switch for turning on and off, depending on the input into the neurons. The selection of the transfer function typically depends on the nature of the input data and the objective of the network (Fausett, 1994). In this regard, there are a number of alternatives, including the step function, sigmoid function, hyperbolic tangent function, and linear function among others. The selection of the transfer function typically depends on the nature of the output of the network (Fausett, 1994). Because the output of this study is continuous in nature and ranges from 0 to 1, this study uses the *sigmoid transfer function* as recommended by Zahedi (1994). This scale is the most suitable if the goal of the neural network is differentiating an object from others.

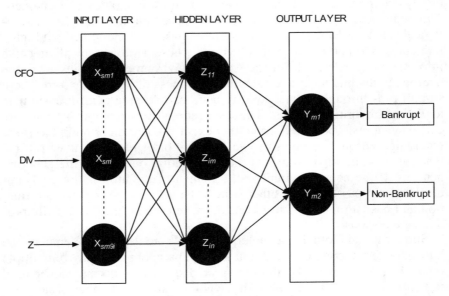

Fig. 7.1. Structure of the Artificial Neural Network

Since the bankruptcy problem is inherently non-linear in nature, it is important to create an ANN that can approximate complex non-linear functions. This approximation is achieved by adding hidden layers (i.e., several layers of sigmoidal functions) that consist of neurons that receive inputs from the preceding cells and pass on outputs to subsequent cell layers (Lippermann, 1987). Although in theory a single hidden layer is sufficient to solve any function approximation problem (Fahey, 1998; Funahashi, 1989; Hornik, Stinchcombe., and White, 1990), as Fausett (1994) notes, some problems may be easier to solve using more than a single hidden layer.

To summarize, each connection in the ANN has weights that are generated from the input values which are converted to an output value by a transfer function. The output value of a neuron is a function of the weighted sum of its inputs. The weights represent the nature of the strength of connection between neurons. A large positive value will influence the next neuron to activate, while a large negative value will inhibit activation of the next neuron. The determination of these weights is a critical component of the learning process and is generated by an iterative training process where case examples with known decision outputs are repeatedly presented to the network. As previously indicated, this study compares the predictive ability of two types of learning techniques, namely, back propagation and genetic algorithms. These two methods are discussed briefly below.

7.2.2 Backpropagation Learning Method

In the case of the BP learning algorithm, the network begins its training with a random set of weights, and a set of input-output relations (represented by data sets). During the feedforward process each input unit (X_i) receives an input signal and sends the signal to each of the hidden units $Z_1....Z_n$. Each hidden unit then computes its activation and sends its signal z_j to the output units. Each output unit computes its activation y_k to form the estimated response of the network for the given input pattern. These estimates are then compared to the desired output, and an error is computed for each given observation. This error is then transmitted backward from the output layer to each node in the hidden layer. Each of the hidden nodes receives only a portion of the error, which is based on the relative contribution of each of the hidden nodes to the given estimate. During this process, it is important to note that the transmission of the signal occurs from layer to layer and not between nodes within any given layer. This process continues until each node has received its error contribution. The accumulated error for all of the input-output pairs is defined as the Euclidean distance in the weight space. The initial weights are then adjusted with the goal of converging towards a minimum error. This process continues until the minimum error value is reached.

7.2.3 Genetic Algorithm Learning Method

This stochastic heuristic optimization search technique is designed after the natural selection process followed in biological evolution; i.e., it follows the nature of sexual reproduction in which the genes of two parents combine to form those of their children. When this technique is applied to problem solving, the basic premise is that an initial population of individuals representing possible solutions to a problem is created. Each of these individuals has certain characteristics that make them more or less fit as members of the population. The "most fit" members will have a higher probability of mating than lesser-fit members and will produce progeny that have a significant chance of retaining the desirable attributes of their parents.

This method is very effective at finding optimal or near optimal solutions to a wide variety of problems because it does not impose many of the limitations required by traditional methods. It is an elegant generate-and-test strategy that can identify and exploit regularities in the environment, and it converges on solutions that are nearly globally optimal. The Genetic Algorithm consists of three fundamental steps, namely: initialization, reproduction, and recombination. These stages are discussed below.

7.2.3.1 Initialize Population and Fitness Evaluation (Initialization)

In the initialization stage the number of genes for each individual and the total number of chromosomes in the population size has to be determined. In a general population of genetic structures, which are randomly distributed in the solution, space is selected as the starting point of the search. Each individual is evaluated using a predetermined objective function. The objective function in this study, the Mean Square Error (MSE), is minimized.

7.2.3.2 Reproduction Stage

On the basis of their relative fitness values, individuals in the current population are selected for reproduction. The selection strategy used in this study was the *Roulette wheel* selection, where a roulette wheel has slots (F) sized according to the total fitness function of the population.

In other words, the candidate for the reproduction is chosen randomly, but the choice probability is proportional to the candidate's fitness. The higher the fitness function values of the individual, the higher its chances of being chosen for the reproduction process. Each chromosome has a certain number of slots proportional to the fitness value. The roulette wheel selection process is based on spinning the wheel pop size times; with each spin a single chromosome is selected for a new population. In accordance to the theory of inheritance, the "most fit" chromosomes will be selected more than once, while the "least fit" will die. As can be observed in Fig. 2, chromosome 1 and 3 were selected once, chromosome 2 was selected twice, while chromosome 4 was discarded.

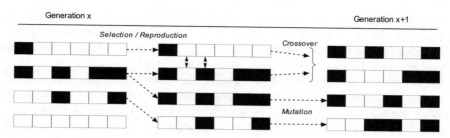

Fig. 7.2. Stages in the genetic algorithm

7.2.3.3 Recombination Stage

As shown in Figure 7.2, the selected parent individuals from the generation x are now recombined using two types of operators to produce the next generation (x+1). The first operator, *crossover,* draws only on the information present in the solutions of the current population in generating new solutions for evaluation. The mates for the crossover are chosen randomly from the initial population with the restriction that no individual can crossover with itself. The number of individuals undergoing the crossover operator increases with population size and as the number of chromosomes per individual increases. The next recombination operator is the *mutation operator* that arbitrarily alters one or more components of a selected structure thus providing the means for introducing new information into the population.

7.3 Developing the Predictive Model

The procedure for developing the predictive model is summarized in figure x. The framework can be divided into six major steps: (i) problem definition, (ii) feature selection, (iii) data representation, (iv) model and architecture development, (v) training and testing the predictive model, and (vi) result interpretation. These stages are discussed briefly below.

7.3.1 Understanding the Problem Domain

The prediction of bankruptcy and financial distress has received considerable attention in the accounting, auditing, and finance literature over the past three decades. Prior research (Chen and Church, 1992) has noted a poor correlation between the issuance of a going concern modified opinion by an auditor and the subsequent filing of bankruptcy by the client. In an attempt to aid auditors in their decision-making, financial distress researchers have relied on a number of statistical methods in the past two decades. These methods include multiple discriminant analysis (MDA) and probit and logit models (Hamer, 1983; Jones, 1987; Zavgren, 1985; Zmijewski, 1984). Hamer (1983), however, noted that differences in predictive accuracy among traditional methodologies were relatively insignificant. With the advent of Artificial Neural Networks (ANNs) in the 1980s, researchers applied ANNs to a variety of problems with special emphasis on bankruptcy prediction. In general, the evidence is mixed. With the exception of Klersey and Dugan (1995), the results indicate that ANNs have higher predictive accuracy than traditional statistical techniques such as logit, MDA, and probit models. The most extensive study was done by Boritz et al (1995), who examined predictive accuracy of two different ANN training methods to a number of statistical techniques (linear, quadratic, and nonparametric discriminant analysis) and logit and probit models. Boritz et al concluded that while ANNs appear to have a higher predictive accuracy, they are sensitive to the proportion of bankrupt firms in the training samples. See O'Leary (1998) for a meta analysis on this literature.

A commonly used learning method in all the above-mentioned ANN based studies was the back propagation algorithm (BP). The use of this supervised learning technique can lead to several problems. The first difficulty is that the method requires an adequate computation of the error to make a reasonable prediction of what the actual outcome should be. The second difficulty is that the global search space is typically too large for the algorithm. Searching for a minimum from zero typically leads the networks to oscillate, thereby reducing the networks, ability to generalize. Curry and Morgan (1997), Archer and Wang (1993), and Lenard, Alam, and Madey (1995) point out that BP and gradient techniques do not provide the best and fastest way to train neural networks and has in many instances resulted in inconsistent performance. This inconsistence can be attributed to the fact that gradient search techniques such as BP are designed for local search, i.e., they typically achieve the best solution in the region of their starting point. In other words, obtaining a global solution is often dependent on the choice of starting values (Schaffer, Whitley and Eshelman, 1992).

An alternate approach to learning is selectionism, which is a complete behavior system generated by an evolutionary process. Evolutionary development has been shown to be an extremely important source for generating more complexity in systems (Smithers, 1992). Neurobiologists proposed it to be the major mechanism underlying new functionality in the brain (Changeux, 1986). A common variant for classifying systems is called Genetic Algorithm (GA). Studies by Varetto (1998), among others, have found this technique to be an effective tool for business diagnosis. In this study, we hope to extend knowledge about ANN predictive accuracy by comparing the predictive accuracy of the ANN using two different learning techniques, namely, back propagation and genetic algorithms.

7.3.2 Feature Selection

Feature selection involves selecting a small subset of variable features that ideally is necessary and sufficient to describe the target concept (Kira and Rendell, 1992). Feature selection is of paramount importance since it can influence the performance of the predictive model.

Past research has focused on the usefulness of accounting numbers and has often ignored non-accounting variables that may contribute to the classification accuracy of the distress prediction models. There is little theoretical guidance concerning which specific variables to select. In this study, we used a combination of qualitative and quantitative characteristics to measure financial distress.

7.3.2.1 Qualitative Measures of Financial Distress

This research diverges from other studies in that we use different criteria to measure financial stress. According to evidence provided by prior research (Gajpal, Ganesh, and Rajendran, 1994; Gilson, John, and Lang, 1990; Giroux and Wiggins, 1984; Turetsky, 1997), this study has used negative operating cash flows, reducing or omitting dividend payments, debt default (including technical default or default on loan payments), and troubled debt restructuring as indicators of financial distress before firms go bankrupt. We use the term qualitative to represent dummy variables. Negative cash flows, reduction or omission of dividends, debt default, or troubled debt restructuring were all represented by dummy variables (1 if yes, they had a negative cash flow from operating activity, reduced or omitted dividends, debt default, or entered into troubled debt restructuring; 0, if these events had not happened). This representation was in accordance with prior studies (Lau 1987; Gilson et al 1990; Turetsky 1997). The justifications for the use of these variables are now discussed in greater detail.

Negative cash flows from operations: Bell and Tabor (1991) note that cash position measures, in particular cash raised from operating activities, are indicators of a company's liquidity position. John (1993) suggests that financial distress results from progressive negative operating cash flows. Giroux and Wiggins (1984) take negative cash flows into account as signaling corporate financial decline. Foster (1986) states that a firm's cash flows provide essential information for investors to evaluate the likelihood of financial distress. A negative operating cash flow, in the author's opinion, implies a tendency toward an insufficient future cash or working capital position. They are symptoms of financial stress that in turn could affect long-term survival of the company. Negative cash flows from operations were measured as a dummy variable, namely, 0 if no negative cash flows from operations and 1 if otherwise.

Dividend reductions or omissions: Dielman and Oppenheimer (1984) noted that a firm's dividend decisions could play an important role in identifying financially distressed firms. Dielman and Oppenheimer note that firms tend to follow a stable dividend policy if financially healthy. DeAngelo, DeAngelo, and Skinner (1994) contend that the financial problems of those firms that omit or cut dividends are more than temporary. Therefore, dividend changes, in particular, significant reduction of dividend, may have the potential to be an important predictor of financial distress. Dividend reductions or omissions were measured as a dummy variable, namely, 0 if the event did not happen and 1 if otherwise.

Debt default: Chen and Church (1992) argued that before a firm fails, its financial ratios deteriorate. However, in their opinion, a clearer signal of potential problems that could lead to bankruptcy would be difficulties a firm may encounter in fulfilling its debt obligations such as compliance with lending agreements or making scheduled payments. In addition, when firms violate debt covenants, creditors may accelerate the maturity of debt and impose heavy re-contracting costs to lenders. Furthermore, technical default will constrain their freedom of action in operating the firm (Smith and Warner 1979). If default in debt agreements are not remedied through renegotiation or firms do not get waivers from creditors, default is more likely to lead to bankruptcy. Chen and Church note that if default has occurred it is a clear signal of financial distress that could possibly lead to bankruptcy. Debt default was measured as a dummy variable, namely, 0 if no debt default and 1 if otherwise.

Troubled Debt Restructuring: Prior studies also regard troubled debt restructuring (TDR) as a distinct stage in a financial distress continuum (Giroux and Wiggins, 1983; Turetsky, 1997). A TDR results from a private renegotiation of debt outside of a chapter 11 filing in order to resolve or remedy debt defaults. As a result, current and future debt-service related cash flows may be improved. Unsuccessful TDR firms may end in bankruptcy. Hence, the current study views TDR as a stage following technical default and the preceding stage prior to a potential bankruptcy filing. TDR can be considered to be a clear signal of financial distress that could potentially portend bankruptcy. TDR was measured as a dummy variable, namely, 0 if the firm did not engage in troubled debt restructuring and 1 if otherwise.

7.3.3.2 Quantitative Measures of Financial Distress-Zmijewski Score

Hopwood, McKeown, and Mutchler (1994) note that financial distress is related to the probability of bankruptcy. Rather than use a multiplicity of financial ratios as in previous studies, we used a model that incorporates ratios measuring profitability, solvency, and liquidity. The model selected is the Zmijewski score. Zmijewski (1984) developed a weighted probit bankruptcy prediction model. This model is used rather than more popular models such as the Altman Z score because of its generalizability (Altman, 1968, 1993). The Altman Z score was developed using a sample of manufacturing companies. Many critics have noted that the Altman Z is not suited for examining the probability of bankruptcy of financial entities. This criticism does not hold with the Zmijewski model as it is not industry specific. Since our study covers both financial and non-financial industries, it was preferable to use a non-industry specific model. The Zmijewski model was developed based on a large sample of New York and American Stock Exchange companies. The b* statistic, a surrogate for the probability of bankruptcy, is calculated as follows:

$$b* = -4.803 - 3.6(ROA) + 5.4 (FNL) - 0.1 (LIQ) \qquad (4.1)$$

Where,

ROA	= Net income / Total assets
FNL	= Total debt / Assets
LIQ	= Current assets / Current liabilities

In this model, a higher value of b indicates greater probabilities of bankruptcy.

7.3.3 Pre-processing Data

Since Turetsky (1997), among others, notes that negative cash flows from operations, omission or reduction of dividends, violation of debt covenants, and troubled debt restructuring are signals of financial distress, we used these criteria to select the financially stressed firms in our control sample. The difference between our experimental and our control groups was that the experimental group filed for bankruptcy while the firms in the control sample, while exhibiting the above mentioned characteristics of financial distress, subsequently survived. The control firms were selected from the Compact Disclosure database for the period covering December

1989 to March 1996 and were selected by a three-step process[2]. The firms' annual and quarterly financial information in the "all text" fields of *Compact Disclosure* was used to validate the occurrence or non-occurrence and timing of events of distress[3]. We excluded from our sample troubled firms that were not publicly traded and incorporated in the United States. We also excluded those firms where information was not available on *Compustat* tapes and firms with incomplete data.

The screening process resulted in 522 firms after merging all sampled firms in the different event years by using the unique CUSIP number provided by *Compustat* and deleting duplicate samples. Our final sample grouping resulted in 265 distressed firms with dividend omission or reduction, 319 distressed firms with technical defaults or default on loan payments, 91 distressed firms restructuring their debt, and 104 firms that filed for bankruptcy. Finally, all the firms were examined to identify if those firms experienced negative cash flow from operations before the first "distress event" had occurred during the period covered by this study. A total of 497 firms in our sample had experienced negative operating cash flows.

7.3.4 ANN Training and Testing

The variables were represented as input data in a format that the neural network can uniquely identify (Zahedi, 1994). To assess the predictive accuracy of the ANN models, the experimental sample of 522 was split into two distinct groups namely, a training sample (418 datasets) and a holdout sample (104 datasets). This 80:20 combination was chosen after experimentation with other combinations. (The combinations included 20:80; 40:60; 50:50; and 60:40.). The 80:20 combination provided the best results.

Neural network research indicates that over training a network can lead it to oscillate thereby reducing the networks ability to generalize (Janssen, 1988). To prevent over-training, the training sample was further partitioned into two subsets. The first subset, the cross validation sample (n=52), was used to determine the lowest error term achieved during train-

---

[2] The provisions of statement of cash flows (SFAS No.95) are effective for annual financial statements for fiscal years ending after July 15, 1988. The earlier starting date of cash flow information prior to the fiscal year of July 15, 1988 could bias whether sampled firms had negative cash flow. Since there is a time lag of reporting financial information, therefore we choose December 1989 Compact Disclosure to initially select data.

[3] All test fields in Compact Disclosure include management discussion, president's letter, financial footnote, corporate exhibits, other corporate events, financial comments, and description of business.

ing, i.e., the cross validation criterion stopped the training process when the lowest error value (in terms of Mean Square Error) was reached. The second subset, the training sample (n=366), was used to estimate the model (i.e., train the network).

Training is the learning process by which the input and output data are repeatedly presented to the network. The ANNs for this study were developed on NeuroSolutions and Genehunter, both Windows-based artificial intelligence software applications. After the networks were trained, the holdout sample (n= 104) was entered into the system, and the trained ANNs were utilized to test the predictive accuracy of the network for the sample.

7.3.5 Interpretation of Results

In essence, the experimental group represented financially distressed firms that filed for bankruptcy. The control group was financially distressed firms that did not file for bankruptcy.

Table 7.1. Predictive Accuracy of Classification Models (Training Sample)

Classification Method	ANN-BP		ANN-GA		MDA	
	Actual Group Membership		Actual Group Membership		Actual Group Membership	
Predicted Group	Group 1	Group 2	Group 1	Group 2	Group 1	Group 2
Group 1	275	10	284	1	171	114
Group 2	11	70	4	77	25	56
True-pos. ratio	95.15%	87.50%	98.61%	98.72%	87.24%	32.94%
Type 1 error	0.04		0.01		0.13	
Type 1 error	0.13		0.01		0.67	
Error Rate	0.16		0.01		0.38	

n   = 366
Group 1   = Non Bankrupt (285)
Group 2   = Bankrupt (81)

Table 7.2. Predictive Accuracy of Classification Models (Cross validation sample)

Classification Method	ANN-BP		ANN-GA		MDA	
	Actual Group Membership		Actual Group Membership		Actual Group Membership	
Predicted Group	Group 1	Group 2	Group 1	Group 2	Group 1	Group 2
Group 1	76	6	84	1	48	36
Group 2	5	14	4	15	10	10
True-pos. ratio	93.83%	70.00%	95.45%	93.75%	82.76%	21.74%
Type 1 error	0.06		0.05		0.17	
Type 1 error	0.30		0.06		0.78	
Error Rate	0.11		0.05		0.44	

        n   = 104
  Group 1 = Non Bankrupt (84)
  Group 2 = Bankrupt (21)

To study the effectiveness of the ANN based classification, the results of networks were compared with the traditional Multiple Discriminant Analysis (MDA). A common measure of predictive models is the percentage of observations correctly classified. Table 7.1 reports the predictive accuracy of the two datasets. As can be observed, the ANN-GA classifier predicted the training sample with 99% accuracy.

This result is not surprising, since the networks were tested with the data set that was used to design the networks. Of greater interest, however, were the results of holdout sample (i.e., datasets that the network had not seen before).

Table 7.2 presents the results of utilizing the three techniques to evaluate the 104 holdout samples in terms of the average percentage of correct classifications. The genetic algorithm neural network (ANN-GA) had the highest accuracy (Group 1, bankrupt firms = 95%; Group 2, non-bankrupt firms = 94%) in predicting the financial status of the company. The back-propagation neural network (ANN-BP) was the next best accurate predictive model (Group 1 = 94%; Group 2 = 70%), while the MDA models had a lower accuracy rate (Group 1 = 83%; Group 2 = 50%) respectively. In general, ANN classification accuracy for the groups that went bankrupt varied from 100% to 90.4%.

7.4 Conclusions

In this study, ANNs utilizing two learning techniques, namely back propagation and genetic algorithms, were developed as tools for predicting bankruptcy. The predictive ability of the models was tested by comparing their predictive ability with that of a MDA model using real-world examples. The results indicate that, overall, ANN models had a higher predictive accuracy than the MDA models. Further, the ANN-GA model had a higher predictive rate than the ANN-BP model. The superior performance of the ANN-GA model over the ANN-BP model could be attributed to the fact that gradient techniques such as Backpropagation have a tendency to converge locally, thus affecting the selection of weights that is needed for the neural network's accuracy. Therefore, since the algorithm tends to get trapped in a local minima, the solution provided by this neural network is not a global solution.

The results of this study compare favorably with other studies. Brockett et al (1994), using a backpropagation neural network, found the ANN to correctly classify 73% of insolvent firms. Fanning and Cogger (1994), using generalized adaptive neural networks (GANNA), reported a 94% success rate. Etheridge and Sriram (1997), using probabilistic neural networks, found accuracy rates of 88% and 96% for their sample of banks for the two ANN models they tested. However, the point is that most studies with the exception of Etheridge and Sriram (1996) used healthy companies as a control sample. Our study used financially stressed companies that had not filed for bankruptcy as the control sample.

Although the predictive models have several advantages and uses, they also have their limitations. The number of variables that can be input into the models is limited. In this respect, rather than use a plethora of variables, this study contributes to the extant literature by developing a parsimonious model that captures liquidity, profitability, solvency and incorporates qualitative signals of distress. The constructs of liquidity, profitability and solvency are measured by the Zmijewski distress score. The Zmijewski distress score has an advantage over other models such as the Altman Z score in that it can be universally applied across industries. Using this parsimonious model, we find that the genetic algorithm neural network significantly outperforms the backpropagation model. The predictive results are superior to prior studies. In addition, the genetic algorithm model had the lowest misclassification error rate.

In summary, the contribution of this article is to extend prior research by incorporating a more parsimonious model and developing and testing a genetic algorithm neural network. The experimental design attempted to incorporate an element of reality by including financially distressed firms in the control sample.

In conclusion, the model cannot, and should not, entirely replace professional judgment. It should be used to provide auditors with objective information to assist with their reporting decision on a client in financial distress and going concern contingencies. Many important qualitative variables such as management ability and future plans, which could potentially mitigate the stress faced by a firm, are not formally incorporated into the models.

8 Visualization of Patterns in Accounting Data with Self-organizing Maps

Eija Koskivaara

Turku Centre for Computer Science, Turku School of Economics and Business Administration, Finland

Abstract. Neural networks are data driven methods. They provide additional information to the decision process as might be left hidden otherwise. Neural networks have already been applied in many different business areas; and they can be used for prediction, classifying, and clustering. They can learn, remember, and compare complex patterns. This chapter shows how a neural network, especially Kohonen's self-organizing map (SOM), can be used in visualization of complex accounting data. The SOM is used for clustering ten years of monthly income statements of a manufacturing firm. The purpose is to show how the data sets of various accounts and years form their own groups. We found that the SOM can be a visual aid for classifying and clustering data sets, and that it reveals if some cluster contains data that a priori should not be in it. Hence, it can be used for signaling unexpected fluctuations in data. Furthermore, the SOM is a possible technique embedded in the continuous monitoring and controlling tool.

8.1 Introduction

Many parties, such as investors, creditors, and managers, are interested in the accuracy of an organization's financial account values. Managers want to estimate the future revenues and expenses in order to optimize the operations during a certain period. Auditors want to assess the accuracy of an organization's financial statements. Creditors want to analyze the organization's payment ability. All these parties may benefit from a tool that monitors and visualizes complex accounting data.

One possible technique embedded in the monitoring tool could be an artificial neural network (ANN). ANNs are not a priori statistical formal techniques but instead they are data driven techniques. ANNs have already been applied in many different business areas; and they can be used for prediction, classifying, and clustering tasks (Vellido *et al.* 1999, Zhang *et al.* 1998). They can learn, remember, and compare complex patterns (Medsker and Liebowitz 1994). They are claimed to be able to recognize patterns in data even when the data are noisy, ambiguous, distorted, or variable (Dutta 1993). They are capable of discovering data relationships. For example, unlike traditional statistical techniques, ANNs are capable of identifying and simulating non-linear relationships in the data without any a priori assumptions about the distribution properties of the data. ANNs learn from examples and then generalize to new observations. They provide additional information to the decision process as might be left hidden otherwise. These features make ANNs potentially suitable for many tasks within accounting. Information technology development and processing capacities of PCs have made it possible to model ANN-based information systems for monitoring and controlling operations.

Researchers have developed a variety of ANN-models to assist in the monitoring and controlling of operations such as detecting material errors in the data (Coakley and Brown 1991a, Coakley and Brown 1991b, Coakley and Brown 1993, Wu 1994, Coakley 1995, Busta and Weinberg 1998, Koskivaara 2000), detecting management fraud (Green and Choi 1997, Fanning and Cogger 1998, Feroz *et al.* 2000), and support for going concern decision (Hansen *et al.* 1992, Lenard *et al.* 1995, Koh and Tan 1999, Anandarajan and Anandarajan 1999, Etheridge *et al.* 2000). ANNs have also been applied to internal control risk assessment (Davis *et al.* 1997, Ramamoorti *et al.* 1999) and financial distress problems (Fanning and Cogger 1994). Material error applications direct users' attention to those financial account values where the actual relationships are not consistent with the expected relationships. A user has to decide whether and what kind of further investigation is required to explain the unexpected results. Material error ANN-models either predict future values or classify data. The results of material error ANN-models seem promising, at least as a supplement to traditional analytical auditing procedures, and offer improved performance in recognizing material misstatements within the financial accounts.

Companies are using or have used ANN applications to support their business. Credit-card companies use ANN technology to reveal fraudulent clients (Mulqueen 1996, Fryer 1996, Fisher 1999). KPMG Peat Marwick has already developed an ANN for bankruptcy prediction (Etheridge *et al.* 1994). Pohjola insurance company has applied an ANN solution to their direct marketing (Sinkkonen and Lahtinen 1998).

In this chapter we show the feasibility of an ANN, especially Kohonen's self-organizing map (SOM), in monitoring account values in monthly income statements of a manufacturing firm. We study whether the SOM is capable of revealing monthly variations and clusters in the data sets in the meaningful matter. The SOM has proven to be suitable for data analysis tasks (Kohonen 1997). Although many papers on self-organizing maps, since its invention in 1981, have been published, few studies have dealt with the use of self-organizing maps for financial analysis. The studies by Martín-del-Brío and Serrano-Cinca (1993) and Back *et al.* (1998) are examples of the application of the SOM for financial analysis. Martín-del-Brío and Serrano-Cinca (1993) studied the financial statements of Spanish companies and attempted to predict bankruptcies among Spanish banks during the 1977-85 banking crisis. Back *et al.* (1998) compared 120 companies in the international pulp and paper industry. In this study, the aim is to receive evidence of this method's suitability to analyze monthly account data. We anticipate that the SOM recognizes the relationships between different account values and reveals the time variation of the data sets. According to our information, the SOM has not earlier been applied to analyzing monthly account data sets.

The remainder of the chapter is organized as follows: Section 8.2 describes the research methodology. This section includes a brief description of SOM, and the choice of the financial account values used in this experiment. Section 8.3 presents the construction of the self-organizing maps, and Section 8.4 presents a detailed analysis of the maps and gives guidelines to implement this kind of model. The conclusions of this paper are presented in Section 8.5.

8.2 Methodology

8.2.1 Self-organizing Maps

The SOM is a clustering and visualization method, and the purpose is to show the data set in another representation form (Kohonen 1997). It creates a two dimensional map from n-dimensional input data. This map resembles a landscape in which it is possible to identify borders that define different clusters. These clusters consist of the input variables with similar characteristics, i.e., in this report, the monthly variation of account values'. The self-organizing training trials continue until two input items that are close in the input space are mapped into the same or neighboring neurons on the map. Output neurons create groups; which together form a map of the input neurons.

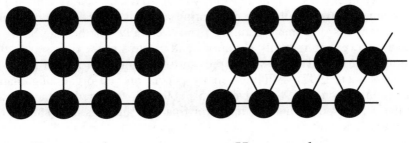

Rectangular   Hexagonal

Fig. 8.1. Forms of lattice

The SOM has six learning parameters, *topology, neighborhood type, X- and Y-dimensions, training rate, training length*, and *network radius*. The network topology refers to the form of lattice. There are two commonly used lattices, rectangular and hexagonal (Fig. 8.1). In a rectangular lattice, each neuron is connected to four neighbors, expect for the ones at the edge of the lattice. In the entire network we used, the output neurons are arranged in a hexagonal lattice structure. This arrangement connects every neuron to exactly six neighbors, expect for the ones at the edge of the lattice. This choice was made following the guidelines of Kohonen (1997), since we expected the SOM to provide some benefit for the monitoring due to its visualization capability. Neighborhood type refers to the neighborhood function used, and the options are Gaussian and bubble. X- and Y- dimensions refer to the size of the map. In too-small maps, differences between clusters are hard to identify; and in too-large maps, clusters will appear to be flat. The training rate factor refers to how much the neuron in the neighborhood of the winning neuron learns from the input data vector. The training length measures the processing time, i.e., the number of iterations through the training data. The network radius refers to how many nodes around the "winning" neuron are affected during the learning process. The training process of the network is split into two parts. In part one, the map is "roughly" trained. In the second part, the network is fine-tuned.

8.3 Data

We used actual data comprising ten years of monthly income statements for a manufacturing company. The company was a medium-sized firm in Finland, and its net sales amounted to approximately EUR 11 million per year. With the help of a certified public accountant (CPA) auditor the accounts chosen represented the major and the most interesting monthly income statement categories. The accounts and their monthly averages in thousand euros are presented in Table 8.1.

Table 8.1. Financial accounts (in EUR 1000)

	90-99	1998	1999
Net sales	916	1325	1250
Materials + Change in inventory	215	297	259
Personnel costs	125	165	161
Gross margin	571	864	830
Administration	58	57	58
Total indirect	340	360	383
Operating profit	215	462	396
Receivables	1450	1630	1591
Trade debt	1468	2563	1965

The reasons for selecting the above accounts for our models are as follows.

- *Net sales* (NS) are a significant value to monitor. In this particular case, variation between July and the other months is big because the company is closed in July. From the management's point of view, it is better if the actual value is bigger than the budgeted value because then there are fewer disappointments. From the auditor's point of view, this scenario might raise doubts about whether all sales are recorded if the actual value is much below the prediction value. On the other hand, if the actual value is much higher than the prediction values, the company might have recorded some fictitious sales.
- *Materials* (Mat) + *Change in inventory* (CinIn) together should tell the total use of material during a certain period. The value should be in alignment with net sales as this is a manufacturing company.
- *Personnel costs* (PC) should be in alignment with production and the total use of material.
- *Gross margin* (GM) is an important value at least from the prediction point of view as well as in seeing how much money is left to cover indirect costs and profit.
- *Administration* (Adm) shows the overall trend of the costs in the company and in the line of business.
- *Total indirect* (TotInd) indicates all fixed costs. This value should be predicted in all cases because these costs do not depend on sales.

- *Operating profit* (OP) is an interesting value at least from the prediction point of view. Furthermore, it is important to see that the operation is profitable in the long run.
- *Receivables* (Rec) are an interesting and important value to follow in order to know how much of the company's money is "outside".
- *Trade debt* (TD) tells how much the company has to pay "outside". Receivables and trade debts should be in alignment with the net sales.

8.4 Clustering with the SOMs

For the clustering purpose, we used The Self-Organizing Map Program Package version 3.1, created by The SOM Programming Team of the Helsinki University of Technology in the network building (Kohonen *et al.* 1995). For the visualization of the results of the SOM, we used Nenet-Demo version 1.1a created by The Nenet Team (Elomaa *et al.* 1999). Nenet is a user-friendly program designed to illustrate the use of SOMs, and it also provides individual parameter level maps and feature planes. This property suits our purposes perfectly, because we want to compare different accounts and months with each other.

We constructed two different kinds of maps with different input vectors. First, we constructed a map so that in a vector there were the monthly data of the account per year as vector items. With this A-map, we wanted to see how different accounts are situated in comparison to each other and to the previous years' values. Second, we constructed a map with the values of a certain month's data as vector values and presented those in a chronological order for the neural network. With this B-map, we wanted to see whether there are any yearly tendencies in the data sets. These map approaches resemble analytical auditing procedures such as a comparison of current information with similar information for prior periods and a study of relationships among the elements of information (Gauntt *et al.* 1997).

There are some guidelines to follow when creating maps. The map ought to be rectangular, rather than square, in order to achieve a stable orientation in the data space. Normally, the x-axis should be about 30 percent greater than the y-axis, thus forming a rectangular output map. Another recommendation is that the training length of the second part should be at least 500 times the number of the network units in order to reach statistical accuracy (Kohonen 1997). We chose one where the layer consisted of 35 neurons arranged in a 5*7 hexagonal grid. As mentioned earlier, hexagonal lattices are good for visualization purposes. The neighborhood function was the bubble. The training length and training rate in the first phase were 1750 and 0.5 and in the second phase, 17500 and 0.05. The neighborhood radius in the first phase was 9 and in the second phase, 1.

To visualize the final self-organizing map, we used the *unified distance matrix (Umatrix)*. This U-matrix method can be used to discover otherwise invisible relationships in a high-dimensional data space. It also makes it possible to classify data sets into clusters of similar values. The simplest U-matrix method is to calculate the distances between neighboring neurons and store them in the matrix, i.e., the output map, which can then be interpreted. If there are "walls" between neurons, the neighboring ones are distant, i.e., the values differ significantly. The distance values are also displayed in colors when the U-matrix is visualized. On the maps, we define the clusters by looking at the color shades of the borders between the hexagons. The dark colors in the walls represent great distances while brighter colors indicate similarities amongst the neurons. The colored borders between the hexagons are of great value when trying to determine and interpret clusters.

By viewing the individual feature planes, it is possible to visualize the values of a single vector column, i.e., in this study, the maps for one month (A-maps) or for one account (B-maps). These feature planes can be visualized in order to discover how the company has been doing according to different months or different accounts. Because we selected accounts that depend on each other, the feature planes of the months should be more or less similar.

8.5 Visualization of the data

Next we show how the outputs of the SOM can be used as a visual aid for classifying and clustering the monthly income statements values over ten years. The user analyzes the clusters of accounts and variations of the monthly feature planes in order to find whether the clusters are close enough to each other or whether there are any significant differences between the monthly feature planes (A-map). The user may also analyze whether the account values are close enough to the previous year's values (B-map). If the difference is significant, the user has to decide how much and what kind of further investigation is needed.

8.5.1 Studying the account cluster

Studying the underlying monthly feature planes of the A-map (Fig. 8.2) and the final A-map (Fig. 8.3), a number of clusters of accounts and the characteristics of these clusters were identified (Fig. 8.4).

The feature planes in Fig. 8.2 show a map for each month in this study where the red color in the bottom left corners represents high values, which in our case imply revenue accounts. Dark colors in the bottom right corners show negative values, which in our case imply a trade debt account. From these feature planes, we see that there is only a little variation between the months. For example, in the feature planes of June and July there are a little lighter neurons in the middle than in the other months' planes. However, the feature planes of the months are so similar that none give any reason for auditing implications. This result means that the relationships between the accounts included in this study are quite stable during the year. If the feature plane of the month differs much from the other feature planes, it is a hint for a user to investigate more.

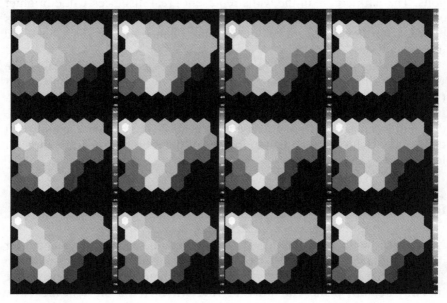

Fig.8.2. The feature planes maps for the months: January, February, March, and April at the top, May, June, July, and August in the middle, and September, October, November, and December at the bottom

In Fig. 8.4, we have named identified clusters according to the accounts these clusters contain. We labeled the last two years' accounts to see whether the accounts are close to each other and to name the clusters. We identified four main clusters: *revenues, margins, costs, and trade debts*. Revenue and trade debt clusters were easy to identify based on the feature planes of the different months. Although the trade debts of the last two years are in the same neuron, the cluster itself is much bigger because the earlier years' trade debt values were more spread out on the map. The revenue cluster could be bigger based on the feature planes on March, June, July, and August; however, the labeling of gross margin and operating profit reveals that these neurons belong to the margins cluster. All the cost accounts in our study are situated in the upper right corner; therefore; we named it the cost cluster. Receivables (Rec), net sales (NS), operating profit (OP), personnel costs (PC), change in inventory (CinIn), administration (Adm), and materials (Mat) of two last years are in the same neuron. The gross margin (GM) and total indirect (TotInd) of 1998 and 1999 are in different neurons. This location indicates that the relative monthly account value's variation of gross margin and total indirect is bigger than that of the other accounts in these years.

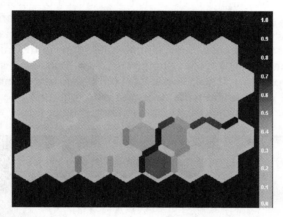

Fig. 8.3. The final A-map

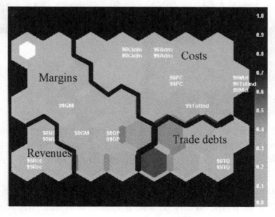

Fig. 8.4. Clusters on the A-map

8.5.2 Studying the yearly tendency

We also let the SOM cluster the account based on the month. With this B-map, we wanted to see whether the months are close to each other and whether the different years are close to each other. We analyzed the B-map with account feature planes (Fig. 8.5) and by labeling all the months on the map. This method found six clusters in a map. The feature planes of net sales, gross margin, operating profit, and receivables are at the top of Fig. 8.5. These accounts present in our sample the income accounts where the red color illustrates high values, which are situated on the left side of the feature planes. The overall outlook of the net sales, gross margin and operating profit seems very similar. The feature planes of materials, change in inventories, personnel costs, and administration are in the middle. Materials and personnel costs have the same general outlook as net sales although the colors are opposite. These accounts should be in alignment. The feature planes of total indirect and trade debts are on the bottom line. In these feature planes; the darker the color gets, the bigger the cost is.

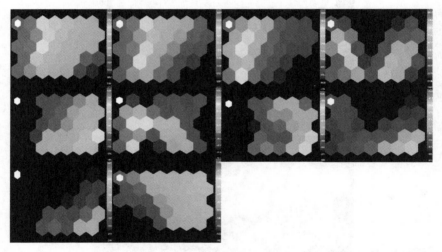

Fig. 8.5. Feature planes of accounts: net sales, gross margin, operating profit, and receivables at the top, materials, change in inventories, personnel costs, and administration in the middle, and total indirect and trade debts at the bottom

In Fig. 8.6, we have counted how many monthly data of the year belong to one cluster in the B-map. We also see a tendency starting from the bottom right corner, where the early nineties data are situated, up towards the top of the map and then to the bottom left corner and once again up towards the top of the map. The best performance seems to be in the bottom left corner where the monthly data from the year 1998 are located. All the July data are in the bottom line neurons. The first seven years of July data are in the ultimate bottom right corner of the map. The July data of 1997-1999 are also grouped at the bottom right neurons of these years' clusters.

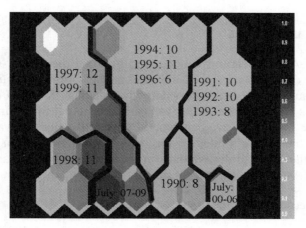

Fig. 8.6. Yearly clusters of B-map

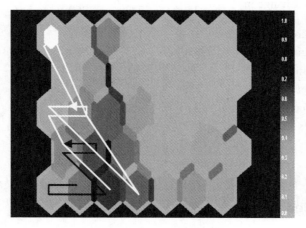

Fig. 8.7. Movements of the 1998 (Black) and 1999 (White) months

We also illustrate with a black arrow the monthly movement in 1998 and with a white arrow the monthly movement in 1999 (Fig. 8.7). From these arrows, we see that the movement of the 1999 monthly data on the B-map is much broader. The reason for the more compact movement of the 1998 data might be that the account values of that year are the biggest in the whole data set; and therefore, they have concentrated in one corner. The same but opposite reason applies to the July data, especially with the years

1990-1996. These account values are the smallest in the whole data set and, therefore, have concentrated in the bottom right corner. We also see from Fig. 8.7 that both arrows start from and end at adjacent neurons.

8.5.3 Account Values

To ease the ANN's learning process and improve the quality of the map, the data are often pre-processed in some manner. We did not use any pre-processing method, because we wanted to calculate the 1999 average account values based on the vector values in the output maps. In Table 8.2, we compare the actual average monthly account values to values calculated from the vector values of the A-map and B-map. On average, it seems that the vector order we have in the B-map is better than the vector order in the A-map if we compare the output vector values.

Table 8.2. Account values

	1999	A-map	B-map	A/1999	B/1999
Net sales	1250	1238	1239	-1 %	-1 %
Materials + Change in inventory	259	273	269	5 %	4 %
Personnel costs	161	123	161	-24 %	0 %
Gross margin	830	873	807	5 %	-3 %
Administration	58	59	56	2 %	-2 %
Total indirect	383	471	361	23 %	-6 %
Operating profit	396	467	394	18 %	0 %
Receivables	1591	1408	1532	-12 %	-4 %
Trade debts	1965	1626	1978	-17 %	1 %

8.5.4 Seeded Error

We seeded an extra use of material in the data in order to see whether the SOM recognizes any difference. We manipulated the data by doubling the use of material in December 1999 to see the effects on maps and feature planes. This effect is very tiny considering that in one map we have all the data from the ten years visible at the same time. In Fig. 8.8, we show how the feature planes of the maps change because of this manipulation. On the left side of the figure, we have the feature planes of the original data; and on the right side, we have the feature planes of the manipulated data. The feature planes at the top of the figure are based on months (A-map), and the feature planes at the bottom of the figure are based on accounts (B-map). The white neurons on the left show the right place for the vector. The white neurons on the right show where the manipulated data vectors are. We have also circled the effects the manipulation has on the whole map. The monthly use of material is situated in the same neuron in both cases (see Fig. 8.8 upper feature planes). However, the color of the adjacent neuron has changed dramatically. On the account feature planes, the change is more radical. The whole feature plane looks very different. The manipulation has turned the whole feature plane inside out. The neuron has changed its place, and the colors of the adjacent neurons have changed.

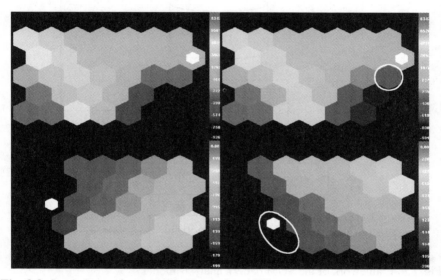

Fig. 8.8. Seeded use of material in December 1999

8.5.5 Implementing the Model

Fig. 8.9 depicts the framework of our SOM-based pattern analysis model in accounting data. In general, this accounting data should illustrate the business process. The SOM takes advantage of the data that already exist in the accounting systems. The SOM utilizes the data and gives a compact and excellent visualization of it. Furthermore, it clusters the data in a meaningful manner. The SOM gives new kind of information to human analysts and, therefore, makes the interaction between a human actor and information system possible. Generally, the human actor may refresh the model in three ways. First, they can make changes in the business processes. For example, allocate more timely the use of material in the accounting system. Second, they can correct the faulty data. For instance, take away all the fictitious sales from the bookkeeping records. Third, a human actor may refresh the model either by changing the parameters in the model or by chancing the variables of the model.

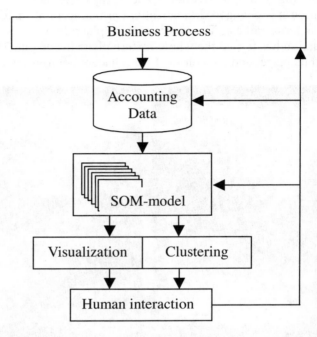

Fig. 8.9. Framework of the SOM pattern analysis model

8.6 Conclusions

In this chapter, we showed how the SOM could be used in the visualization of the monthly income statement values. The SOM was used for the clustering of the data sets, and the purpose was to show account values in another representation form. We let the SOM cluster a manufacturing company's monthly account data from ten years. We found that the SOM is a tool for classifying these data sets and similar accounts form their clusters close to each other. We argue that the SOM can assist users by visualizing irregularities in the data and guiding the user to the heart of the problem. The SOM utilizes the entire data and finds homogenous groups in the data. With the SOM embedded in the monitoring system, it is possible to plot a picture on screen from complex data sets, for example once a month, and give a visual aid for analyzers of the business data. We used monthly values of account, but the SOM could also be used for analyzing all the transactions of certain accounts.

The development and assessment of advanced analysis methods like ANNs in an accounting context and for continuous monitoring and controlling is important in order to supply users with more efficient and effective means of monitoring account values. This monitoring is one way of restoring the public confidence in the capital market system and accounting profession, which was shaken by the collapses of Enron and Arthur Andersen etc.

9 Visual Representations of Accounting Information

Richard B. Dull[1], David P. Tegarden [2]

[1]School of Accountancy and Legal Studies, Clemson University, South Carolina

[2] Department of Accounting and Information Systems, Virginia Tech, Virginia

Abstract. Modern accounting information systems provide decision-makers with such a large volume of accounting data, it can overwhelm even the most sophisticated accounting decision-maker. The result may be underutilization of relevant information. Advances in information visualization technologies provide an effective alternative to address the current and future volume of accounting information. This chapter addresses the theoretical background of visualizations, describing the literature that supports the use of visualizations. The application of information visualization to accounting is discussed, followed by a description of variety multidimensional visualizations techniques.

> *Information, once rare and cherished like caviar, is*
> *now plentiful and taken for granted like potatoes.*
> - The First Law of Data Smog, David Shenk, 1997

9.1 Introduction

Today's accounting information systems provide decision-makers with such a large volume of accounting data, it can overwhelm even the most sophisticated accounting decision-maker. With the increasing trend to use enterprise-wide systems, such as ERP and CRM systems, and the use of multidimensional data to support decision-making, e.g., on-line analytical processing (OLAP), knowledge discovery, and data mining (Adriaans and Zantinge 1996; Fayyad, et al. 1996; Thomsen 1997), the volume of data that the decision-maker could face in the future is even greater. Therefore, the decision-maker needs tools to extract the actual information from the flood of data that is available.

Recent advances in information visualization technologies provide one avenue to address the current and future "glut" of accounting information facing the decision-maker. Current information visualization technologies allow the decision-maker to use their visual/spatial abilities to solve the abstract problems found in business. These technologies already have been deployed in finance, litigation, marketing, manufacturing, training, and organizational modeling (Brown, et al. 1995; Chorafas and Steinmann 1995; Grantham 1993; Markham 1998; Schroeder, et al. 1998; Thierauf 1995).[1] Furthermore, multidimensional information visualizations may better support the decision-maker that must use multidimensional data (Dull and Tegarden 1999).

The remainder of this chapter is organized as follows. In the next section, we provide a definition and purpose of information visualization, a short history of visualization, and a justification of why information visualization is appropriate for accounting decision-making. The third section provides an overview of information visualization research in decision-making and accounting. In the fourth section, we detail some of the tools that can be used in accounting information visualizations and describe a set of metaphors for accounting information visualizations. In the final section, we explore directions for future research and applications in accounting information visualizations.

9.2 Background

What exactly is meant by visualization? According to The Dictionary of Computer Graphics and Virtual Reality, visualization is "the process of representing data as a visual image." (Latham 1995, p. 148) The data being visualized may represent concrete objects, such as rooms or cars, or abstract objects, such as profit, sales, or cost. Information visualization deals with transforming non-spatial or behavioral data (i.e., abstract data)

---

[1] For a more complete description of visualization examples and issues, see Bertin (1983), Card, et al. (1999), Cleveland (1993, 1994), Jones (1996), Kosslyn (1994), and Tufte (1983, 1990, 1997).

into visual images that represent an analogy or metaphor of the problem space. If the data are abstract, then a visual analog must be created, such as a pie chart or line graph.

According to Grinstein and Ward (1997), the purpose of information visualization is *not* to replace solid quantitative analysis but instead to allow the quantitative analysis to be focused. Information visualization technologies:

- allow the human visual system to be exploited in order to extract information from data,
- can provide an overview of complex data sets,
- aid in identifying the structure, patterns, trends, anomalies, and relationships in data, and
- provide a means to identify the areas of "interest."

When used appropriately, information visualization technologies support the decision-maker in deriving the information from the data.

9.2.1 Visualization History

Visualization has been used for a long time. For example, cave drawings in France are over 20,000 years old and maps existed in China in the 12th century. The first multi-dimensional representations appeared in Europe during the 19th century. In one early example from 1854, Dr. John Snow plotted cholera deaths in central London (Fig. 9.1). He marked the location of deaths with dots and of water pumps with crosses. Based on this visualization, he realized that nearly all occurrences of cholera occurred among those who lived near the water pump on Broad Street. From this observation, he had the handle from the pump removed and ended the cholera epidemic (Tufte 1983).

According to Tufte (1983), Minard created possibly the best statistical graphic ever drawn in 1861. This graphic portrays the losses suffered by Napolean's army during his invasion of Russia in 1812. (Fig. 9.2). The width of the band across the figure represents the size of his army. The lighter color band represents the invasion, while the darker band represents the retreat. At the beginning of the invasion (seen at the left of the graphic) the size of his army was approximately 422,000. When Napoleon reached Moscow, the army had dwindled to about 100,000 men. His army shrunk to about 10,000 men by the time it reached the Polish-Russian border. Furthermore, the temperature scale and dates of the retreat are shown at the bottom of the chart (Tufte 1983).

Fig. 9.1. Snow's Cholera Graphic (Tufte 1983, p. 24, © Graphics Press)

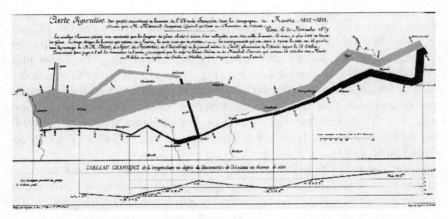

Fig. 9.2. Minard's Graphic of Napoleon's Moscow Campaign of 1812 (Tufte 1983, p. 41, © Graphics Press)

9.2.2 Why Information Visualization?

Even though decision-makers suffer from information overload, due to the high volume of data produced by modern accounting information systems, they tend to underutilize large amounts of relevant information. Since a majority of the brain's activity that processes sensory data deals with analyzing visual images, visualization technologies can help resolve this dilemma. (Chorafas and Steinman 1995). In this section, we describe why visualization technologies may be appropriate for accounting decision-making by summarizing visual cognition, the cognitive fit model, and the types of tasks for which visualization is appropriate.

9.2.2.1 Visual Cognition

From a visual cognition perspective, research shows that visualizations can improve problem-solving capabilities. Miller (1956) reports on a set of non-business results that imply a human's input channel capacity is greater when visual abilities are used. The reported results demonstrated that decision-makers that required unidimensional or multidimensional data are more efficient using their visual abilities. Based on these results, information visualization technologies should be able to enhance the capability of a decision-maker to process information that is either unidimensional or multidimensional. Furthermore, visual imagery researchers (Kosslyn 1980; Shepard and Cooper 1982) have shown that visual recall outperformed verbal recall. However, visual recall is dependent on perception, i.e., how the objects were learned (visual images on visual perception; auditory images on auditory perceptions, etc.).

9.2.2.2 Cognitive Fit Model

The Cognitive Fit Model (CFM) suggests the effectiveness of the problem-solving process is a function of the relationship between the problem-solving task and the problem representation (Umanath and Vessey 1995; Vessey 1991,1994; Vessey and Galletta 1991). Using the CFM, Vessey (1991) provides an explanation for the mixed results in the "tables versus graphs" literature. When the problem representation "fits" the problem-solving task, a preferable mental representation of the problem will be realized; and the speed and accuracy of the problem-solving process will be improved. In other words, the better the "fit" between the task and the representation, the more effective and efficient the problem-solving process will be. Therefore, accounting information visualizations must be created with the problem-solving task in mind. It also should be emphasized that when mismatches do occur between the task and the representation, decision-making performance will suffer in terms of speed, accuracy, or both. When considering multidimensional data, this union becomes even more crucial.

9.2.2.3 Visualization Tasks

According to Grinstein and Ward (1997), there are three types of problem-solving tasks that are amendable to information visualization: exploratory, confirmatory, and production. With exploratory tasks, decision-makers normally search the visualization for structure or trends to extract or they attempt to create or test hypotheses about the underlying data. Decision-makers attempt to confirm or refute hypotheses with confirmatory tasks. Decision-makers perform production-based tasks when they already have validated a hypothesis and are using a visualization-based report. Depending on their job, accounting decision-makers may perform all three types of tasks.

9.3 Information Visualization Research

Historically, the majority of the research in accounting information visualizations has been related to report format and presentation of accounting information. Even though the report formats used in most accounting information visualization research differ significantly, one common theme emerges: the presentation format of information affects the decisions that are made (Anderson and Kaplan 1992; Anderson and Reckers 1992; MacKay and Villarreal 1987; Stock and Watson 1984). Before jumping in to accounting and information visualization research, we will provide an overview of information visualization research in decision-making.

9.3.1 Decision-Making and Information Visualization

The behavioral disciplines have had many research studies relating to the topic of visualization (Colet and Aaronson 1995; Cooper 1990, 1995; Schkade and Kleinmuntz 1994). This interest is in part due to the recognition that one's experiences are based on observations from a three-dimensional world (Cooper 1990). A second reason for the interest relates to usefulness of information visualizations in recognizing relationships among data. Information visualizations can be used as a tool to direct the process of mathematical modeling when investigating these relationships (Colet and Aaronson 1995). Yu and Behrens (1995) developed their framework of using visualizations in statistical analysis to assist in "balancing noise and smoothing in statistical analysis" (p. 264).

Beyond the general statistical analysis uses of visualizations in psychological literature, numerous studies have investigated human interactions with visualizations (Cooper 1990, 1995; Lohse et al. 1994). Cooper looked at the connection between two-dimensional and three-dimensional views of an object (1990) and the concept of mental imagery (1995). The 1990 study suggests that when confronted with two-dimensional representations of structural objects, individuals will mentally create a three-dimensional representation of the object. This research is significant in reporting the mental connection between two-dimensional and three-dimensional representations.

Psychological researchers also have investigated decisions made based on the type of representation. For example, Schkade and Kleinmuntz (1994) found a significant effect on the decision process based on the information format used during information acquisition. Furthermore, Larkin and Simon (1987) found that diagrams were superior representations to textual ones and suggested three reasons for these results:

- diagrams group related information together,
- diagrams use location to aid in information search, and
- diagrams aid in many perceptual inferences.

As such, they concluded that diagrams seem to support more efficient computational processes than their written counterparts when the user is capable of using diagrams to acquire information.

In another study, Jones and Schkade (1995) found that decision-makers sometimes "translate" information in an unfamiliar format into a more familiar one and base their decision on the new format when the information representation did not match problem representation. This best format concept is supported by the cognitive fit model (Vessey 1991).

Wickens et al. (1994) indicate that for questions requiring an integrative knowledge of information, extraction and retention of data is superior for 3D images over 2D images. In addition, they concluded that rotation was used more by subjects when answering questions that were relatively more integrative. As such, multivariate representations may produce varying levels of decision effectiveness based on the perception and interpretation of data (McCormick et al. 1987). Therefore, information users may have an advantage using information presented in a multidimensional format.

There are many variables that must be considered when presenting multidimensional information. For instance, Pani (1993) reports that the angle of rotation affects the comprehension of an object that is presented within a 3D representation; if an improper angle is used, the data may be distorted. Generally speaking, as the dimensionality of the representation increases, approaching the dimensionality of the data, the task of understanding the representation should be less intensive, allowing faster decisions.

In general, the above studies suggest that multidimensional visualizations should be useful in decision-making; such visualizations can help information users to recognize relationships among data. If these visualizations fit the problem and problem-solving process, the speed and accuracy of the problem solving should benefit.

9.3.1.1 Color in Business Visualizations

One variable that has been extensively studied is the use of color to aid in representing multidimensional data. In a study relevant to accounting decision-making, Benbasat and Dexter (1985) introduced the use of color to the "graphical decisions" business literature. The study used an experimental decision model to optimize profit.[2] Their study compared results for subjects that used one-color versus multi-color graphs to make a promotional budgeting decision that resulted in changes in profits. The graphs that were tested displayed the functional relationship between promotion/profit for multiple territories. One factor that was controlled was time; one group of subjects had five minutes to make the decision, and another group has fifteen minutes. They found that by simply using multiple colors to implement the graphs, the decisions were better[3] for the group having only five minutes to complete the task. It should be noted that their use of color was redundant; all of the information was available without the use of color.

Benbasat and Dexter's (1985) results were consistent with Hoadley's (1994) research regarding color supplanting other information. The supplanting functions used by Hoadley's subjects included: 1) discriminating, 2) organizing, 3) disembedding, and 4) quantity visualization. However, since Benbasat and Dexter's experiment used redundant data and differences were only found for the lower time group, one cannot conclude that color alone made the difference.

There have been several other studies in the management information systems literature relating to the effect of color. Hoadley (1990, p. 121) summarized the results of the color research by noting that color improves performance in recall tasks, search-and-locate tasks, retention tasks, and decision judgment tasks. Color also improves comprehension of instructional materials.

Lohse (1993) confirmed previous research that color aids decision-making when using graphs but equally important suggested that the decision usefulness of a visualization depends on the task being investigated. This theory is consistent with the results described with the Cognitive Fit Model (Vessey 1991). Much of the previous business research focused on

---

[2] Benbasat et al. (1985, 1986, 1986a, 1986b) studied color in decisions under a variety of assumptions.

[3] " Better" is operationally defined as a higher profit in decision case used.

the existence of color, rather than the importance of color(s) used in the representations. Tufte (1990) summarizes his view of the complexity of the color selection process for visual displays by stating:

"The often scant benefits derived from coloring data indicate that even putting a good color in a good place is a complex matter. Indeed, so difficult and subtle that avoiding catastrophe becomes the first principle in bringing color to information: *Above all, do no harm*". (Tufte 1990, p. 81)

One does not generally think of the introduction of color as potentially harmful however, but any part of a visual representation that detracts from the data may be detrimental to understanding or decision-making.[4]

9.3.2 Accounting and Information Visualization

Many visualization problems have been investigated relative to accounting information. Areas of interest include financial forecasting and time series information (Bouwman et al. 1995; Carbone and Gorr 1985; DeSanctis and Jarvenpaa 1989) and auditors' effectiveness (Kaplan 1988; Moriarty 1979). Goldwater and Fogarty (1995) looked at cash flow predictions based on the format of information presentation. Much of the past accounting information visualization research is based on two-dimensional graphs. Two factors are primarily the cause of this direction of the research. First, the availability of technology to create multidimensional representations has been limited until recently. Second, much of the research interest was based on the relationship between two variables; until this basic level was understood, it would not have been natural to progress to multidimensionality issues.

Generally, most of the multidimensional research was performed using Chernoff Faces.[5] Most results indicate that representation format may improve decisions (MacKay and Villarreal 1987; Moriarty 1979; Stock and Watson 1984); however, MacKay and Villarreal (1987, 536) indicate that using faces may reduce the content validity of a visualization and therefore, limit its usefulness as a decision aid. Additionally, Amer (1991) reports that using Chernoff Faces and radar charts (Harris 1996) in an integrative decision-making task provided no differences when compared with bar charts and tables.

---

[4] Tufte (1990, 80-95) provides an excellent group of guidelines and examples to enhance the use of color in a variety of visual representations Rheingans and Landreth (1995) also give several details effective use of color in visualizations.

[5] Chernoff used facial characteristics as variable representations for multivariate analysis (Chernoff, 1973).

In another study, Dull and Tegarden (1999) showed that subjects using a multi-dimensional visualization, a 3D trajectory graph, of momentum accounting information (Ijiri 1982, 1986, 1989, 1990) produced more accurate predictions than when using a set of two-dimensional visualizations for an integrative decision-making task. However, from a practical perspective, momentum accounting information systems do not exist. As such, it is not possible to make any generalizations to the effectiveness of 3D graphical representations of accounting information.

In other publications, the significance of visualizations of non-accounting information in annual reports has been recognized (Graves et al. 1996; Preston et al. 1996). If decision-makers obtain useful information from this source, there may be an opportunity to provide them with similarly easy to comprehend financial information.

In summary, many types of accounting-based decisions have been used to examine representations of accounting information. With regard to these decisions, representation format has been shown to be important to the decision-making process. In some instances, two-dimensional representations have been shown to assist in superior decisions over tabular presentations of data. However, much of the multidimensional visualization research in accounting provides only mixed results. With today's information visualization technologies, using most desktop computers, one can represent multidimensional data by generating complex graphics rather than by limited formats such as the faces, radar charts, and 3D trajectory graphs.

9.4 Information Visualization Tools and Metaphors

The area of visual representations has been fueled by the dramatic decreases in the cost/power ratio for hardware and software (Wolff and Yaeger 1993). Today, desktop computers are available with multiple processors, gigabytes of long-term storage, megabytes of dynamic memory, and powerful graphic capabilities. This power has allowed the development of large complex programs capable of producing a variety of visual representations in relatively short periods of time. Many of these programs have been directed at the end-user of a system, generating more interest in the use of visual representations. Until recently, it was not technically feasible for end-users to develop complex visual representations. To draw a graph, one had to write programs to plot each data point, function and axis. In today's environment, the user may only have to specify the data and work through prompts, selecting the details of their representation from lists of options. This "user friendliness" is made possible through the availability of extensive graphics libraries, 4GL programming languages and turnkey visualization software (Brown et al. 1995).

9.4.1 Visual Metaphors/Representations for Accounting Information Visualization

One of the most difficult aspects of creating accounting information visualizations is the choice of visual metaphor. The difficulty resides in deciding what is a good cognitive fit between the decision task and the visual representation for the abstract accounting information used in business decision-making. However, information visualization designers have created visual metaphors that can serve as a beginning point in creating new information visualizations.

A good starting point for the accounting decision-maker is to look at business charting techniques. Business decision-makers are already familiar with bar charts, line graphs, pie charts, and other typical business diagrams. These fundamental charts can form the basis of usable multidimensional accounting information visualizations. However, much research remains to be done in this area. In this section, we describe a sample of the multidimensional visual metaphors created by information visualization designers based on recognizable business charts. These include: Kiviat diagrams, parallel coordinates, 3D scattergrams, 3D trajectory graphs, floors and walls, maps, and surfaces.[6]

Kiviat diagrams (Fig. 9.3) depict relationships among multivariate data. Originally developed to support computer performance evaluation (Kolence and Kiviat 1973), each measure's value is shown on its own individual axis. For example, if we have nine separate measures, the diagram would have nine distinct axes (radii). The value for each measure for the entity of interest is plotted on the appropriate axis. The points are then connected. The information visualization is the pattern formed when "connecting the dots." To compare one entity to another, one simply compares the patterns of the separate entities. These diagrams are also known as radar charts, star graphs, spider graphs, and star glyphs. One area in which Kiviat diagrams could be beneficial is using financial information for ratio analysis. Using one axis for each financial ratio, one could easily compare across companies or time periods. Parallel Coordinates (Fig. 9.4) is another multivariate technique that has been used for a long time (Inselberg 1997). Like a Kiviat diagram, each measure's value is plotted on its own individual axis for each entity.

In this case, the pattern is a line instead of a polygon, which makes looking for similar patterns across multiple entities straightforward. For example, looking at the last two variables in Fig. 9.4 demonstrates two separate groupings of entities - one in red and one in blue.

---

[6] For a more complete set of examples see Harris (1996) and Jarett (1993).

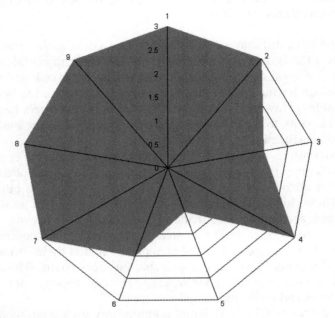

Fig. 9.3. Kiviat Diagram

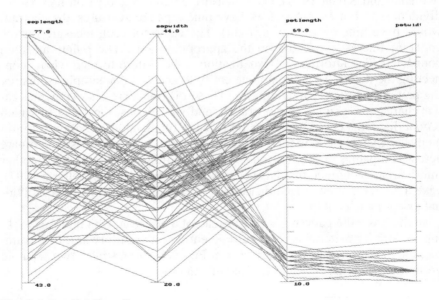

Fig. 9.4. Parallel Coordinates

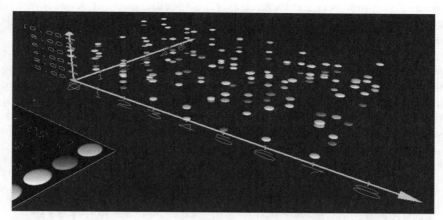

Fig. 9.5. 3D Scattergram

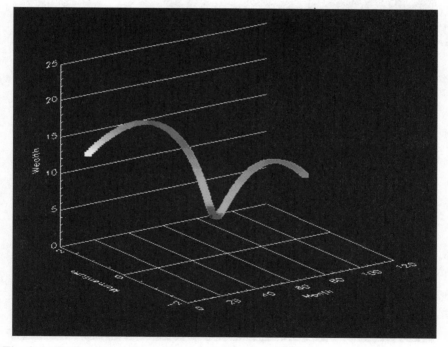

Fig. 9.6. 3D Trajectory Graph (Dull and Tegarden 1999)

A 3D scattergram (Fig. 9.5) is an extension to the typical 2D scatterplot. In this case, one can represent up to four separate measures on each entity: one for each axis (x, y, and z) and color. However, due to the difficulty in determining precisely the location of each specific value, it is necessary to add reference data, e.g., lines from each value to their respective axis values and the addition of a color map.

A 3D trajectory graph (Fig. 9.6) allows the representation of up to four separate measures for the entity of interest. This graph is an extension to the typical 2D line graph. In this case, the line spirals through the three dimensions (x, y, and z). As the fourth measure changes, the color of the line changes. In this case, since only one entity is graphed at a time, the results are easier to interpret than the 3D scattergram. However, like the 3D scattergram, this metaphor necessitates the addition of reference data and a color map to be usable.

Fig. 9.7. Floor and Walls (courtesy Visible Decisions, Inc.)

The floors and walls metaphor (Fig. 9.7) uses a room-based representation. In this metaphor, information is assigned to various business graphics and is displayed on a wall or floor of the room. This representation allows a great deal of information to be placed in a relatively small space. Furthermore, the decision-maker is already familiar with the underlying charts used in the room, e.g., pie charts, bar charts, and line graphs.

The map metaphor (Fig. 9.8) potentially could be a "natural" representation for entities that can be analyzed geographically. For example, if a regional (state) manager would like to see how their region (state) is performing in comparison to other regions (states) in terms of retail sales, the manager could look at a map-based "bar" chart type of visualization. One drawback of this particular visualization is that generally only one measure can be visualized at a time.

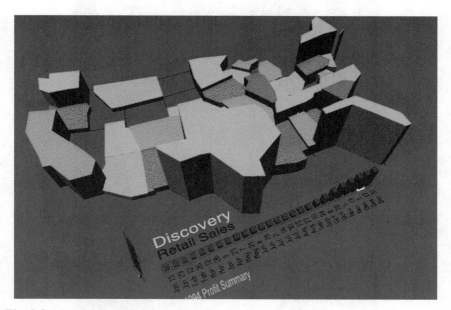

Fig. 9.8. Maps (courtesy Visible Decisions, Inc.)

Surface metaphors (Fig. 9.9) have been used primarily with scientific visualization. However, the idea of traversing the peaks and valleys of a business information landscape to find "interesting" patterns is appealing. Since surface representations are continuous in nature, not discrete, they should only be used when representing a continuous variable. However, since most traditional accounting information is discrete, their usefulness is currently limited.

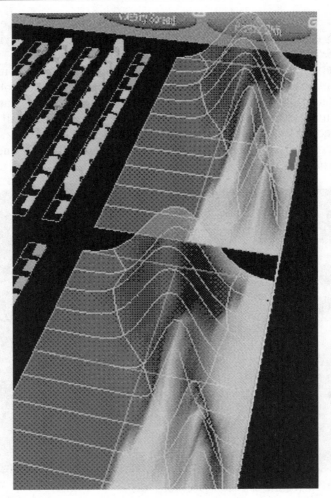

Fig. 9.9. Surfaces (courtesy Visible Decisions, Inc.)

9.4.2 Software Products for Accounting Information Visualization

Today, many software products that support information visualization are available to implement the visual metaphors/representations described previously. The products range from spreadsheets to spreadsheet add-ins, to user-friendly stand-alone information visualization packages to sophisticated object-oriented class libraries that can be incorporated by programmers using Visual Basic, C++, or Java.

As with most computer programs, visualization software continues to progress, with even the simplest of tools enhancing user-friendliness and allowing increasingly complex visualizations. This trend will allow more decision makers to use relevant visualizations when addressing a rising number of financial issues.

9.5 Future Research and Applications in Accounting Information Visualizations

Over the years there has been discussion regarding the decision-usefulness of annual and quarterly reporting. These academic and regulatory discussions regarding improvements in the decision-usefulness of financial information suggest increasing the frequency of reporting to "continuous" or "near-continuous" financial reporting.[7] As reporting requirements change, and financial data are reviewed continuously, auditors will need new tools to analyze data to form opinions. Visualizations may provide the tools to view trends and identify anomalies in real-time, allowing the investigation of an anomaly near the time of occurrence. Such visualizations may be continuations or adaptations of graphics discussed previously in this paper; additionally, new visualization concepts may be created (or adapted from other problem spaces) and applied to accounting.

As regulatory authorities move to increase reporting frequency, it will also be necessary to develop tools that can assist financial information users in the analysis of higher volumes of financial data. Using information visualizations is an obvious method of addressing this issue. Investors and creditors could use visualizations with only minor adjustments based on the frequency of information distribution.

The usefulness of visualizations is not limited to decision-makers external to an organization. For example, within organizations that use ERP systems, continuous data is already available for decision makers. For such companies to be competitive, it is imperative that good decisions are made based on timely data. Large ERP systems can have thousands of data tables, tens of thousands of data fields, and millions of individual data items, creating an environment ripe for information overload. Companies must look for the proper tools to sift through these data, without looking at each item, due to the obvious time limitations. Such a volume of data can be a valuable asset; using it effectively can provide great benefits.

---

[7] See http://raw.rutgers.edu/continuousauditing.

A strength of using information visualization is the ability to evaluate large sets of data and interrelated data items to spot trends or anomalies, allowing for additional investigation of those specific items of interest, rather than all items. As companies move into more mature ERP installations, we should expect visualizations to play a part in using these vast datasets.

As the accounting and information systems communities continue to develop larger systems, and decision-makers are faced with timely processing of voluminous amounts of information, there will be an increase in the quantity of decisions to be made and the speed with which those decisions will be made. These issues may be appropriately addressed using information visualizations. When using properly developed visualizations to address large volumes of data, decision makers can make high quality decisions in a timely manner, frequently resulting in an improvement in the overall decision-making process.

10 Alignment of AIS with Business Intelligence Requirements

Andreas I. Nicolaou

Department of Accounting and MIS, Bowling Green State University, Ohio

Abstract. An important issue in the fields of accounting and management decision-making concerns the alignment of the accounting information system with an organization's needs for conducting business intelligence activities. The present research identifies sources of requirements for business intelligence activities that are contingent on the degree of organizational formalization, information interdependence among functional areas, and dependence in interorganizational information sharing. Results of the empirical study indicated that, as hypothesized, the alignment between the accounting system design and the requirements for business intelligence resulted in a more successful system.

10.1 Introduction

An important issue in the fields of accounting and management decision making concerns the alignment of the accounting information system (AIS) with an organization's needs for conducting business intelligence (BI) activities. An AIS is defined as a computer-based system that processes financial information and supports decision tasks in the context of coordination and control of organizational activities. Organizational scholars demonstrate that an important step for the design of effective information systems is the collection and organization of strategy-focused information (Drucker 1998). Competitive intelligence (CI) in organizations is an activity that helps in the analysis and transformation of externally-oriented data into useful information, which is able to support business decisions (McGonagle and Vella 2002). Business intelligence (BI) is synonymous to a competitive intelligence activity that is designed to support business strategy. BI thus creates needs for collecting, analyzing, and reporting on data at the interface between internal and external activities in an organization's supply chain. While prior accounting research has examined issues on the alignment between an AIS and contingencies in organizational tasks, structure, and environment (Chenhall and Morris 1986; Kim 1988; Mia and Chenhall 1994), research has not examined system alignment issues in relation to BI activities and has not investigated their effect on system effectiveness.

Past literature on strategic management accounting has focused its attention on how management accounting systems can assist managers in externally-oriented functions, such as the design of systems for assessment of competitors in a firm's supply chain (Guilding 1999; Shank 1989; Simmonds 1981). Professionals also emphasize the importance of designing systems and processes that contribute to the strategic goals of an organization (Love 2003), while professional societies have expressed interest in the design of accounting systems that support strategic BI activities. For example, the Society of Management Accountants of Canada has developed guidelines for the design of competitive intelligence activities that are linked to strategic management accounting systems (Howell 1996).

The present study adds to this body of literature by developing a specific system design construct, "AIS Integration," and by examining its functional relationship with perceived system effectiveness. AIS Integration, in turn, is hypothesized to be a function of a number of contingency constraints that are due to business intelligence requirements. AIS integration refers to a particular design state where the system, in its implemented form, can provide output information that may be effectively used to address BI requirements. Contingent variables, such as (a) the degree of formalization in the structure of an organization (Hage and Aiken 1969; Simons 1987), (b) interdependencies in information requirements between functional areas within an organization (Govindarajan and Fisher 1990; Thompson 1967), and (c) dependencies due to inter-organizational information sharing and electronic data interchange (EDI) links (Bakos 1991; Srinivasan et al. 1994; Zaheer and Venkatraman 1994), influence the extent to which organizations experience different levels of BI needs or requirements. AIS integration can resolve difficulties in BI activities that are created by these contingent variables.

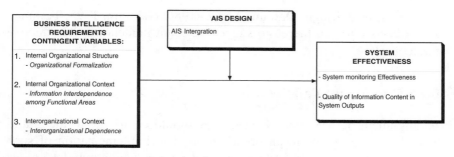

Fig. 10.1. Research Model for the study

The purpose of this study is to empirically examine the relationship between AIS integration and perceptions of system effectiveness (see Fig. 10.1). Specifically, it is hypothesized that to the extent that AIS design provides for system integration, as necessitated by the three contingent variables mentioned above, the system would be perceived as effective. This hypothesis is tested with data collected from firms in the United States using the survey research method. Results partially confirm the hypothesis that the degree of alignment between AIS integration and the contingent variables predicts AIS effectiveness. There is stronger support for the hypothesis when AIS effectiveness is defined by decision makers' satisfaction with the accuracy and monitoring effectiveness of output information than by the more traditional definition of satisfaction with quality of information content in system outputs.

10.2 Theoretical Framework

The research issues central to the organizational literature relate to the design of internally consistent organizational mechanisms that will ensure managerial and economic effectiveness (Galbraith 1995; Zimmerman 1995). AIS are considered an important organizational mechanism that is critical for effective decision management and control in organizations (Jensen 1983; Zimmerman 1995). As indicated by such contingencies as organizational context and structure, differences in requirements for organizational coordination and control across organizations, are likely to result in differences in accounting systems (Jensen 1983, p. 325). As Otley states, "Accounting systems are an important part of the fabric of organizational life and need to be evaluated in their wider managerial, organizational and environmental context." (1980, p. 422) The contingency theory of organizational design (Daft and Lengel 1986; Galbraith 1995; Tushman and Nadler 1978) can therefore suggest relevant models for the effective design of AISs.

10.2.1 Contingent Variables

The alignment of AISs and BI processes should contribute to the attainment of strategic goals in an organization. The implementation of such systems is sometimes justified on financial returns, which may lead to erroneous decisions because strategic benefits to the organization are likely to be ignored (Love 2003). For example, data warehousing applications provide support for BI activities. A recent survey reports that about four out of every ten such projects fail because of alignment problems. Systems do not meet end-user expectations, designers and users do not have a clear view of the business problem, business processes are not clear to technology experts, and the quality of available data is debatable (Connor 2003). As a result, a properly aligned system should minimize redundancies, promote increased consistency among data elements used in different functional areas within the organization, enhance data organization, and promote a cross-functional view within the organization (Cook and Eining 1993). Requirements for system alignment are directly related to the BI needs in the organization, which in turn place constraints on such contingencies as organizational formalization, internal organizational interdependence, and interdependence with other organizations.

Interdependence denotes the extent to which different organizational segments within a subunit depend on one another to carry out their tasks (Thompson 1967). Interdependence can occur at any level, including the individual, departmental or functional, subunit, or organizational level (Fry 1982). Prior research in management accounting has examined this variable as an aspect of task technology both within business subunits (Chenhall and Morris 1986; Kim 1988) and among subunits (Govindarajan and Fisher 1990; Hayes 1977; Macintosh and Daft 1987). Task interdependence within subunits was also reported to have a significant association with system integration, that is, the provision of information that integrated the effects of decisions from different functional areas (Chenhall and Morris 1986). Given the interest in this study to examine interdependence as a constraint in BI activities, the concept of interdependence is defined here as the "required information sharing" that takes place among different organizational functions in carrying out their tasks.

Organizational formalization refers to the extent to which an organization uses rules and procedures to prescribe behavior (Fredrickson 1986; Hage and Aiken 1969). A more formalized organization or one where many rules exist will tend to be associated with tight control where rules and control procedures are embedded within organizational routines and systems, and there is an increased need for monitoring organizational actions on an ongoing basis. In such situations, the AIS becomes a tool for control and must provide integrated information at the organizational level in order to support control requirements.

The introduction of information sharing systems that cross organizational boundaries (Bakos 1991) can also significantly increase the degree of complexity in the operating environment of an AIS and necessitate important changes in AIS design in order to integrate inter-organizational information (Barrett and Konsynski 1982). Inter-organizational systems (IOS) facilitate communication between two or more organizations by providing a highly efficient and error-free electronic information link (Bakos 1991). These benefits of electronic integration, however, may create dependencies between two different organizations that rely on each other for the procurement of resources.

Resource dependencies emerge from asymmetries in the control of critical resources (Pfeffer and Salancik 1978). Pfeffer and Salancik's (1978) model of resource dependence posits that the following factors are critical in determining the dependence of one organization on another: (a) the importance of the resource or the extent to which the organization requires it for continued operation and survival, and (b) the extent to which the organization has discretion over the resource allocation and use (Pfeffer and Salancik 1978, p. 45). In cases where resource dependence is present and significant, the integration of interorganizational information processed through EDI systems with internal accounting systems can provide significant benefits to the organization in terms of improved BI activities.

10.2.2 AIS Effectiveness

Past research in information systems has defined system effectiveness in terms of "user information satisfaction" or perceptions of system users about the extent to which the information system available to them meets their information requirements (Ives, Olson and Baroudi 1983, p. 785). User information satisfaction has been generally accepted as a surrogate for utility in decision making.

A semantically similar concept of "information usefulness" has also been extensively examined in the accounting literature (Chenhall and Morris 1986; Fisher 1996; Gul and Chia 1994; Kim 1988; Mia and Chenhall 1994). The whole set of "information usefulness" studies in accounting draws on a common base of information concepts that were originally developed to capture report users' reactions to qualitative characteristics of accounting information.

AIS effectiveness, therefore, is defined in this study in terms of the decision makers' perceptions that the output information available to them through an accounting information system meets their BI requirements.

10.2.3 Relationship between AIS integration and AIS effectiveness

AIS integration has been defined above as a system design state that influences the ability of the system to provide output information, which can be effectively used to respond to BI requirements. At the conceptual level, therefore, AIS integration is related to AIS effectiveness.

Increased system integration has been suggested to improve communications both within (Huber, 1990) and across organizations (Malone et al. 1987). Huber (1990) argues that improved coordination due to system integration can improve the quality of decision making. The relationship between the use of integrated systems and user evaluations of "task-technology fit," that is, the degree to which a technology assists an individual in performing his or her portfolio of tasks, has been empirically demonstrated by Goodhue (1995). Electronic integration among interorganizational (EDI systems) and internal information systems has also been reported to have a significant association with a perceptual measure of user information satisfaction (Premkumar et al. 1994). In conclusion, system integration is shown in past research to be an important construct that is influenced by contextual factors. As a result, this study examines the effect of contextual influences on AIS integration and on its relationship with system effectiveness.

The congruence of AIS integration with the contingent variables implies that an interaction exists between the two sets of concepts (Drazin and Van de Ven 1985). An interaction hypothesis is advanced that predicts the effect of system-context alignment on AIS effectiveness. Following Venkatraman's (1989) argument, "fit" in this study is conceptualized in terms of how strongly the relationship between AIS integration and AIS effectiveness is affected by the presence or absence of the contingent variables. The three contingent variables, therefore, jointly influence the relationship between AIS integration and AIS effectiveness. The following research hypothesis is advanced:

The alignment of AIS integration with BI requirements, as defined by the joint effect of information interdependence among functional areas, organizational formalization and interorganizational dependence, will have a positive association with perceptions of AIS effectiveness.

10.3 Research Method

10.3.1 Sample and Data Collection

A cross-sectional sample of 600 organizations was randomly selected from the *Phillips Business Information EDI Yellow Pages Directory*. Each selected organization was mailed one copy of the research instrument for completion by the financial controller or chief financial officer. The research instrument was evaluated by expert panels, including faculty members and an individual from the target population (Dillman 1978, pp. 155-158). The final response rate from all mailings was 22 percent. About half of the respondents were from the manufacturing industry, another 18 percent from wholesale and retail trade, about 10 percent from transport, and the rest from miscellaneous industries. Responding firms had an average size of $669 million in annual revenues (standard deviation: $1,054 million) and on average employed 3,524 employees (standard deviation: 5,730 employees).

10.3.2 Measurement of Research Variables

The study measures AIS effectiveness using a number of items that relate to the satisfaction of system users with the quality of information outputs. A previously validated instrument (Doll and Torkzateh 1988) was used to measure user satisfaction (a surrogate measure for AIS effectiveness). The instrument encompasses five related sets of information concepts: information content, accuracy, format, ease of use, and timeliness. In addition to these items, two additional items were included in the instrument in order to measure user perceptions about the monitoring effectiveness of the system.

174   Andreas I. Nicolaou

At the operational level, AIS integration is defined in terms of the following two characteristics: (a) the degree of integration in internal AIS applications (Davenport 1998; Davis et al. 1998; Scapens et al. 1998) and (b) the degree of integration between the interorganizational EDI systems and the internal AIS applications (Cathey 1991; Kogan et al. 1997). The integration of AIS applications was measured by the extent of standardization in coding schemes and by the extent to which application systems adhere to standard coding schemes. Another six items were used to measure the extent of integration of the AIS with information provided by EDI systems, with one item for each of the following organizational areas: accounting, procurement, shipping/distribution, reporting/budgeting, payments (financial EDI), and production planning.

Information interdependence is defined as the extent of required information sharing between pairs of organizational functions that are supported by AIS applications. Applications in AIS are identified to relate to the following four areas: (a) accounting, (b) procurement, (c) shipping/distribution, and (d) reporting/budgeting. The resulting six pairs were used to measure information interdependence. An existing scale, developed by Hage and Aiken (1969), was employed to measure organizational formalization. The scale measures the extent of use of formal policies and procedures in the organization, the monitoring of compliance to established policies and procedures, and the existence of penalties in case procedures are not followed. The dimensions from Pfeffer and Salancik's (1978) resource dependence model were used as measures of interorganizational dependence. The first dimension measured resource importance (RES-IMP), while the second dimension measures discretion over resource access and use (RES-ACC).

10.4 Results

10.4.1 Construct Validity and Reliability of Measures

New items were developed in this study to measure the constructs of resource accessibility (RES-ACC), information dependence (INF-DEP), AIS integration (AIS-INT) and the two items of user perceptions about the monitoring effectiveness of the system. Exploratory principal component analysis on RES-ACC and INF-DEP resulted in satisfactory single-factor structures, while the results on the Cronbach coefficient of internal consistency were also satisfactory.

The validity of existing measures was evaluated by confirmatory factor analysis (CFA). Maximum likelihood estimates of the CFA model were obtained using the LISREL program. With the exception of the RES-ACC scale, all other latent constructs exhibited adequate levels of reliability and construct validity. Due to the poor reliability and weak construct validity of the RES-ACC scale, the three individual items that comprised the scale were used in hypothesis testing instead of the summated measure.

10.4.2 Results on Hypothesis Testing

The research hypothesis was tested using a deviation score approach (Drazin and Van de Ven 1985). The first step in the deviation score analysis involves the estimation of the linear relationship between AIS-INT and the contingent variables, that is, INF-DEP, FORMAL, RES-IMP, and the three items of RES-ACC. The absolute value of the residuals from this model represents the extent of system fit. Table 10.1 presents the results of the regression of AIS-INT on the four contingent variables.

The research hypothesis was tested by estimating regression models of UIS and PME on SYSTEM FIT, that is, the absolute value of the residuals from the previous regression of AIS-INT on the contingent variables. The variables determining system fit (or alignment) were also included in the regression in order to partial out the main effects from the effect of the fit variable. Two regression models were estimated in order to test the research hypothesis. Table 10.2 presents the results of regression models estimated for UIS, and table 10.3 presents the results for PME, the second dependent variable.

The research hypothesis predicts that the degree of alignment of AIS integration (AIS-INT) with the joint effect of information interdependence (INF-DEP) among functional areas, organizational formalization (FORMAL), and interorganizational dependence (RES-IMP, RES-ACC1, RES-ACC2, RES-ACC3) will be positively associated with UIS and PME, the two factors of AIS effectiveness. The hypothesis was partially supported by the data. As can be seen from table 10.2, the estimated coefficient of system fit was marginally significant ($t_{(101)}$=-1.70, $p<.10$) in the regression of UIS on system fit. In the regression of PME on system fit, however, the estimated coefficient of system fit was highly significant ($t_{(101)}$=-3.22, $p<.01$). This result is shown in table 10.3 and provides strong support for the hypothesis advanced earlier in the study. In both regression models, the direction of the effects was as expected. The coefficient of system fit is negative, indicating that, as expected, a lower deviation in the relationship between AIS-INT and the joint effect of the contingent variables is associated with a higher level of UIS and PME, that is, AIS effectiveness.

Table 10.1. Estimated Regression Model of AIS Integration on Contingent Variables

Independent Variable	Parameter Estimate	(t-statistic)	Standardized Coefficient
Intercept	-.29	(-0.57)	
INF-DEP	0.19	(2.36**)	0.21
FORMAL	0.13	(2.15**)	0.19
RES-IMP	0.42	(4.43***)	0.41
RES-ACC1	-.02	(-0.35)	-.04
RES-ACC2	0.04	(0.93)	0.09
RES-ACC3	-.01	(-0.25)	-.02

$F_{(6,103)}=8.39***$
Model $R^2=0.33$
Model Adjusted $R^2=0.29$

* Significant at the 0.10 level
** Significant at the 0.05 level
*** Significant at the 0.01 level

Table 10.2. Estimated Regression Model of UIS on System fit

Independent Variable	Parameter Estimate	(t-statistic)	Standardized Coefficient
Intercept	3.08	(7.77***)	
System Fit	-0.30	(-1.70*)	-.16
INF-DEP	0.11	(1.70*)	0.16
FORMAL	0.14	(2.85***)	0.26
RES-IMP	-0.14	(-1.73*)	-.18
RES-ACC1	-0.03	(-0.90)	-.10
RES-ACC2	-0.01	(-0.30)	-.03
RES-ACC3	-0.06	(-1.55)	-.14
AIS-INT	0.18	(2.22**)	0.23

$F_{(8,101)}=5.10***$
Model $R^2=0.29$
Model Adjusted $R^2=0.23$

* Significant at the 0.10 level
** Significant at the 0.05 level
*** Significant at the 0.01 level

Table 10.3. Regression of PME on the System fit

Independent Variable	Parameter Estimate	(t-statistic)	Standardized Coefficient
Intercept	4.92	(8.79***)	
System Fit	-0.40	(-3.22***)	-.30
INF-DEP	0.25	(2.72***)	0.25
FORMAL	0.22	(3.18***)	0.29
RES-IMP	-0.33	(-2.84***)	-.26
RES-ACC1	-0.10	(-1.88*)	-.20
RES-ACC2	-0.03	(0.66)	0.07
RES-ACC3	-0.03	(-0.63)	-.06
AIS-INT	0.16	(1.44)	0.15

$F_{(8,101)}$=5.78***
Model R^2=0.31
Model Adjusted R^2=0.26

* Significant at the 0.10 level
** Significant at the 0.05 level
*** Significant at the 0.01 level

10.5 Conclusions

This study examined the relationship between the degree of alignment be-tween organizational requirements for business intelligence with the de-sign of an AIS and perceptions of effectiveness about the system. Contin-gency theory served as the basis for the development of the hypothesis in the study. The results of the study indicated that internal dependence due to (a) required information sharing across organizational functions, (b) or-ganizational formalization, and (c) interorganizational dependence in terms of both resource importance and accessibility had a significant ef-fect upon the requirements for business intelligence that should be met by the design of the system. The alignment between AIS design and those re-quirements significantly contributed to perceptions of monitoring effec-tiveness and to perceptions about the accuracy of information outputs. System alignment, however, failed to exhibit a strong effect on user in-formation satisfaction, that is, on the perceived quality of information con-tent available in system outputs.

The overall results are consistent with the theoretical perspectives un-derlying the concepts examined in the study. The theory of resource de-pendence (Pfeffer and Salancik 1978) explains the behavior of organiza-tions in cases where one organization is dependent upon another for critical resources. As interorganizational EDI links become more prevalent and organizations depend on them for survival, the requirements to share information and control internal activities that support business decision-making become more intense. The alignment of the system with those BI requirements has been shown to contribute to satisfaction with the accuracy of system-generated information, as well as with satisfaction with monitoring effectiveness.

The results of the study are also consistent with information processing theory, (Daft and Lengel 1986; Galbraith 1995; Tushman and Nadler 1978) which posits that, in the face of uncertainty, organizations will incorporate information processing capacities in their structures in order to match information processing requirements. Interdependent processes among functional areas can create requirements for information sharing and the design of integrated AISs that will satisfy such requirements. Adherence to rules and procedures may lead to an increased need for ongoing evaluations and these results have shown that, in such cases, AIS design must be responsive to those requirements in order for the system to be perceived as effective. The design of integrated systems, as a response to such requirements, may satisfy the need for improved accuracy in information sharing and continuous monitoring and thus result in more effective systems.

System tools that support BI activities have spread widely in the past few years. According to a recent survey, overall spending on BI software is expected to reach $30 billion by 2006, as compared to $17 billion in 2001 (Adams 2002). The mere size of such an investment in BI software tools suggests that business professionals should consider the extent to which they lead to effective decisions. With the increase in investments to support BI activities and the resulting need for alignment of BI requirements with accounting system design, firms hope to obtain useful information that can improve decision making. Improved decision-making should, in turn, improve organizational performance.

This study has examined AIS effectiveness as a proxy of organizational performance. The results demonstrate that AIS effectiveness is a valid proxy of such performance indicators and is also directly affected by the alignment of the system with organizational contingencies. Contingent factors in an organization's internal and external environment were also found to be important. Such factors represent those conditions that differentiate the level to which different organizations are capable of aligning their systems with BI requirements so that they can effectively utilize those systems in order to support business strategy.

In conclusion, the central issue of system alignment examined in this study has been demonstrated to be an important concern. The construct of AIS integration successfully captures the effect of specific contextual influences on AIS design, thus leading to an alignment between system design and business intelligence requirements. Business intelligence requirements are validly related to an organization's specific context, since this context may be determined by inter-organizational agreements, internal team-work, or cross-functional decision-making units. The design of integrated systems to provide support for such requirements is a critical issue for system effectiveness. This study only represents the start of a series of conceptual and empirical investigations into these important issues that are faced by current businesses.

11 A Methodology for Developing Business Intelligence Systems[1]

Bay Arinze[1], Onuora Amobi[2]

Department of Management, Drexel University[1], Pennsylvania

Kaiser Permanente[2], California

Abstract. Recent years have seen significant advances in systems development methodologies. Structured systems analysis and design approaches have been complemented and often substituted by a variety of new approaches such as prototyping, Object-Oriented Analysis and Design methodologies (OOADM), and Rapid Application Development (RAD), among others. System development methodologies and methods have always reflected the available toolsets, e.g., Fourth Generation languages and CASE tools, which enabled rapid application development. Organizational focus has also shifted over the years from Transaction systems to decision support and competitive intelligence. The frequent, expensive occurrences of implementation failures are a stark reminder of the need for appropriate methodological approaches to implementing BI systems. This chapter examines the peculiar methodological needs of BI systems and contrasts those systems with earlier transactional and reporting systems. Based on this comparison and analysis, a methodological framework and approach is proposed for effectively developing and implementing BI information systems.

[1] This material is based upon work supported by the National Science Foundation under Grant No. 0227802."

11.1 Introduction

In recent years, organizations have spent increasing amounts on business intelligence. Business intelligence (BI) software consists of three subcategories that include ad hoc query and analysis, reporting/OLAP, executive information systems and analytical applications. IDC has estimated the size of this market to be $5.5 billion in 2002. By the year 2005, IDC expects this market to nearly triple, reaching $15.7 billion annually. The motivation behind these huge expenditures is the desire of companies to improve their employees' decision-making by effectively using real-time business information in innovative ways.

In the analytical applications area, new applications such as Customer Relationship Management (CRM), Supplier Relationship Management (SRM), and Supply Chain Management (SCM) have proliferated as firms seek to gain on their competition. However, there appears to be a low success rate in organizational BI implementations. Tellingly, the Gartner Group reports that more than 50 Percent of CRM implementations are considered failures from the customer's point of view. A major reason for these failures and disappointments is the lack of appropriate methodologies for selecting and deploying BI technologies in the varied contexts in which they are used (Hayes, 2002; Johnson, 1999). In fact, many BI systems are deployed with little idea of their effectiveness or even an understanding of costs.

Given the increasing BI budgets across virtually all industries, an important question for IT departments and theoreticians alike is how best to select appropriate BI tools and technologies for specific contexts (Vedder, 1999). Other questions are: What form of organizational support is needed to guarantee the success of BI projects? Can traditional structured methodologies and newer OO-based methodologies be used to develop BI systems without modification? Currently, methodologies are applied haphazardly, determined mainly by the experience (or lack thereof) of the business consultants involved in the project.

The argument espoused in this paper is that methodologies for successfully developing BI systems will differ from those used to develop other types of systems in key aspects. They will embody elements of RAD, incorporate best-of-breed subsystems, utilize open systems and standards, and involve users in very different ways from transaction and other types of systems. First, system development methodologies and their evolution are reviewed, followed by a description of BI systems. The requirements for BI systems are then placed within a framework and the methodological implications examined. Finally, a methodological approach to developing BI systems is proposed.

This paper has important implications for both practitioners and academics alike. Practitioners will better understand the important elements of development methodologies for their BI systems. They will also be better able to avoid pitfalls in BI deployment, saving time and money during the development process. On the other hand, researchers will better understand, within a methodological framework, how BI system development approaches both resemble and differ from current IT methodologies.

11.2 A Review of Systems Development Methodologies

Structured system analysis and design methodologies (SSADM) have been a staple in the world of systems development since the 1970s. They were a reaction to the often-haphazard process of developing information systems up until that time, which resulted in failed systems. Prior experiences were often lost, system concepts were not consistently applied, and few benchmarks or techniques were available to the developer as opposed to those available to engineers developing engineering artifacts.

By introducing systems concepts into the development process, researchers and practitioners alike injected various models and techniques to bring greater rigor and repeatability into the process of systems development. Structured systems development envisaged a life cycle, where general statements of system capabilities were transformed into functional requirements then more specific design specifications prior to the development of the system itself. Design took place in top-down fashion with a sidewise expansion of requirements in succeeding stages.

The tools dimension was, and is, closely related to development methodologies. Third-generation development tools such as COBOL were commonly used with structured development methodologies. The use of system concepts was valuable in articulating and planning new systems. Further, such tools as Dataflow Diagrams (DFDs) helped to standardize the expression of functional specifications in a way that was easily understandable to users and analysts alike. Design specification tools and techniques such as Structure Charts, Entity-Relationship Diagrams (ERDs), flowcharts and pseudocode have helped developers create tightly defined design specifications with little room for ambiguity by programmers.

As technology improved with fourth generation languages (4GLs), Integrated Development Environments (IDEs), CASE tools, and Object-Oriented Development (OOD), a greater number of methodologies emerged largely due to these new toolsets. 4GLs, in particular, led to the rise of quicker system development. Three specific approaches are:

1. **Prototyping**. In prototyping, developers were able, via 4GLs, CASE tools and shrink-wrapped software, to quickly develop systems in an iterative fashion. This iteration is done in close cooperation with the user community using rapid review cycles. System modifications are suggested and implemented until the form and function of the system is agreed upon. The fully functional version of the system may be developed thereafter.
2. **Joint Application Development (JAD)**. This form of organization usually supports prototyping, although JAD could be used to support other development approaches. It defines the composition of the development team, with membership from the user, managerial, and developer communities. It also outlines the organization and operation of such development teams.
3. **Rapid Application Development (RAD)**. This formal methodology ties together process (prototyping) with organization (JAD) in order to develop systems in much shorter development cycles than the traditional SDLC process.

Also worth mentioning are Object-Oriented (OO) tools, techniques and even methodologies. These are corporately used to develop systems under the OO paradigm, with rapid development and code reuse being important features. Increasing amounts of system development are being done using Unified Modeling Language, a design and specification formalism for OO systems, and Java, the leading programming language for developing OO systems.

Over the past decade, an unmistakable trend has been the widespread use of shrink-wrapped software. This trend represents an instance where technology has again acted to reshape development methodologies. Enterprise Resource Planning (ERP) software has arguably had the greatest recent impact on organizations. ERP software suites are not merely a new class of software that produces incremental change to organizational information systems. ERP systems have, in fact, introduced to the organization an unprecedented degree of integration of processes and data (Legare, 2002). Activities on the supply chain are linked such that transactions taking place in one functional area immediately impact other areas. These systems also give users the ability to view activities all along the supply chain and thereby offer new opportunities to work more collaboratively and efficiently. Sauter (1999) highlights this insatiable need for data and process 'visibility' in organizations. Most IT managers agree that ERP-based systems are radically different from the various information system types that preceded them.

ERP Systems development of necessity takes a different path from systems developed by the organization or an outsourced firm (Arinze, 1991;

Arinze and Anandarajan, 2002). Shrink-wrapped software in general and particularly enterprise software experienced changes in all aspects of the systems development life cycle. The effort typically spent on creating functional and design specifications, coding, and testing, together with maintenance and operations, is dramatically affected by the use of ERP systems.

Most BI systems are also shrink-wrapped and purchased from various vendors. The software categories with BI capabilities include *ERP, CRM, Data Warehousing, Data Mining, Online Analytic Processing (OLAP)* and *statistical software*. As this software becomes increasingly critical in determining the success of firms, a key topic is the form of the methodology required to successfully deploy these systems. BI systems are discussed next, followed by methodological requirements for deployment and use.

11.3 Business Intelligence (BI) Systems

BI involves the use of data from internal and external sources to feed a powerful suite of analytical tools in order to discover strengths and weaknesses within an organization as well as opportunities and threats in the organization's environment (Hoelscher, 2002). BI systems are used to generate knowledge that has value to organizations. It enables improved decision-making at all levels of an organization that in turn leads to better products, services, supply chain management, and logistics. As earlier mentioned, the majority of BI software is pre-configured, with many vendors producing software to accomplish BI-related functions.

Acquiring data in usable form is an essential component for successful BI systems. These data come from a multitude of internal and external sources and must be recombined in data warehouses, data marts, and other repositories (Koutsoukis et al., 1999). This remodeling requires powerful data extraction, transformation, and load (ETL) software capabilities (Arinze and Banerjee, 1992). These capabilities are rarely programmed from scratch by the using organization, as hundreds of tables may be involved with associated data cleansing. Instead, off-the-shelf software is the best choice, using specialized software developed by vendors for this purpose.

BI is now understood to be more than the creation and interrogation of multidimensional data warehouses—a technique known as Online Analytic Processing (OLAP). Here data are pre-aggregated into data cubes along various dimensions, e.g., store sales by time, categories, regions, etc. More contemporary uses of these data repositories include data mining using neural networks (Inmon, 1996; Vedder, 1999). These complex algorithms are used to find related items or patterns of data in large data repositories.

Other BI techniques use similarly sophisticated algorithms for analytic processes. It is inefficient and impractical to attempt to program rule induction, genetic algorithms, decision analyses, simulation and other approaches used within BI systems from scratch. Corporations will instead purchase analytic software from any of a variety of vendors to supply these capabilities. The other factor against hand coding of BI software is the often short timeframes required for the development of BI-based systems. Coding such systems in house would require years, not the months mandated to develop many such systems.

Another factor that relates to the methodological approaches needed for BI systems is the intended set of BI system users. Prior generations of analytic software were directed mainly at middle-to upper-level management and often used staffers or the IT department as intermediaries between users and the systems. Contemporary BI systems provide a wide range of capabilities to support decisions of employees at virtually all levels of the organization (Shim, 2002). The capabilities also typically come at a significant cost—up to several million dollars for enterprise-strength BI analytic applications.

The cost of BI systems adds pressure for appropriate methodological approaches to lessen the risks of system failures. By categorizing BI system requirements and comparing them to other common types of (primarily transactional and reporting) systems built using 3GLs and 4GLs, a means is created to derive the essentials of a methodology for BI systems.

11.4 BI Requirements and Methodology Framework

A framework for BI systems development requirements is outlined below. This framework represents a tool to compare and analyze the methodological requirements of systems developed for transactional and managerial reporting using 3GLs and 4GLs and those of "packaged" BI systems.

- **Tools**. This dimension illustrates the tools used to develop each category of system. It includes such 3GLs as COBOL and C; 4GL Integrated Development Environments (IDEs), such as Java and VB.NET; and examples of packaged BI tools, e.g., SAP R/3 Business Warehouse (BW) and SAS.
- **Sources**. Under Sources, the typical origination of the software is listed. For both 3GL and 4GL-based systems, the coding and testing is done in-house or outsourced to an external organization. BI software is typically purchased from a vendor or through an Application Service Provider (ASP).

- **Emphasis**. 3GLs and 4GLs are primarily used to develop transactional and reporting systems. Some 4GL tools, e.g., Java and VB.NET, are also used to develop Internet-based versions of these applications. Packaged BI systems are mainly not used for analytical applications that support decision making at all but rather tactical and strategic levels in the organization (Keen and Scott Morton, 1978).

- **Prototyping**. Most 3GL tools are not readily amenable to the prototyping approach, as development time takes too long. 4GL environments are much more conducive to prototyping. Packaged BI systems are also used for prototyping but of a different type. The focus is more on a gap-fit analysis and testing by configuring the product, not also on code correctness, as in 4GLs (which must deal with both).

- **Cost of the Software**. The cost of software ranges from low (3GLs), moderate for 4GLs, and more expensive still for BI software, which incorporates best practices, more configurable functionality, and has been exhaustively tested.

- **Cost of Personnel**. Similarly, the cost of personnel is lower for programming using 3GLs, higher for 4GLs, and the highest for those who install and configure BI software.

- **Speed of Development**. Using 3GLs, such as COBOL, for system development can result in system lifecycles of many months to many years. 4GLs can result in shorter system life cycles and are thus appropriate for prototyping. Packaged BI systems can be installed, tested, and operational in weeks or months. Requirements can be rapidly tested through configuration.

- **Planning Emphasis**. With 3GL and 4GL-based systems, all aspects of feasibility are relevant and must be performed—financial, organizational, and technical feasibility. With BI systems, the focus is mainly on financial and organizational feasibility. Technical feasibility is seldom evaluated for the core BI product, but its interfaces with ERP and other organizational systems and databases are evaluated.

- **Functional Specifications**. During development, analysts create detailed functional specifications for 3GL-based systems. Some formalisms include DFDs and flowcharts. Detailed functional specifications are also required for 4GL-based systems, although a working prototype might also serve as an additional specification. BI-based functional specifications are very high level as the software functionality is prewritten.

- **Design Specifications**. Similarly 3GL system design specifications are typically detailed using formalisms such as structure charts and ER diagrams. 4GL-based systems frequently add a prototype to the design specifications. BI-based systems describe design specifications only at a high level, given the prewritten nature of the software.

- **Implementation**. For 3GL and 4GL-based system, implementation comprises the three steps of *program design—coding—testing*. The code must be documented extensively for maintainability. For BI-based systems, the process is *installation—configuration—testing*. Occasionally, some code development is needed as an adjunct to the configuration process, e.g., ABAP programming in SAP R/3.

Table 11.1. Comparing 3GLs, 4GLs and Packaged BI Systems

	3GL Developed TPS and MIS	4GL Developed TPS and MIS	"Packaged" BI Systems
Tools	COBOL, C	Visual C++, Java, VB.NET	SAP R/3, Siebel, SAS, SPSS, MicroStrategy
Sources	Internal, Outsourced	Internal, Outsourced	Purchased, Application Service Provider (ASP)
Emphasis	Transactional & Reporting Systems	Transactional & Reporting Systems, Internet-based Systems	Analysis and Reporting Systems at Tactical & Strategic Levels
Use in Prototyping	Limited	Typical, using Toolsets	Typical, via configuration
Cost of software	Low	Low—Moderate	High
Cost of Personnel	Low	Moderate	High
Speed of Development	Slow	Faster	Fastest
Planning Emphasis	Financial, Organizational, & Design Feasibility	Financial, Organizational, & Design Feasibility	Financial & Organizational Feasibility
Functional Specifications	Detailed Functional Specifications	Detailed Functional Specifications, Prototype	High Level Functions
Design Specifications	Detailed Design Specifications	Detailed Design Specifications, Prototype	High Level Functions
Implementation	Program Design— Coding—Testing	Program Design— Coding—Testing	Installation— Configuration— Testing

11.5 BI Case Studies

Three case studies below illustrate the use of Business Intelligence software in three very different organizations. In each case, the company's background and the problems faced are provided, together with the BI solution selected and results.

11.5.1 Case Study #1 - Aegis Communications Group

Aegis Communications Group is a Teleservices Outsourcing company that was the result of a 1998 merger between ATC (Irving) and IQI (Los Angeles). They provide inbound customer care, help desk and acquisition, data management and analysis, and outbound acquisition and surveys. They had 11 domestic call centers, an overseas partnership, and 5100 workstations to support.

In Aegis' competitive environment, they faced several IT business challenges, namely: (a) reducing the overall development cycle from weeks to days, (b) improving reporting capabilities through standard and user-customizable reports, and (c) transitioning to an e-CRM Solution.

They chose to use a vendor solution (PeopleSoft CRM) in order to quickly expand service offerings and avoid high costs of development. The implementation of PeopleSoft CRM met their requirements, providing more functionality than originally expected and providing ROI relatively quickly.

11.5.2 Case Study #2 - Lufthansa Airlines

Lufthansa is Germany's leading online travel site. With more than 240 aircrafts, they are one of the most modern airline fleets in the world. They have over 30,000 employees worldwide and fly to 729 destinations in 94 countries, in cooperation with their Star Alliance. With eight call centers worldwide supplying 24x7 support, they serve 8 million customers, including 5.4 million frequent flyers. Their network includes 500,000 agents and 235,000 companies as customers.

Their objective was to create a central data Warehouse in order to reinforce their call center infrastructure. To accomplish this goal, they integrated their systems architecture to provide one consistent view of their customer data via a CRM package. The deployed CRM package provided interoperability with other application systems and a base architecture for further integration applications. Deployed successfully, it also provided open and modern interface standards and connectivity to legacy systems.

11.5.3 Case Study #2 Philadelphia Housing Authority (PHA)

Established in 1937, the PHA is the nation's fourth largest public housing authority. It is funded by the Federal Government and chartered by the state of Pennsylvania. There is also local oversight by the city of Philadelphia and Board of Commissioners.

The PHA's mission is to provide quality affordable housing for low-income people. Its strategy is to add value to Philadelphia through private-sector partnerships and market-driven development practices. The PHA has 2,600 employees, 100 offices, 14 divisions, and 734 vehicles. Their challenge was to efficiently manage high-volume, complex real estate/property management transactions and diverse customer support services.

The PHA's strategic plan aligned goals with key principles for improving property management and fostering a higher degree of public safety. These goals also included creating partnerships to advance the provision of economic opportunities and services to residents and to leverage technology for infrastructure upgrades.

Infrastructure-wise, the PHA sought to upgrade from standalone legacy systems to an integrated, web-enabled environment. They deployed PeopleSoft, specifically V7.51 Financials and HRMS applications. PHA was the first public housing authority in the country to implement a full ERP suite of applications.

In the future, PHA seeks to use PeopleSoft CRM to support integrated call center operation, automate call routing and tracking, and provide on-line accessibility to a full view of key resident information. It will also replace their existing work order system and track and report on the progress of public safety complaints and investigations (via case management). Finally, CRM Help Desk will be used to support ISM operations and enable new applications deployment. In the future PHA hopes to use PeopleSoft for fundraising.

11.6 BI System Development Methodologies

From the preceding framework and an analysis of various case studies, it is possible to propose the form and detail of a methodology from the development of BI-based systems. Key aspects of such a methodology include:

- **Comprehensive Fit-Gap Analysis**. Since such systems are almost always prewritten, focus shifts from coding based on design specifications to performing Fit-Gap analysis—matching the system capabilities to user requirements.

- **Rapid Application Development**. This method is standard in today's environments, where systems are required in extremely short time frames.
- **Key Analytic Personnel Skills**. These are mandatory for BI's specialized applications. Developers must understand the analytic tools supplied in BI software, such as neural networks, simulation, and data warehousing. Other experts will require product configuration skills.
- **Automated Project Management Tools**. These tools ensure automatic generation of system documentation and are contained in such tools as SAP R/3 and PeopleSoft.
- **Lifecycle User Participation.** For BI system projects, users should be involved throughout the system lifecycle. This participation is required due to the customized and decision supporting nature of such applications. Absent such involvement, the risk of failure is increased.
- **Focus on Data.** In BI systems, a greater emphasis on data stems from the diverse sources of data from internal and external sources used to populate the data repository.

The form of the proposed methodology is shown in Fig. 11.1 below. The broad eight-stage model is iterative in nature. Each of the stages is described in detail below.

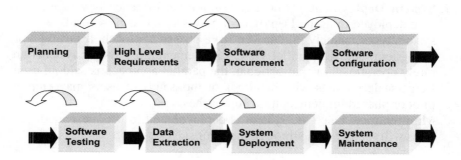

Fig. 11.1. The Proposed Methodology for Developing BI Systems

1. **Planning**. In the planning stage, the general problem or user requirement is defined in broad terms. Feasibility analyses determine the *business benefits* of the proposed system the *alignment with organizational imperatives* and *technical feasibility*. The system's stakeholders (e.g., managers, users, owners, champions) are identified, and the first stop/go decision is made. The project team is set up, and resources are allocated to the project.

2. **High Level Requirements**. Requirements are defined at a high level following a decision to proceed. Critical success factors (CSFs) are defined, along with system components: hardware, software, data, people, and procedures.
3. **Software Procurement**. Here, the high level requirements and CSFs are used to define evaluation criteria for prospective software. Requests for Proposals (RFPs) are followed by vendor bids and product evaluations. The software is then procured along with vendor and/or consultant services.
4. **Software Configuration**. Following software acquisition, specialists configure it based on Fit-Gap analysis. This phase will typically include user involvement and the generation and loading of test data to test the system's functionality and user interface.
5. **Software Testing**. The BI software is then tested not only for technical accuracy (e.g., for calculations) but also for usability, interfaces to other systems, satisfaction of functional requirements, and performance metrics. Developers may cycle back through configuration to fine tune the software's functionality.
6. **Data Extraction**. Full Extraction, Transfer, and Load (ETL) activities take place with data loaded from internal and external data sources. A data dictionary will be created to store data mappings and definitions.
7. **System Deployment**. After the system's performance is verified, it is then deployed to users. Deployment may take the same 4 forms as other system types, namely (a) cutover, (b) a phased approach, (c) using a pilot system, and (d) parallel system implementation. As BI systems are rarely operational or transactional, the parallel approach is seldom used. Large-scale projects with hundreds or thousands of users may employ pilot or phased implementation approaches.
8. **Maintenance**. Once the system is deployed and in use, new modifications will rapidly cycle through the prior stages.

11.7 Financial Aspects of BI Systems

The major impetus for deploying BI systems is financial. Companies deploying various types of BI systems expect financial benefits from the use of the software, either via cost reductions or through increased profits. Benefits from BI systems are notoriously more difficult to cost-justify compared to transactional systems although analysis methods are improving. Much of the benefit of BI systems comes from improved information for decision-making, which can often be difficult to quantify. However, BI systems remain one of the fastest-growing areas of software expenditures, reflecting the importance attached to them by organizations.

While difficult, estimating benefits from BI systems is not an impossible task. Based on a growing number of successful implementations, metrics are now being better understood and cost-benefit analyses more precise. Several areas that commonly result in savings are as follows:

1. **Greater Supply Chain Efficiencies**. Implementing ERP systems and specialized supply chain software translate into measurable dollar benefits. Lower inventories translate into lower carrying costs; and faster delivery, billing, and payments result in improved cash flows. Other advancements include improved forecasting accuracy, which translates to fewer stockouts, and more efficient transportation planning for deliveries.

2. **Cost Avoidance**. Another major area of financial benefit is that of cost avoidance in the realm of reporting. When deploying data warehouses, for example, companies are able to reduce costs incurred by decision makers in three separate areas, namely: (a) cost/effort of locating information, (b) cost/effort of interpreting information, and (c) cost in integrating and synthesizing information. Studies of workflows before and after implementation quickly reveal these efficiencies.

3. **Improved Decision Making**. This area must be carefully handled to avoid attributing savings to BI software that actually arose from some other source. However, performance targets by managers can be estimated beforehand and measured afterward to see if the use of BI software has resulted in more targets being met or exceeded. These targets include faster reaction time, more customers acquired, fewer lost customers, and greater individually attributable revenue.

4. **Improved Customer Relationships**. BI systems, particularly CRM systems, have a precisely targeted set of benefits that can result from their use. They include: (a) *Lowered costs of database marketing*. Better analytics can identify how best to expend efforts on individual versus market segments. In addition, CRM software combines marketing information from various channels. These all result in lower costs of marketing with greater 'yield' from marketing dollars spent (b) *Limiting or eliminating unprofitable contacts*. Banks have been able to use CRM software to great effect by directing marketing efforts and services to their most profitable customers and increasing fees to 'unprofitable' customers. This change has increased their profits overall.

At the heart of all BI systems; therefore, is the aspect of cost-justification. The good news is that frameworks and metrics have improved over the years. With the growing database of case studies, rigorous cost-justification for BI systems is not only desirable, but also imperative. Its importance is not only to seek approval from top management but also to clarify the purpose of the system in the minds of developers and eventual users of such systems.

11.8 Summary

This paper has examined the evolution of system development methodologies and the need for a defined methodological approach for implementing Business Intelligence Systems. With BI technologies becoming widely used across many organizational types, it is important to understand the form BI deployment methodologies should take to avoid costly system failures. The paper began by comparing BI systems development to systems development of transactional and reporting systems created using 3GLs and 4GLs. These earlier systems and tools required lengthy development cycles with a frequent disconnect between user requirements and eventual system functionality. Later, 4GLs and other new tools allowed rapid development approaches, such as prototyping and RAD. Users could now be integrated into the development process, using Joint Application Development.

ERP systems introduced prewritten software into organizations across many industries over the last two decades. Shorter development cycles became possible and changes in system development strategy became necessary. The emphasis switched to configuration versus coding and fit/gap analysis versus transforming requirements into code. Best of breed software often led to adoption of the best practices embodied by the software.

As demands for access to data repositories grew, Online Analytical Applications (OLAP) also became widespread, using multidimensional databases to support managerial decision-making. The field of BI incorporates OLAP but also includes newer techniques such as data mining using neural networks, genetic algorithms, and others. The need for a methodology for developing these more recent systems has only grown from those needs experienced with ERP deployments. Some major reasons are the cost of such projects and the increased for competitive intelligence in more challenging global business environments.

This paper has proposed the form of a methodology for developing and deploying BI systems. It involves prototyping and user involvement in the development process, due to the capabilities already incorporated in the software. In its short, iterative cycles, requirements are described at a high level. Also, focus is placed on product selection and matching functionality to user requirements. Fit/gap analyses take center stage as a means of ensuring that best of breed methods are used to provide the capabilities users need. There are twin emphases on extraction and cleansing of data and prototyping as a means of sharpening the match between functions and system capabilities.

Cost justification of BI systems has grown in importance over the last few years. Once seen as systems with 'intangible' benefits, BI development approaches now include improved frameworks and better metrics for estimating and measuring hard benefits. Cost-benefit analyses are important in order to justify BI systems before top-level management but are just as important to clarify their objectives and goals prior to deployment.

As BI systems become a staple in more organizations, the need for better, more efficient methodologies will become more important to avoid costly system failures and to ensure that deployed systems achieve maximum effectiveness. The methodological approach taken in this paper will be valuable to IT theoreticians and practitioners alike who are seeking to deploy BI systems more effectively. Further research directions will involve testing and benchmarking new methodologies such as these we have described in actual BI implementation settings.

12 An OO Approach to Designing Business Intelligence Systems

Kathleen S. Hartzel[1], Trevor H. Jones[1], Valerie C. Trott[2]

[1]Department of Information Technology, Duquesne University, Pennsylvania

[2] Department of Accounting, Duquesne University, Pennsylvania

Abstract. While standard accounting needs tend to be relatively static, the demand for corporate managers to be constantly aware of changing business dynamics is ever present. Consequently, support systems, technical or otherwise, must be up to the challenge of responding to the demands of their users by incorporating available accounting data. This chapter explains how organizations can use object-oriented analysis and design techniques to more effectively create systems to respond to escalating business intelligence needs. Towards this end, we discuss the differences between business intelligence systems and operational accounting systems. We explain basic object-oriented software principles and how data and procedures are viewed within the object-oriented paradigm. We demonstrate how object-oriented systems can evolve more quickly in response to changing business intelligence needs than systems developed using more traditional (structured) methods. Finally, we provide an example demonstrating the application of these principles. The example demonstrates how the collection of retail sales data and the separate recording of advertising expenditures can be combined to address specific business intelligence questions. This allows us to demonstrate how data collected for specific accounting purposes can be rapidly manipulated and combined, to be used in a decision support, as opposed to the regulatory reporting, role.

12.1 Introduction

Accounting data, reported in the traditional formats, have a largely regulatory and static format. While useful to external agencies, standard accounting reports have limited value to internal constituencies for the purposes of operational analysis and decision support, often referred to as business intelligence. Business intelligence systems are designed to cater to a variety of sophisticated, real-time, specialized information needs. Business intelligence is "thinking abstractly about an organization, reasoning about the business, and organizing large quantities of information about the business in order to define and execute a strategy (Giovinazzo, 2000)". Not surprisingly, the analytic capabilities of technology, such as online analytic processing (OLAP) and data mining tools, bind the extent to which a business analyst can query existing systems. However, a more systemic problem is the ability of organizations, and more specifically the technologists providing the support systems, to modify or create systems that can respond to those new queries in dynamic business environments. This problem is particularly true for systems tasked with the extraction and manipulation of operational data upon which executives rely for input to their short-term decision-making processes.

This chapter explains how organizations, in an increasingly competitive environment spearheaded by expanding markets and emerging technologies, can use object-oriented analysis and design techniques to more effectively view accounting data in response to escalating business intelligence needs. To accomplish this objective, we first present the fundamental differences between business intelligence systems and operational accounting systems. We discuss the problem of identifying and extracting the auxiliary data necessary to supplement accounting data for business intelligence activity. Second, we explain object-oriented principles and how data and procedures are viewed within the object-oriented paradigm. We also analyze how object-oriented systems can evolve more quickly in response to changing business intelligence needs than systems developed using more traditional (structured) methods. Finally, the introduction to object-orientation is followed by an example illustrating the application of these techniques. The example demonstrates how the collection of retail sales data and the separate recording of advertising expenditures can be combined to address specific business intelligence questions. This case allows us to demonstrate how data collected for specific accounting purposes can be rapidly manipulated and combined to be used in a decision support as opposed to the regulatory reporting role.

12.2 Operational Accounting Systems vs. Business Intelligence Systems

First, we should understand that the fundamental difference between these two types of systems is not the technologies that drive them. The fundamental difference is the data requirements and the need to manipulate it in order to provide alternative views of the data. Typically, accounting requirements center around repetitive time-based aggregations, whereas business intelligence needs are more dynamic and require sophisticated models.

Operational accounting systems are designed to support traditional reporting requirements such as balance sheets, income statements, and cash flow statements. Data are captured and maintained at the transaction level and later summarized for specific reporting periods. Additionally, accounting data requirements tend to be relatively short-term, again to support the most recent statement reporting. Once the data have been processed and the accounting period closed, the data are archived.

On the other hand, business intelligence information is structured to provide real time data that are essential in current decision-making processes. The transactional data collected by traditional accounting information systems are useful but are not a complete source of data for business intelligence. In today's organizations, data collection goes beyond the accounting data, and it is often stored in distributed and heterogeneous environments. Consequently, business intelligence requirements create significant data storage and manipulation problems that are not encountered in standard accounting reporting. Furthermore, the short-term availability of data for accounting requirements, because of its archival, is contrary to the data needs of business intelligence, which tend to require longer time periods (e.g., to support trending and comparative analysis) as well as the need for complex modeling processes. To create useful information, the accounting data must be aggregated and supplemented by data from other sources that describe the organizational environment.

12.2.1 Data Warehousing and Data Marts

One of the trends that has encompassed the collection and use of data over the past few years is the use of a massive volume of historical data to create an environment that facilitates time-based analysis (business intelligence). The manipulation of such large quantities of data, in and of itself, presents an operational problem. Consequently, data warehousing systems came into being. Data warehouses allow sophisticated analysis of large amounts of time-based data, independently of the systems that process the daily transactional data of the organization.

A data warehouse typically contains time-based summarizations of the underlying detailed transactions. Only necessary attributes are extracted from the original source data. Then the data are transformed to conform to the format of the data warehouse and also "cleansed" to ensure quality. In order to create these summary "snapshots", the level of summary detail for the data components must be pre-defined; and it is fixed for the life of the warehouse, ensuring consistent analysis. This level of summarization is called the granularity of the warehouse. This granularity then determines, for all subsequent data retrieval, the level of transactional detail available for any potential analysis. Aggregating the data reduces the overall number of records necessary to perform specific analyses.

A major challenge in designing a business intelligence system stems from the relationship between the detailed operational and the aggregated data warehouse systems. The data warehouse model creates a design and implementation situation where the supply of data has been predefined (legacy accounting systems, other internal data collection systems, and external data repositories); but the user requirements have not been defined. User requirements tend to be ambiguous and require significant flexibility to respond to changing competitive requirements (unlike standard accounting reporting). To address this problem of incongruent levels of granularity among systems, data marts have been employed. A data mart is a more limited data collection, designed to address the needs of specific users, as opposed to the more general audience of the warehouse. The data mart, however, still draws data from the general data warehouse and consequently is still governed by the granularity and scope restrictions dictated for the warehouse. Fig. 12.1 shows the general relationship among operational data, data warehouses, and data marts.

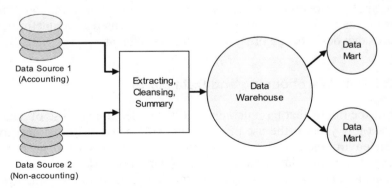

Fig. 12.1. Relationship among operational data, data warehouses, and data marts

12.2.2 The Time Dimension of Business Intelligence

Remember, the goal of business intelligence is to provide the necessary information to define and execute strategy. Strategic activity is geared toward finding new and better ways of conducting business. Discovering novel insight requires new perspectives and often-new views of organizational data to confirm or uncover patterns. A business analyst's analytic processes and data requirements cannot be fully anticipated. As the business analyst studies an organization's data and environment, the activity itself creates additional informational requirements that are not met by existing data warehouses and data marts.

Given the strategic nature of business intelligence, time can be of the essence. As business intelligence needs emerge, a methodology should exist to ensure those needs are met. To respond to this challenge, operational systems and the data extraction processes must be able to quickly adapt to emerging intelligence needs. Although operational and business intelligence systems both rely on corporate data, the program code supporting either activity need not be intertwined. Therefore new, on-demand analytic tools (systems) can be developed independently of legacy systems to advance this objective.

The underlying system design is transparent to the users. For example, from a user standpoint, queries in an object-oriented environment will not appear fundamentally different than those in a non-object-oriented environment. However, technologists in an object-oriented environment are in a better position to increase the range of queries that can be answered. Even though it is transparent to the user whether a system is or is not object-oriented, it is painfully obviously how quickly and at what expense a system can be developed or maintained to meet emergent needs. Thus, it is imperative that these on-demand systems are object-oriented, because object-oriented systems are more flexible and adaptive than systems developed using procedural methods. Therefore, analytic tools that are inherently object-oriented can be developed or modified more quickly than non-object-oriented tools. Quicker development means faster decision-making and increased organizational agility. Therefore, using object-oriented development methods can be important in sustaining effective business intelligence systems. The following section explains the fundamentals of the object-oriented approach. This section is presented to help the reader understand why object-orientation leads to more flexible systems and quicker implementation.

12.3 The Object-Oriented Paradigm

12.3.1 Objects

Central to the object-oriented development approach is the object class. The class is a template for creating a collection of objects with the same attribute and operation definitions. Attributes are atomic data describing the 'thing' the object represents. Operations are pieces of program code used to create, delete, or manipulate data within an object. The data and program code are physically stored within the object and hidden from other objects. An object is graphically depicted as shown in Fig. 12.2. This figure shows an object named Sale (top section), which might represent a single sale transaction. The second section shows one attribute called Date, representing the date of the sale. The bottom section shows operations, in this case an operation named getZip() that might be responsible for identifying the zip code of the store associated with this sale.

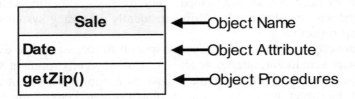

Fig. 12.2. Components of an object class

12.3.2 Message Passing

For a business system to work, multiple objects must work together, each fulfilling a particular function within the system requirements. As objects require other objects to perform some function, they send triggering messages containing any required parameters. In reality, these messages are nothing more than programming code feeding parameters to other pieces of programming code, which are then initiated to perform some additional action. The ability of objects to "communicate" with each other is depicted in Fig. 12.3. The line between the Sale and Store classes on the diagram shows that objects in the two classes can communicate. Specifically, the object Sale uses the getZip operation to send a message to Store object, which accepts the zip request and uses the giveAttValue operation to return the specific zip code belonging to the store associated with the Sale.

The symbols on the connecting line represent the number of associations that can take place. In this example, one sale can be associated with only one (1) store, while each store object can be associated with multiple (*) sales. The number of possible associations among objects is called multiplicity.

12.3.3 Encapsulation

The process of hiding data and program code is called encapsulation. Encapsulation allows an object to be viewed and developed as a single, independent piece of the system. When one object needs another object to execute some portion of its program code, it does not need to know the details of how the second object is designed, only the name and relevant parameters of the message used to initiate the execution of the code (see message passing, above). Because the data and programming code are encapsulated within the objects, changes in data structure and programming logic are usually isolated within one or a small number of object classes, thus reducing development and maintenance effort.

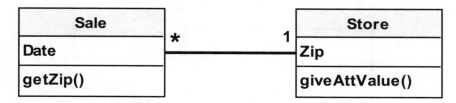

Fig. 12.3. Message passing

12.3.4 Inheritance

Inheritance is another feature of object-oriented methodologies that reduces development and maintenance effort. An object class hierarchy is defined to establish common data and procedures among object super-classes and sub-classes. Sub-classes inherit attribute definitions and programming code (operations) from their super-class. Thus, the attribute definitions and programming code need only be defined once in the super-class. The data definitions and programming code in the sub-class can be modified to meet the unique needs of the sub-class. Changing inherited data definitions and programming logic is called "overriding inheritance."

12.3.5 Polymorphism

Objects essentially remain dormant until they receive a message that triggers them into action. Any number of different object classes can be designed to receive the same message. However, each object class may respond differently to that message. The ability of different object classes to receive the same message but exhibit different behavior is called polymorphism. For example, in Fig. 12.4, the two sub-classes IncomeStatement and SalesAd contain the operation displayReport(). These operations are named the same but generate different results; the first creates an income statement, and the second creates a custom-defined report combining sales data with advertising data.

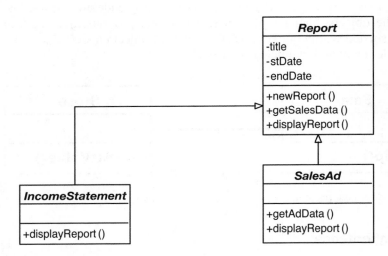

Fig. 12.4. Example of polymorphism

12.3.6 Object-Orientation Summary

Encapsulation, inheritance, and polymorphism are the features of object-oriented development techniques that facilitate more rapid development and maintenance of systems[1]. Object-oriented systems are more flexible and adaptive because the 'pieces' of an object-oriented system, the objects, data and procedures that are contained within them, are relatively inde-

---

[1] For a more comprehensive description of object-oriented principles and UML see John W. Satzinger and Tore U. Ørvik, The Object-Oriented Approach: Concepts, System Development, and Modeling with UML, Course Technology, Boston, MA, 2001.

pendent from the other 'pieces' of the system. Technically stated, objects are loosely coupled. Thus changing the behavior of an existing system typically developed around the interaction of independent objects requires modifying only an isolated area of a software program. Whereas, in the traditional environment, software components requiring similar attributes and programming logic to describe and manage their function may result in the duplication of data descriptions and programming logic. Furthermore, modifications to an existing system may have a ripple effect, where the same or similar changes must be made multiple times throughout a system. However, when object interactions have been defined and object class hierarchies have been established, shared attribute definitions and programming logic are defined only at the super-class level or within the specific objects as needed. When definitions are changed in a super-class, all sub-classes will automatically inherit the attribute definitions and programming code of their super-class. Polymorphism simplifies intra-program communications by allowing the same message to be used by a myriad of object classes. Consequently, the cognitive and development load on the programmer is reduced.

Using encapsulation, inheritance, and polymorphism, a system's functionality can quickly be extended or modified in response to changing business needs. Because accounting applications built using object-oriented development methods and tools are more adaptive to changing business needs than those built using traditional process models and development tools, object-oriented applications can evolve more quickly to fill voids in business intelligence systems.

12.4 An Object-Oriented Example

To demonstrate how object-oriented techniques can be used to design business intelligence systems that are both stable and flexible, we employ a simple example. This case conceptualizes how an organization can integrate data from its accounting system and departmental marketing databases to better understand how its marketing campaigns are affecting sales revenues and profitability. To complete this task, data must be extracted from both the accounting and marketing databases.

The example uses two Unified Modeling Language (UML) diagrams (see Fig. 12.5 and 12.6). UML is the industry standard language for analyzing and designing object-oriented systems. It is a set of notations, semantics, and syntax used for documenting software systems. The first diagram presented, a class diagram, identifies and describes the attributes and operations of classes and how the classes are associated with one another. The second diagram, a sequence diagram, shows how objects interact with one another. In order to keep our example simple, we have only identified the classes, attributes, and operations essential[2] to supporting our argument. These diagrams in no way represent the full level of complexity that would be found in a project.

12.4.1 Diagram – Notation and Syntax

The class diagram (Fig. 12.5) displays the classes and their associations. The association lines between classes that do not have an arrow on either end are used to tell us that the objects in these classes can send messages to each other. The association lines with the arrowhead are used to represent inheritance. The class to which the arrows are pointing is the superclass. In our example this superclass is the *Report* class. IncomeStatement and SalesAd are both subclasses of *Report*. Therefore, each is a special type of report that is in some way different than the other subclasses. Each subclass has inherited the attributes and operations of *Report*.

The superclass, *Report*, is an abstract class. We know this because its name, found in the first section of the class symbol, is italicized. All of the other classes found on the class diagram are concrete classes. A concrete class is a class used to instantiate objects. In other word, a concrete class has objects. An abstract class does not have objects. The attributes and operations found in an abstract superclass are physically instantiated in the concrete subclasses. Using an abstract class is a way that a developer can define once the structure, attributes, and behavior of a number of similar classes while maintaining the distinctions among classes.

Objects interact by sending messages from an operation in one object to an operation in another object. Sequence diagrams show the order in which these messages are passed Fig. 12.6 shows our sequence diagram. The objects are indicated by rectangles listed across the top of the diagram.

---

[2] Using the word "essential" is intentional in this context. Describing the essential use of the system means that only the basic business use of the system is initially considered. Delaying the task of dealing with the details of the design until they are necessary is part of the prevailing philosophy in UML-based design methods. However, the same diagrams initially used to capture the essence of the system are used and evolve throughout the development process. As the effort progresses, they become increasingly more detailed and implementation specific.

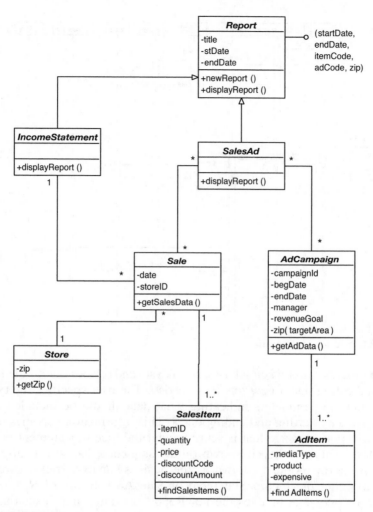

Fig. 12.5. Class diagram

12.4.2 Diagram – Semantics

To fully understand appreciate a system's design, we must study both the static (class diagram) and behavioral (sequence diagram) models. The following example incorporates both types of diagrams to demonstrate how object-oriented design techniques aide in developing business intelligence in accounting.

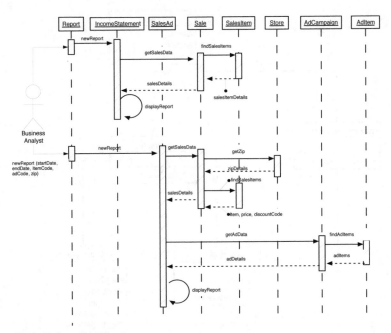

Fig. 12.6. Sequence diagram

The process starts when a business analyst sends a message to the *Report* class indicating that a new report is needed. The user specifies the type of report and the parameters indicating what data should be included in the report, such as starting and ending dates. This information becomes part of the newReport message that is sent to either the IncomeStatement or SalesAd class. This message is shown on the sequence diagram. It originates from an interface object (shown as the business analyst stick figure) and flows to either the IncomeStatement or SalesAd subclass of *Report*. The newReport message invokes the newReport operation that instantiates either an IncomeStatement or SalesAd object. The class diagram shows that *Report* is an abstract class with two concrete subclasses. It also contains the list of available attributes and operations. However, we have to reference the sequence diagram to see that the newReport message is sent from the user interface to a *Report* subclass to start this process.

When the business analyst requests an income statement, the newReport operation instantiates an IncomeStatement object. All the necessary information which is needed for an income statement is found in the accounting data[3], which are encapsulated in the Sale and SalesItem objects. The new IncomeStatement object sends a message, getSalesData, to the Sale class to invoke the getSalesData operation, which is responsible for accumulating the appropriate dollar totals and items counts for items sold. The Sale object must in turn find the details about the items included on that sale. Hence, the Sale object sends the findSalesItems message to the SalesItem class invoking the findSalesItems operation. The findSalesItems operation finds the SalesItem objects associated with the Sale object and returns the needed data values to the requesting object using the salesItemDetails reply message. Then these values are returned via the salesDetails reply message to the IncomeStatement object where the displayReport operation accumulates the values for the Sale objects.

We have described the classes, objects, operations, and messages necessary to create the income statement report. We can see how the objects encapsulate both data and operations. Furthermore, we have described how the messages between the objects that invoke operations that allow objects to exhibit behavior. The remainder of this example will show how object-oriented design techniques allow the addition of new functionality within a stable, yet flexible, system.

Assume that after the accounting portion of the system was built, the business analyst realized that integrating these data with information from the marketing database would provide valuable insight into the effectiveness of the organization's marketing campaigns. Because of the class hierarchy we have established, where *Report* is the superclass and IncomeStatement is the subclass, additional report types can be easily added. The addition of the SalesAd class does not impact the IncomeStatement class. We do not need to worry about "ripple effect" changes. This addition is an example of the stability inherent in object-oriented techniques. Furthermore, the labor required to add the new report type is limited because many of its attributes and operations are inherited from its superclass. This inheritance is an example of the flexibility inherent in object-oriented techniques. This example demonstrates that new functionality can be added "relatively" quickly without adversely affecting the existing system.

In order to create a report showing sales level and advertising initiatives within a given time period, data must be pulled from both the accounting database and the marketing database. As we observed above, the Sale and

---

[3] Other types of transactions that must be included in the accounting data, such as expenses, are not shown in this example. The philosophy behind the example is not to accurately represent a complex accounting system but to present a clear picture of an object-oriented model and to demonstrate the benefits of object-oriented methods.

SalesItem objects encapsulate the accounting data. The marketing data are encapsulated within the AdCampaign and AdItem objects. When a business analyst requests a sales and advertising report, a SalesAd object is instantiated. The initial operations performed are similar to those described above. The SalesAd object also needs the accounting data so it sends a message to the Sales object, which in turn sends a message to the SalesItem object. These messages and operations are identical to those described in the income statement scenario. However for the sales and advertising analysis, we also need to know where the sale occurred to understand which advertising campaigns have a significant effect on sales. The marketing campaign data contain the zip code information of where the promotions were run, but the accounting data do not. Nevertheless, the accounting data includes a store identifier. Address information describes the store, not the sales; and therefore, the zip is stored in the Store objects. However, each Sale is associated with a Store as depicted in the class diagram. Therefore, the zip is readily available for the analysis. Therefore, the Sales object must send a second message, getZip, to the Store object to know the geographic region of the store that made the sale.

In addition to accounting sales data, the SaleAd object also needs marketing information. Therefore, we will use the data and operations found within the AdCampaign and AdItem objects. These objects were not needed to generate an income statement. The objects are also not directly associated with the accounting sales data. However by using good object-oriented design principles, their inclusion has a minimal impact on the rest of the system.

In order to retrieve the marketing data, the SalesAd object sends a getAdData message with the parameters to AdCampaign objects. The AdCampaign objects send the findAdItem message to the AdItem objects, which returns the adItems reply message. Then the adDetails message is returned to the SalesAd object to be summarized and displayed by the displayReport operation.

As stated before the presentation of the retail store marketing example, encapsulation and polymorphism are the properties of an object-oriented method that lead to the creation of systems that are both stable and flexible. Encapsulation protects objects in one class from changes in other classes. Inheritance allows the addition of new report types with minimal labor and expense. Polymorphism allows each subclass of *Report* to respond in different ways to its newReport message. Object-oriented design leads to systems that are both stable and flexible.

12.5 Conclusion

Within corporate cultures, standard accounting data are not sufficient to respond to the data demands of sophisticated decision-making problems. As functional business subsystems and the technologies that support them have been integrated through concepts like Enterprise Resource Planning (ERP), there has been a demand for more comprehensive access to these data sources. There has been a steady advance of the technologies to support these initiatives. Data warehouses and data marts have opened up new avenues for viewing corporate data over time. Previously, the lack of logical integration among enterprise-wide data created by different functional business areas seemed to create an insurmountable challenge for those trying to understand the data as a single corporate resource. However, data warehouses and data marts have successfully tackled much of this challenge. Unfortunately, the usefulness of these technologies is limited by the design choices of the creators. The level of granularity and attributes included in a system define which analyses can and cannot be performed. By design, data warehouses are not flexible in their abilities to respond to unexpected data queries.

The ability to query data in the accounting environment is critical in decision-making. Generally speaking, user-executed queries are not routine or standardized. If they were, they should be institutionalized in a canned report. Therefore, the user query is intended to provide insight into the operations of the business that exceeds the initial specification of the system. It is the ability to intelligently and creatively view data through ad hoc queries that allows the business analyst to contribute to the competitive and strategic advancement of the organization.

Toward that end, small, stand-alone analytic systems can be created as a supplemental resource for business intelligence. State of the art object-oriented development methods and tools can be used to generate flexible data retrieval and manipulate systems relatively quickly. Applying object-oriented methods to generate this type of system can be a valuable supplement to data warehouses and data marts in supporting accounting business intelligence.

Within this chapter, we have provided a foundation for understanding the object-oriented paradigm. This foundation includes definitions and examples of the basic structures and concepts, as well as how these components allow the conceptual and physical development of changes and additions to systems. We have attempted to show how this approach lends itself to efficient systems redesign through the non-duplication of system components, specifically data and operational definitions and instantiation. These requirements are crucial to facilitate rapid design and development response. To reinforce the understanding of the application of these concepts, we have used an example showing how basic accounting data (sales) can contribute but must be supplemented (advertising revenues by zip code) to produce valid intelligence (correlation between advertising expenditures and sales generated). The example serves to show not only the implicit nature of business intelligence but also the object-oriented approach for dealing with the implementation of a system that provides valuable data for analysis. While standard accounting needs tend to be relatively static, the demand for corporate managers to be constantly aware of changing business dynamics is ever present. Consequently, support systems, technical or otherwise, must meet the challenge of responding to the demands of their users.

13 Evaluating Business Intelligence: A Balanced Scorecard Approach

Barbara M. Vinciguerra

Management Division, Pennsylvania State Great Valley School of Graduate Professional Studies, Pennsylvania

Abstract. Adoption of new information technology often has an indirect effect on an organization's bottom line; however, many organizations require some minimum financial return on investment before undertaking a major investment. The return on investment in business intelligence (BI) such as data warehouses, data marts, reporting and query tools, and analytic applications are even more challenging to measure since many of the benefits are intangible. How can a company objectively measure the value of improved communication and information for decision-making?

It has been noted that traditional financial performance measures do not measure the increase in value when companies improve their capabilities through the use of new technology. Further, traditional financial measures such as return on investment (ROI) appear to show improvement even when the technology is not being used effectively. In this chapter, we discuss the nature of the Balanced Scorecard and illustrate how it can be used as a measurement tool to evaluate the return on an investment in technology such as BI.

13.1 Introduction

Operating in the information age requires new capabilities for competitive success. Advances in computing technology have changed the nature of the accounting function, resulting in steady decreases in the time it takes to do traditional accounting tasks such as recording transactions and preparing the monthly financial reports. In addition, with the advent of enterprise resource planning systems and database capabilities, managers have more data and data sources at their command than ever before. The challenge for modern companies and their finance departments is to convert this *data* into *intelligence* that mangers can use to effectively run their organizations. According to Intelligent Enterprise Top 10 Trends for 2003, the "performance measurement mantra" for 2003 will be "it's not just having the data; it's what you do with it" that creates strategic advantage (Burriesci et.al. 2003).

The information needed for effective management of resources and managerial decision-making has also undergone a significant change. The financial structure of organizations has evolved from primarily manufacturing companies with "bricks and mortar" assets toward more technology and service organizations, which have primarily intangible "knowledge" assets. Citing research studies conducted by the Brookings Institute and Professor Baruch Lev at New York University, Kaplan and Norton (2001) note that there has been a dramatic shift in the ratio of tangible assets to market value; from 62 percent of market values in the 1980's to an estimated 10 to 15 percent of a market value by the year 2000 (Kaplan and Norton 2001, p. 2).

BI capabilities can create organizational value; however, the benefits of BI are often intangible and difficult to measure in financial terms. Traditional financial metrics do not include valuations for many of an organization's intangibles; therefore, managers have been challenged to find ways to better measure the contribution of intangibles such as competitive advantage from BI capabilities, leading edge IT skills, a motivated workforce, and satisfied customers on the bottom line.

Investments in BI can be costly, and many corporate CFOs won't support an investment in any project unless there is a clear financial return on investment. In the current business environment, "business is demanding value for each dollar" invested in technology, and many contend that IT value results only when investments in technology are successfully aligned with corporate strategy (Love 2003). The same can be said for investments in BI. Business intelligence creates organizational value when the initiatives support an organization's overall strategy. The challenge is to measure how these investments in BI technologies contribute to the organization's financial goals.

13.2 Traditional Methods of Evaluating Investments in Technology

Traditionally, organizations require that investments in information technology, just like investments in other types of assets, are expected to meet some minimum return on investment (ROI) before committing to a project Ross and Beath (2002) refer to this as "making the business case" for an investment in technology. Methods for computing the return on investment vary, from simple payback period computations to more complicated calculations such as economic value added (EVA) and real options valuation (For an excellent summary and description of ROI methods in IT, see Mayor 2000, and Betts 2003). A *Computerworld* online survey found that 94% of respondents required some sort of ROI calculation when deciding to make a major IT investment. The required calculations include payback period (32%), internal rate of return (21%), Net present value (20%), economic value added (12%), balanced scorecard (7%), other (2%), and None (6%).

The ROI methods, above, differ in the specifics of the calculations, for example, some require the discounting future cash streams, while others require the use of a capital charge for the minimum required cost of capital. What all of the methods have in common is that they all require some sort of estimated cost savings or revenue enhancements compared against the upfront cost of the investment. For example, calculation of the payback period on the installation of ATM machines at a bank would include an estimate of the cost savings from the elimination of teller positions compared against the cost of the ATM hardware. A project with a cost of $1,000,000 with an annual cost savings of $250,000 would have a payback period of four years (Example from Anthes 2003).

Computations of cost savings and/or revenue enhancements work well for IT projects that have clear cost savings as in the case where positions are eliminated, processes are streamlined, or customer service systems are improved. Estimates of savings or revenue enhancements are much tougher to come by when the benefits are less tangible and therefore not easily quantifiable. For example, an investment in BI, such as a data warehouse, will provide a common repository of data. This can be expected to streamline the reporting process and allow for a levels and types of data analysis not previously achievable. It may be possible to estimate the cost savings associated with streamlining the reporting process; however, this is only a small portion of the potential benefits achieved by this investment. Many of the benefits of BI are not objectively measurable. For example, how do you accurately measure the financial benefits of the availability of better information on which to base decision-making? How do you measure the value of improved organizational communication? Estimates of this type of savings are "soft" numbers at best; however, failure to account for these benefits may result in an achieved payback that falls short of organizational standards.

Eric Brynjolfsson of MIT's Sloan School of Management specializes in IT effectiveness. He notes that his research indicates that 90% of the costs and benefits of IT are in intangibles and suggests that firms who focus too heavily on the short-term financial returns of projects may sacrifice long-term potential (Ambrosio 2003). In a study of IT funding practices, Ross and Beath (2002) found that 25 out of the 30 companies surveyed said that they traditionally relied on "making the business case" to justify investments in IT Most, however, noted that they have funded at least one initiative without a business case where the project was deemed strategic (Ross and Beath 2002, p. 52).

Ross and Beath (2002) categorize IT investments as transformation, renewal, process improvement, and experiments. Investments in BI fall into the transformation category *Transformation investments* are driven by an infrastructure that is inadequate for the desired business model. They are triggered by the growing need for integrated customer data, end-to-end processing, and platforms that provide around the clock support. Examples of these initiatives include ERP implementations and data warehouses. *Renewal investments* are introduced when a company's infrastructure becomes outdated and includes initiatives such as purchasing additional capacity and upgrading technology standards. *Process improvement investments* are triggered by the need to improve operational performance, and include initiates such as shifting data capture to customers and streamlining cycle times for processes. *Experiments* are driven by the availability of new technologies, new products, and new business models. These initiatives include testing demand for new products and learning if customers can self-serve. The authors suggest that traditional measures of ROI are well-suited to renewal and process improvement initiatives; however, they suggest that a high-level strategic funding approach is needed for transformation and experiment initiatives because the payoffs are not easily quantifiable.

Given the strategic nature of investments in BI and the difficulty in accurately and objectively quantifying the financial benefit associated with these investments, we propose the use of the Balanced Scorecard as a means of quantifying and expressing the benefits of BI.

The balanced scorecard is a multi-dimensional approach to performance measurement that emphasizes the cause and effect linkages between performance measures and strategy. It attempts to describe how intangible assets get transformed into customer value and financial outcomes (Kaplan and Norton, 2001). The Balanced Scorecard approach uses a combination of financial metrics (lag indicators of performance) and non-financial metrics (lead measures of performance) to assess the measurement of organizational effectiveness. Specifically, using this approach requires organizations to consider the cause and effect linkages from four key perspectives: learning and growth, internal perspective, customer perspective, and financial perspective.

The remainder of the chapter is organized as follows. First, we describe the origin and logic of the balanced scorecard. Next, we describe a BI application, the decision to adopt data warehouse technology and the type of intelligence that the organization can capture using the information contained in the data warehouse. Finally, we provide an illustration of a balanced scorecard used in a bank that has implemented data warehousing and front-end BI technology.

13.3 The Balanced Scorecard

A major hurdle in undertaking and promoting a significant technological investment relates to the issue of how to measure its benefits. As noted by Kaplan and Norton (2001), information technology has a third order effect on an organization's bottom line making the direct return on investment difficult to assess. For example, what is the financial return when a company makes a major investment in data warehousing technology that allows for improvements in the speed and accuracy of reporting and enables the company to capture financial and non-financial data that improves decision making capabilities of its managers? Improvements in data availability may allow a customer service rep to have deeper knowledge of the customer's relationship with the organization. For example, the system may be able to identify whether or not a particular is a profitable customer. This will allow the representative to make more informed decisions regarding services to offer or whether to waive fees. This information may improve customer satisfaction and increase customer loyalty, which in turn may result in an increase in long-term sales.

Unlike traditional ROI measures, the balanced scorecard approach to performance measurement highlights the strategic linkages between people, systems, and customers on financial value creation. Using the balanced scorecard approach demands that proposals for new technology must show a clear link to the organization's key strategic initiatives. Aligning IT with corporate strategy can enable the organization to focus its technology efforts to achieve the highest payoffs.

The Balanced Scorecard has its roots in France under a system referred to as *tableau de bord* (Lebas, 1994; Epstein and Manzoni, 1997). In the U.S it was popularized and further developed as a concept by Kaplan and Norton (1992; 1996; 1997; 2001). The Balanced Scorecard includes financial measures of performance and also adds measures from three additional perspectives: customer, internal business processes, and learning and growth. These four perspectives collectively form the framework from which the organization defines the cause and effect relationship of organizational strategy on performance outcomes. Examining organizational performance from four perspectives allows the use a variety of measures to achieve a balance between short-term and long-term objectives, outcomes and drivers of those outcomes, and objective and subjective measures (Kaplan and Norton, 1996).

The balanced scorecard has a top down logic, beginning with the organization's strategy, determining how the strategy is translated into financial and customer outcomes and moving to the business processes and infrastructure that are the drivers of change (See Fig. 13.1).

The key to applying the balanced scorecard is an articulation of the organization's strategy. One of the noted benefits of the Balanced Scorecard is that it provides a framework to describe and communicate strategy in a meaningful way (Kaplan and Norton, 2001). The articulation of the strategy is followed by the development of performance measures specifying the financial objectives for growth and productivity. Next, the customer perspective is considered. The organization must identify its target customers, consider their objectives, and determine how to measure success with them. As part of this process, the organization defines the way that they provide customer value, i.e., the factors that differentiate the organization from its competitors.

The next perspective, internal business processes, defines the activities that the organization needs to achieve the desired customer value and financial objectives. This perspective considers the organization's effectiveness at providing innovative products and services, efficiency and effectiveness in delivering existing products and services to customers, and satisfying customers in the post-sale. Finally, the learning and growth perspective recognizes that the ability to execute the business processes effectively depends on the organization's infrastructure, i.e., the skills, capabilities, and knowledge of employees, as well as the technology that they use and the environment in which they work (Kaplan and Norton, 2001, p. 76).

In summary, the Balanced Scorecard translates business strategy into objectives and measures across a balanced set of perspectives. While it still tracks the financial perspective, it also measures the factors expected to lead to superior future financial and competitive performance through its focus on customer, internal processes, and organizational learning Atkinson et. al., (1997) note that corporate executives can use the scorecard to measure how their business units create value for current and future customers, how they must build and enhance internal capabilities, and the investment in people and systems necessary to improve future performance.

We suggest that organizations can use the balanced scorecard to measure how investments in BI, when part of an organization's strategy, can translate into improved financial performance. Specifically, we describe how an investment in a data warehouse can be linked to organizational strategy and the achievement of financial goals.

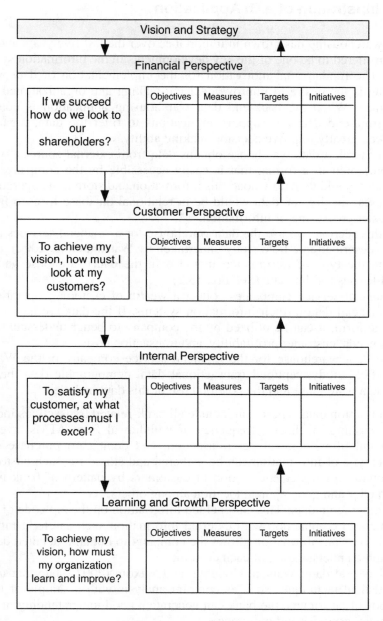

Fig. 13.1. Defining the Cause and Effect Relationship of the Strategy (Kaplan and Norton 2001)

13.4 Illustration of a BI Application

Data warehousing has grown in importance over the last five years and can be considered to be one of the key developments in the information system field. The fundamental motivation for the implementation of data warehousing is the desire to improve decision-making and organizational performance. When the back-end data warehousing application is coupled with front-end decision support applications to filter the data, organizations can greatly improve decision-making ability.

In general, a data warehouse obtains data from external sources, which is then stored in a format that is easily accessible by the company. The company would then download this information and store in its operational databases. Ideally, the data would be in relational database form to facilitate faster processing of information.

In this section, we use the data warehouse for a financial services company, (described in a field study undertaken by Watson, et. al. 2002), to illustrate the type of information included in the data warehouse and the possible uses for that data (See Fig. 13.2).

Financial service companies collect a wealth of customer, operational, and financial data in their information systems. If the data are held in accessible form, it can be utilized by the company to better understand customer needs, customer profitability, and transaction costs.

The data warehouse for the financial service company in the Watson et.al., field study, captured transactional data, demographic data, behavioral data warehouse and the potential use of this data include:

- Transaction data: These can include all bank-related transactions including cashing of checks, frequency of withdrawal from ATMs, average amount of withdrawal per transaction, and debit card purchase data. This type of information can be gathered and stored for each customer, allowing for the categorization of customers by pattern of bank usage behavior and geographical location among others.
- Demographic data: This can include information on the zip code of customers in conjunction with external information such as credit ratings. This type of information allows the company to obtain a detailed demographic understanding of each customer.
- Behavioral data: Watson, Goodhue and Wixom (2002) state that using statistical techniques such as conjoint analysis with a sample of thousands of customers, the bank can generate a good understanding of customers' attitudes and preferences.
- Revenue and cost data: These can include revenue and cost data for each product in the company's product line. Customer profitability analysis can be done by generating revenue by customer or key customer group

and cost by customer or customer group. Product or service profitability can also be generated through knowledge of revenue by type of service, (granting of personal loans etc) and the costs of providing each type of service. This allows the financial service company to focus its sales, marketing, and customer service efforts.

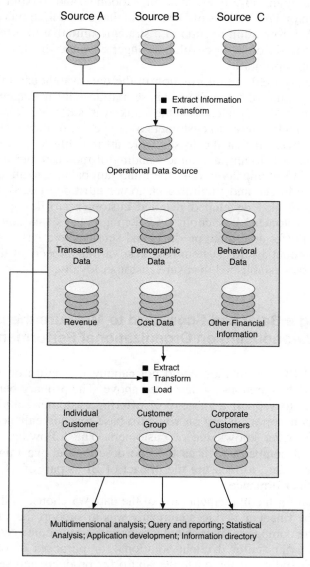

Fig. 13.2. Data Warehousing Architecture for a Bank

The data in the data warehouse can be accessed for the above purposes using BI applications including multidimensional analysis, online query and reporting, statistical analysis, and for the preparation of standardized financial and non-financial reporting.

Information obtained through the data warehouse can be used to meet a variety of strategic objectives. Watson, Goodhue and Wixom (2002), in their research on applications of DW, found that the bank in this case study used the DW information to support a strategic initiative to offer "tailored client solutions" in order to develop stronger customer-bank relationships and long-term profitability.

The company used the information in the data warehouse to better understand the nature of the customer base and account management costs. Their data analysis revealed that the bank was suffering losses on free checking accounts offered to customers over age 55; further analysis of the information revealed that the losses were attributable to customers with low balances. Developing this understanding of the customer and product costs allowed the company to raise the minimum balance to an amount that would reduce losses and minimize customer attrition. The financial services company also developed detailed customer profiles generated by analysis of customer transactions and demographic data. These profiles were used to offer additional products and services to a targeted group of customers, and an awards system based on various aspects of the banking relationship was established to ensure customer loyalty.

13.5 Using a Balanced Scorecard to Measure the Effects of Data Warehousing on Organizational Performance

A traditional ROI calculation could not capture the return on the investment in the data warehousing described above. The primary benefit of the investment is to support a strategy of offering customer solutions; however, there is no prior history on which to base revenue enhancements resulting from better knowledge of customers. The following section describes how a company such as the one described above might use the Balanced Scorecard to measure the impact of BI as part of its overall organizational performance.

The reason for the implementation of the data warehouse and related reporting in the financial services company was to support the strategic initiatives of the company. Their stated strategy was to become 'customer intimate' and offer 'tailored client solutions' for purposes of obtaining a better understanding of the customer and offer products and services that are tailored to customer needs, thus building stronger customer relationships. The company believed that achievement of these goals would lead to long-term sustainable profits (Watson, et. al., 2002).

The first step in the balanced scorecard process is to articulate the strategy and develop a strategy map (Kaplan and Norton, 2001). The strategy map identifies the hypothesized strategic linkages between the four key perspectives: financial, customer, internal, and learning and growth. A strategy map supporting the organization's stated strategy is included in Fig. 13.3.

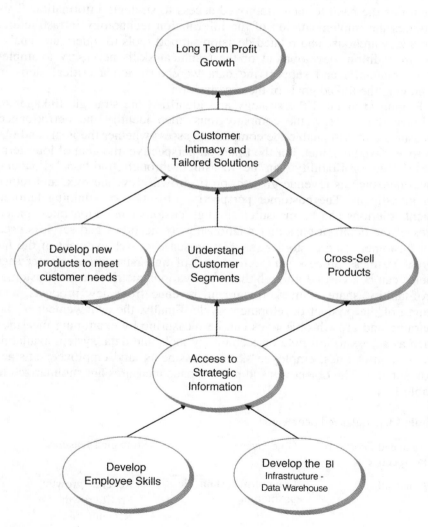

Fig. 13.3. Strategy Map

Having identified the financial objective of long-term sustainable profits and the customer value proposition of providing tailored client solutions and customer intimacy, the strategy map then must focus on the internal processes necessary for the strategy to succeed. The financial service company noted that they needed to develop an understanding of who their "good" customers were so that they could offer product solutions geared toward profitable customers. Three processes were identified: understand customer segments, develop new products to meet customer needs, and cross-sell products. The learning and growth component of the scorecard identifies the need to have improved access to strategic information. This requires the implementation of the information technology infrastructure, the data warehouse and related decision support tools for query and analysis. In addition, development of the technical skills necessary to implement, maintain, and support the data warehouse are a critical steps in achieving the linked goals of the organization.

Having articulated the strategy and identified the strategic linkages to achieve the strategy, the company must then identify the performance measures that will enable the company to assess whether the goals and objectives have been met. For the financial perspective, the goal of long-term sustainable profitability can be measured through traditional financial measures such as revenue growth, profit growth, revenue mix, and return on investment. The customer perspective objective of attaining tailored client solutions can be measured through customer retention rates, measures of the depth of customer relationships (# accounts and services used per customer), and customer satisfaction surveys. Achievement of the internal business process perspective goal of understanding customer segments can be assessed through the use of various metrics such as customer profitability, share of market segment, revenue from new products, and length of the product development cycle. Finally, the achievement of the learning and growth objectives can be measuring by examining measures such as access to information technology tools and data, system availability, response times, employee skills assessments, and employee satisfaction surveys. The objectives and performance measures are summarized in Table 13.1.

Table 13.1. Balanced Scorecard

Balanced Scorecard Perspective	Objectives	Strategic Measures
Financial	Long-term sustainable profitability	Revenue growth Profit growth Revenue mix Return on investment

Table 13.1. (cont.)

Balanced Scorecard Perspective	Objectives	Strategic Measures
Customer	Tailored customer solutions	Customer retention rates
		Depth of customer relationships (# accounts per customer, # services per customer)
		Customer satisfaction
Internal	Understanding customer segments	Profit by customer segment
		Share of market segment
		Revenue from new products
		Length of the product development cycle
Learning and Growth	Development of information systems and employee skills	Access to information technology tools and data
		System availability
		IT response times
		Employee skills assessments
		Employee satisfaction surveys

13.6 Conclusions

Organizations must consider how the use of BI fits into the overall organizational strategy and must determine the key metrics to assess achievement of these strategies. Most BI applications are relatively new information technology tools that enable companies to gain access to much greater and more detailed information than ever before. These tools can then help companies filter their data to enable more informed decision-making. The high cost and complexity of many BI applications cause organizations to consider it a high-risk investment.

The balanced scorecard is a performance measurement system that recognizes that using only financial performance measures may result in suboptimal decisions for firms. To get a true measure of organizational performance, firms must link performance measures to strategy and consider the achievement of organizational goals through the financial, customer, internal process, and learning and growth perspectives. By assessing the impact of new BI technology on the achievement of goals in all four of the perspectives, an organization will be able to capture the benefits that accrue from investment in BI technology.

The use of the balanced scorecard to show the strategic linkage between key technologies and organizational success can be an effective means to measure and assess the potential value of adopting BI technology.

14 A Stakeholder Model of Business Intelligence

Claire A. Simmers

Department of Management, Saint Joseph's University, Pennsylvania

Abstract. The 21st century organization is evolving from a bureaucratic form based upon hierarchy to a new-form based on knowledge and networks. This chapter explores the role of business intelligence in this new-form organization. It develops a model that positions business intelligence as the primary source of explicit knowledge within a stakeholder perspective, integrating with human and social capital (tacit knowledge sources). Stakeholder theory provides a useful theoretical basis for this model as it offers a comprehensive way to depict business intelligence as a pathway, which enables and captures knowledge. The stakeholder model of business intelligence helps to predict value creation in organizations characterized by indistinct organizational boundaries, information overabundance, and fast-paced change.

14.1 Introduction

The firm's ability to take advantage of data and information as part of knowledge construction and utilization becomes more complex with the increasing volume of both internally and externally generated information. Firms are experiencing unparalleled environmental change resulting from the new economics of information (Evans and Wurster, 2000) and the increasingly dynamic and global nature of competition (D'Aveni, 1994). Organizations invest in information technology in an effort to handle the information glut - gathering, analyzing, and sharing knowledge that can be leveraged for competitive advantage. Organizational survival depends on the construction and integration of knowledge fostering adaptation to the environment. However, organizations can also stimulate environmental change with their knowledge and business practices (Dijksterhuis, et al., 1999).

One of the signs of this changing competitive landscape is the movement from hierarchical bureaucratic organizational forms toward a new organizational form that is sensitive to vertical, horizontal, and external challenges and opportunities. This new structure has been labeled the radix or new-form organization (Schneider, 2002) and is characterized by network-like interfaces up and across functions within the organization. In new-form organizations, firms recognize that exchanges outside the organization, that is, along the value chain with suppliers and customers and with others in the external environment, are critical to organizational survival and growth

This chapter builds on Schneider's (2002) response to Daft and Lewin's (1993) challenge for theory regarding the new-form organization Schneider (2002) developed a model for organizational leadership effectiveness based on an organization-environment coevolution framework using the stakeholder theory to predict leader effectiveness in organizations characterized by nebulous organizational boundaries, flattened hierarchies, and contract work relationships. This chapter applies similar theoretical development to another research question: *How does the new-form organization affect the integration of business intelligence to enhance value creation?*

A knowledge-based theory view of the firm (Grant, 1996) posits that the primary role of the firm is the creation and application of knowledge that will lead to sustainable competitive advantage. Several perspectives of how firms behave and why firms are different are integrated into this knowledge-based view including the resource-based view (Barney, 1991; Conner, 1991; Eisenhardt and Schoonhaven, 1996), organizational learning (Crossan, Lane, and White, 1999; Fiol and Lyles, 1985; Huber, 1991; Senge, 1990), and competencies (Helleloid and Simonin, 1994; Reed and DeFillippi, 1990; Leonard-Barton, 1992; Prahalad and Hamel, 1990). A knowledge-based theory defines knowledge as broader in scope than information, weaving facts with ideas and understanding with action. Thus knowledge can be viewed as information combined with social innovative capacities and applied to decisions and actions. There are two distinct streams of research using the knowledge-based view of the firm, each with distinct theories and constructs. These are: 1) the information processing view from the information technology literatures, and 2) the behavioral processing view from the strategic management and organizational theory literatures. Knowledge that is formalized and codified is called "explicit knowledge" and is often equated with the information processing view. This knowledge is captured in tangible records, documentation, rules, databases, etc. Recent advances in information technology, such as business intelligence and enterprise resource planning systems, offer fast, inexpensive ways to capture, apply, and disseminate explicit knowledge. Business intelligence is identified as an amalgamation of reporting, data mining and online analytical processing applications (Hoelscher, 2002). Business intelligence is particularly useful in customer relationship marketing (CRM), which requires a massive database engine for conducting complex analyses of customer behavior (Boon, 1998). Business intelligence is concerned with responding more quickly and flexibly to an increasingly turbulent and competitive environment

The social and cognitive skills embedded in the minds of employees and organizational routines are called "tacit knowledge" and are equated with the behavioral processing view of knowledge. This tacit knowledge is intangible and difficult to formalize but is "visible" in action and emanates from two sources – a social source and a cognitive source. The social component is often referred to as communities of practice. Communities of practice are nodes for the exchange and interpretation of information, emphasizing the learning that people have done together rather than the unit they report to, the project they are working on, or the people they know. They can retain knowledge in "living" ways, unlike a database or a manual, preserving the implicit aspects of knowledge that formal systems cannot capture. The cognitive component centers around expertise or skills built up over time in actions. Know-how (capacity or learning) is more than experience (things undertaken before); it is the cumulative adjustment to experience that improves performance over time. It is not just the doing, but also the enhancement or fine-tuning of doing

Traditional information processing knowledge theories have assumed that the key to knowledge creation rests primarily on hardware and software platforms efficiently processing information and knowledge internal to the firm. Behavioral knowledge theories have focused on resources that are unique and not easily imitated as a way to create knowledge; the domain of organizational members is largely internal, with few in boundary-spanning roles (Thompson, 1967). The rapidly changing environment and modifications in business practices in response to these conditions have increasingly blurred the heretofore generally separate domains of explicit and tacit knowledge and the two corresponding theoretical frameworks. How are the explicit knowledge bases and the tacit knowledge bases integrated in the new-form organization? What is the role of business intelligence in this integration? How is integration success measured in a new-form organization?

In the attempt to answer these questions, recent theorizing about the new-form organization is reviewed. A model is developed in which an integrated explicit and tacit knowledge base is shown to both respond to and induce environmental change. Stakeholder theory is drawn upon as the basis for the stakeholder model of business intelligence, which may include those inside or outside the firm and the integration of tacit and explicit knowledge bases. A review of business practices associated with the new-form organization is given next, from which we see the decline of independent silos of information and knowledge and the increase in coordination and reliance among parts in a connected system. Propositions are developed regarding business intelligence, based on the changes in the business intelligence role and relationships because of the movement to the new-form organization and the need to coordinate within and outside the firm.

The stakeholder model of business intelligence contributes to both information technology and management literatures. It is matched with ongoing organizational trends in which knowledge is increasingly developed and used in nonhierarchical relationships, internal and external to the firm (Barley, 1990; Davidow and Malone, 1992). The model expands the application of stakeholder theory and extends research regarding business intelligence (specifically) and explicit and tacit knowledge bases (generally) to the new-form organization.

14.2 Business Intelligence and the Coevolution of Organizations and Environments

Business Intelligence (BI) has grown in importance, as organizations increasingly perceive the value of their intellectual capital and the potential profits of unlocking this capital. This intellectual capital comes in the form of the processes, solutions, expertise, and heuristics of individuals and groups within the organization that have value in solving problems, identifying opportunities and threats, and improving organizational effectiveness harvested from the data provided by BI. Business intelligence is neither an Information Technology technique nor a technology. It is a combined organizational effort aimed at satisfying the information requirements of the organization. The aim is to provide access to data that has been integrated and cleaned; and then, it can be analyzed, manipulated, transformed, and combined to discover correlations, trends, and patterns that offer new insights and aid decision making (Boon, 1998). This chapter looks at the relationship of business intelligence with knowledge, through the lens of the coevolution framework (Lewin et al., 1999).

The new-form organization reflects the transformation from the industrial to the postindustrial or knowledge-based age. While interest in knowledge can be traced back to ancient times, recognition that we are evolving into a "knowledge society" has been rising since the mid-1960s (Drucker, 1968). The increasing importance of knowledge coincides with innovations in, and widespread adoption of, information technologies and the acceptance of information as the newest factor of production (Boisot, 1999). Knowledge differs from other factors of production (land, labor, and capital) since it is not subject to diminishing returns; output associated with knowledge accumulates at an increasing rate (Boisot, 1999). The information processing view defines knowledge as the process of acquiring, organizing, sharing, retrieving, and updating content throughout an organization to all who need it for action (Albert, 1998; Hibbard, 1997). Polanyi (1964) called this dimension explicit knowledge that is knowledge which is formalized and codified. This knowledge is captured in records; and the recent advances in information technology offer fast, inexpensive ways to capture and apply explicit knowledge. Business intelligence is a major component of an explicit knowledge base (Malhotra, 2000).

Knowledge also resides in human capital, those who are employed to think rather than to merely do (Pfeffer, 1996). Knowledge is also the property of a collective; this social capital is based on relationships. Organizations are characterized as cognitive enterprises that learn and develop knowledge as a collective (Crossan, Lane, and White, 1999). The organization's ability to generate collective knowledge is a function of how it combines its infrastructure, culture, and processes with its explicit knowledge base. The organization's capacity to generate value for customers is increasingly linked to its treatment of human capital, creation of social capital, and use of business intelligence to recognize and to manipulate environmental factors thus promoting and improving an organization's competitive position.

The new-form organization is firmly anchored in creating value for the customer that is seamless across multiple products, regions, and customer groups. Thus it is characterized by permeable boundaries (Kantor, 1990), elasticity and nimbleness (Volberda, 1996), and horizontal connections across functions, divisions, and geographic regions (Galbraith, 1994). It is more open and adaptive than the bureaucratic designs that characterized the industrial age (Wheatley, 1992). The new-form organization is well informed about other firms located along the value chain and looks to utilize contractual agreements rather than takeover activity whenever possible to enhance strategic opportunities, thus maintaining flexibility. Organizations extend relationships outside of traditional boundaries accumulating tacit and explicit knowledge sources. These knowledge sources make possible and sustain these relationships. Business intelligence facilitates the connections in the new-form organization, bringing real-time information to centralized repositories to create rich and precisely targeted analytics that can be exploited at every horizontal and vertical level within and outside the firm.

The coevolution framework makes use of multidirectional causality and multiple environments in explaining new organizational forms. Multidirectional causality illustrates how business intelligence pressures, and is pressured by, the environment (See Fig. 14.1). The framework divides the environment into extra-institutional, institutional and industry. The extra-institutional forces of technological advances, globalization, and institutional forces that are nation-specific differences in political/legal forces, capital markets, and demographic/socio-cultural factors help explain variation in and acceptance of the new-form organization. The industry is the competitive dynamics that require and reward speed, flexibility, creativity, and adaptability in relation to current and potential competitors. The internal organizational aspects of the coevolution framework include strategic intent, managerial action, and leadership.

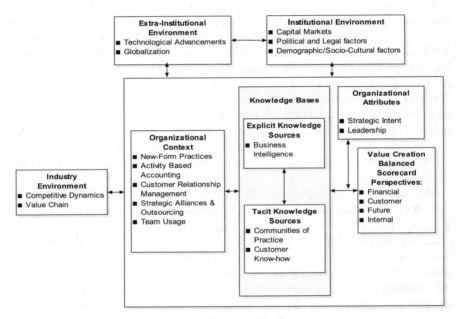

Fig. 14.1. A Stakeholder Model of Business Intelligence

Since the new-form organization is primarily a network, the generation and use of information, human capital, and social capital are critical to knowledge creation and competitive position. Business intelligence is the pathway that enables and captures this capital development. Traditionally, business intelligence has been a function and tool primarily of information technology experts. This view should be modified, and stakeholder theory contributes the needed theoretical basis for placing business intelligence in the larger context of the new-form organization.

14.3 Applying Stakeholder Theory to Business Intelligence

Stakeholder theory conceptualizes the firm as a series of groups with inter-locking relationships (See Fig. 14.2). Stakeholders consist of internal and external members, and the organization is viewed as a collection of coop-erative and competitive interests each possessing intrinsic worth. The stakeholder theory does not simply describe existing situations; it also ad-vocates attitudes, structures, and practices. It requires as its key attribute, simultaneous attention to the legitimate interests of all appropriate stake-holders in establishing procedures, goals, and in day-to-day decision-making (Donaldson and Preston, 1995). Since the purpose of the stake-holder theory is to both explain and guide the structure and operations of the organization through which numerous and diverse participants accom-plish multiple and not always congruent purposes, the theory can be inte-grated with literature regarding business intelligence.

Fig. 14.2. The Stakeholder Model

Stakeholders have the potential to be influenced or affected by the organi-zation and/or to influence or affect the organization (Freeman, 1984). They pressure the organization through their capability to help or hurt the or-ganization's ability to create value. The bargaining power of these stakeholders influences their appropriation of the profits associated with value creation (Schneider, 2002). Effective business intelligence will gather data, analyze it, and disseminate information to these stakeholders to minimize threats and maximize potential benefits. For example, a supplier may present the chance for a cooperative alliance into a new market where data collected on the demographics and psychographics of the market indicate a potential market.

In keeping with much of strategic management theory, the stakeholder model of business intelligence has value creation as the dependent variable. Consistent with the knowledge-based theory of the firm, knowledge bases should translate into enhanced value creation. Evaluating and measuring value creation is multifarious and the balanced scorecard approach is a promising way to capture this complexity Robert Kaplan, an accounting professor at the Harvard Business School, and David Norton, president of the Renaissance Strategy Group, co-developed the balanced scorecard approach (Kaplan and Norton, 1996). The purpose of the scorecard is to identify and track the key elements that drive performance, providing measurement from four perspectives. The financial perspective focuses on traditional measures of profitability. The customer perspective centers on evaluations of an organization's relationships with its customers. The future perspective assesses the firm's ability to innovate and to learn for future value creation. The internal perspective appraises employees and operations. The balanced scorecard approach provides a collection of metrics that have the potential to focus on a clear and manageable set of relevant performance factors. The balanced scorecard reflects the new-form organization and the modern business environment based on co-evolution and includes multiple perceptions and measures of firm performance (See Fig. 14.1).

In order to outline the independent variables within the model, the next two sections specify how practices associated with the new-form organization both influence and are influenced by knowledge bases. The sections correspond to two major bases of knowledge: explicit knowledge and tacit knowledge. Each section discusses how evolution to the new-form organization has affected knowledge. The section on business intelligence develops a proposition regarding the breadth of business intelligence and value creation. Immediately following is the section on tacit knowledge, which includes a discussion of communities of practice and customer know-how. Propositions are developed regarding tendencies to participate in communities of practice and the breadth and depth of customer know-how and value creation. The final section on organizational attributes, proposes some organizational attributes positioned to be particularly critical to value creation.

14.4 Business Intelligence within the Stakeholder Model of Business Intelligence

14.4.1 The Literature on Business Intelligence

Information technologies play a central role in today's knowledge-intensive environment. The watchwords for enabling knowledge sharing are convergence and integration. The IT systems must be able to merge and integrate disparate organizational systems to provide seamless, consistent data flow, connecting individual processes so that data are useful for decision-making throughout the entire business system in a timely fashion. In the information processing view of knowledge, two technologies have been key to improving the quantitative and qualitative value of knowledge available: business intelligence and knowledge management. Business intelligence has applied functionality, scalability, and reliability of database management. Knowledge management technologies combine content management systems like enterprise resource planning (ERP) with the World Wide Web to derive more value from textual information. While these systems have historically been separate, these systems are blending over time with technological advances (Cody et al., 2002). We have seen some evidence of this mingling in the area of mobile communication with phones, digital cameras and personal organizers being incorporated into a single device.

Business intelligence has evolved from data warehousing with its focus on static reporting to a spotlight on intelligence; shifting from data transformation into information as a focal point to data transformation into intelligence. Over the past half of a decade, the data warehouse (DW) has become a standard component of the architecture and strategic direction of most businesses. There is a driving need for businesses to assess and improve their competitive position in the marketplace manifesting itself in the race to collect information, analyze results, predict future trends and make well-informed tactical and strategic business decisions. These decisions affect a myriad of corporate subjects, from customers to products to suppliers and distributors, for a wide range of industries from retailers and manufacturers to banks, healthcare providers and airlines (Moncla, 2000).

In summary, business intelligence has evolved through a series of stages from single-department content to multi-departmental collaboration, then to an enterprise view, and finally to the business value chain. It has moved from reactive to proactive (Moncla, 2000). However, as important as business intelligence has become, there has been little theoretical development and a dearth of empirical studies on either the antecedents or the outcomes of business intelligence. The rise of the new business practices in conjunction with the rise in business intelligence creates an opportunity to map these relationships.

14.4.2 New Business Practices and Business Intelligence

To specify the characteristics of knowledge associated with value creation within the stakeholder model, this section examines the key business practices that have developed in the knowledge-driven age. Their effects include the expansion of business intelligence to include new stakeholders, increased demands for information, and increased codification and sharing of knowledge brought about through extension into multiple internal and external environments.

14.4.2.1 Activity-Based Cost Accounting

Activity-based cost (ABC) accounting differs from traditional systems by modeling the usage of all organizational resources on the activities done by these resources and then linking the cost of these activities to outputs such as products, services, and customers (Cooper et al., 1992). The allocation of past expenses to products, mainly for inventory valuation purposes, is the focal point of traditional accounting systems. In ABC, the costs of resources used to perform organizational activities are measured. An ABC system allows contemplation of how resource demands change as decisions get made and enables management of business activities by providing a cross-functional view of the organization ABC's link to decision making is the major departure from traditional accounting systems. The use of ABC allows for accurate cost reporting matched with work performed, facilitating decisions about outsourcing, eliminating, and streamlining activities (Cooper et al, 1992). Business intelligence facilitates and is facilitated by ABC; but more importantly, this relationship enhances value creation.

14.4.2.2 Customer Relationship Management

Customer Relationship Management (CRM) is a range of marketing and sales concepts and techniques that requires a massive database engine for conducting complex analyses of customer behavior and defining and monitoring micro-segments of the market CRM manages and optimizes customer interactions across organization's traditional and electronic interfaces (Ragins and Greco, 2003). It validates that customers are primary stakeholders and is used to glean better insight into customers' buying behaviors, helping to build competitive advantage. Success of CRM depends on a customer-focused strategy implemented with legacy systems and processes and but often with new processes and systems (Hansotia, 2002). Failure of CRM is often linked to a lack of focus on business objectives and the poor identification and management of scope (Stimpson, 2003). The adaptation functionality of business intelligence is well matched with the evolving demands of CRM.

14.4.2.3 Strategic Alliances and Outsourcing

A characteristic of the existing business setting is that many organizations form cooperative interorganizational relationships (Ring and Van de Ven, 1994). Strategic alliances are driven both by strategic needs to develop or enhance competitive advantage and by knowledge opportunities (Eisenhardt and Schoonhoven, 1996). Cooperative opportunities, whether for joint maximization of complementary assets or for the pursuit of new opportunities, present the challenge of coordinating information and creating a shared knowledge base. Membership in alliances results in interorganizational boundary spanning where having common information systems heightens productivity and efficiency.

Outsourcing is having external sources for activities that were previously performed inside the firm. Organizations should outsource those activities in which the firm has no special capabilities or which are not critical (Saunders et al., 1997). Activities that are outsourced still need to be coordinated and integrated by the home organization. As use of external parties increases, knowledge coordination facilites the efficient achievement of goals. Outsourcing results in enhanced roles for business intelligence and increases its role complexity. For example, organizations may decide that outsourced activities need access to aggregate demand levels for certain products or product groups in order to make better manufacturing planning decisions.

14.4.2.4 Teams Usage

Organizations have increased their reliance on teams (Stewart and Manz, 1995). A team is a collection of task-interdependent individuals who share responsibility for outcomes and increasingly manage across organizational boundaries. Team effectiveness measured by achievement of organization, team and individual goals consists of organizational and team environment elements such as reward systems, organizational leadership, communication, and information systems, team design, and processes, such as team size and cohesiveness. Teams are frequently cross-functional with different expertise and are often working from different locations. The use of virtual teams is rising (Solomon, 2001). Team usage is associated with the expansion of reliance on electronic communication and the ability to not only share but to create and store information since team members may work in different locations at different times and under intense time pressures to complete work assignments (Arthanassiou and Nigh 2000).

It is proposed that those organizations that are viewed as effective across multiple stakeholders will tend to engage successfully in the business practices outlined here. As organizations develop business practices that best suit the environment, the breadth of business intelligence will increase. Thus the coordinated movement to the new-form and the corresponding reliance on business intelligence will heighten the chances of value creation.

PROPOSITION 1. *There will be a positive relationship between the breadth of business intelligence to include multiple new-form practices and value creation.*

14.5 Tacit Knowledge within the Stakeholder Model of Business Intelligence

The review of the new-form organization's business practices indicates that, contrary to bureaucratic models, explicit knowledge is no longer static, reactive and contained within discrete units; indeed, the very nature of business intelligence suggests an integration of explicit and tacit knowledge bases within and outside the organization. The next section reviews the literature on tacit knowledge, particularly communities of practice and customer know-how, to ascertain the linkages within the stakeholder business intelligence model.

14.5.1 Communities of Practice and Business Intelligence

The concept of communities of practice refers to a theory that builds on learning as social participation (Love and Wenger, 1991). Communities are a way of thinking about how work is done and express the idea that people learn on the job and learn from working together. Communities are not isolated; they interact with each other and can be geographically dispersed. The core principles are simple: learning is social and learning happens on the job (Stamps, 1997). Communities of practice have been deeply rooted in the face-to-face world; it has been generally thought that the concept of communities of practice do not transfer to the virtual world (Roberts, 2000; Stamps, 1997). However, more recently, communities of practice have been described as "a group whose members regularly engage in sharing and learning, based on their common interests." (Lesser and

Storck, 2001: 831) Lesser and Storck (2001) suggest that communities of practice are engines for the development of social capital and that members may not be collocated. Critical dimensions include: structural (individuals must perceive themselves to be part of a network); relational (a sense of trust needs to develop); and cognitive (common interest). While face-to-face interaction is important for developing trust, shared repositories and discussion databases also contribute to the creation and maintenance of trust. Business intelligence provides fertile ground for the learning and interest sharing, which characterize communities of practice Lesser and Storck (2001) further posit that communities of practice create organizational value, identifying four areas of organizational performance: decreasing the learning curve of new employees; responding more rapidly to customer needs; reducing re-work; and fostering new ideas for products and services. In keeping with the development of tacit knowledge through communities of practice, I propose that value creation will be enhanced when communities of practice and business intelligence are utilized. They enhance human and social capital, the building blocks of the new-form organization.

PROPOSITION 2a. *There will be a positive relationship between the breadth of communities of practice and business intelligence.*

PROPOSITION 2b. *There will be a positive relationship between the breadth of communities of practice and value creation.*

14.5.2 Customer Know-How

This source of tacit knowledge is a complex construct derived from collaborative know-how examined by Simonin (1997). Customer know-how is the capacity to manage customers; it represents the skill to access and internalize new strategic assets from customers. It is knowledge that is embedded in the minds of employees and organizational routines and represents organization-wide culture and expertise about customers' current and future needs which cuts across departments, individuals and time. Since organizations with customer know-how are better able to avoid mistakes and to resolve problems, they are more likely to develop trust and reputation with customers, building more customer know-how. I propose that business intelligence as an explicit knowledge base and customer know-how as a tacit knowledge base mutually benefit each other. They are in co-evolutionary relationships and continue to mingle. Researchers have increasingly drawn attention to the links between learning as represented by customer know-how and actual firm performance (Nass, 1994).

PROPOSITION 3a. *There will be a positive relationship between the breadth of customer know-how and business intelligence.*

PROPOSITION 3b. *There will be a positive relationship between the breadth of customer know-how and value creation.*

14.6 Organizational Attributes within the Stakeholder Model of Business Intelligence

Attributes of the organization may also play a moderating role in the relationships proposed. They set the backdrop for the enactment of business intelligence in the stakeholder model.

14.6.1 Strategic Intent

The leveraging of the firm's internal resources, capabilities, and core competencies to achieve an organization's goals in the competitive environment is strategic intent (Hamel and Prahaladl, 1989). Concerned with winning competitive battles, strategic intent implies a significant stretch for the organization. It describes the resolve, stamina, and commitment of the organization, emanating from the leadership throughout the organization to strive to be the best (Finkelstein and Hambrick, 1990). It is the dream that challenges and energizes the organization (Hamel and Prahalad, 1994). Using the stakeholder model implies that the strategic intent must be broad enough to include relevant current and future stakeholders. It should not be narrowly focused on maintaining position but on competing for the future and providing the best for the customer. Strategic intent is consistent with and drives the new-form organization business practices. Business intelligence is a way to disseminate, as well as coordinate, this strategic intent not only within the organization but also throughout the organization's stakeholders.

14.6.2 Leadership

Leadership roles, relationships and leader attributes may influence how an organization acts in the new-form organization. Effective leaders will be able to assess stakeholders' respective abilities and whether extra-institutional and institutional forces represent opportunities or challenges. To the extent that leadership is able to discern the importance of often conflicting stakeholder interests and demands, the organization will be better able to enhance value creation. Leaders need to possess significant cognitive, emotional, and behavioral abilities to cope with their complex environments (Schneider, 2002). Organizations with successful leadership can assess the importance of stakeholders, have interpersonal skills to enhance human and social capital, and are better able to envision the potential of business intelligence. Thus they will be more likely to contribute to value creation.

In summary, value creation is enhanced when strategic intent and leadership look beyond the traditional organizational model of bureaucracy and embrace the practices of the new-form organization emphasizing human and social capital that is enabled by business intelligence. Thus I propose that the breadth of strategic intent and leadership in terms of stakeholders will enhance value creation.

PROPOSITION 4. *There will be a positive relationship between the breadth of strategic intent and leadership and value creation.*

14.7 Conclusion

On one side, business intelligence exists because of changing environmental conditions that affect the organization. Additionally, the emergence of the new-form organization has increased the need for business intelligence to respond to shifting environmental surroundings. The stakeholder model of business intelligence is different from the dominant conceptualization of business intelligence that developed under industrial age bureaucracy. Traditional IT theories apply within an organizational context of clear organizational boundaries, a tendency toward hierarchies, and a reliance on back office, closed IT architecture. The stakeholder model of business intelligence applies to the 21st century comprised of nebulous boundaries within and outside the firm, horizontal organizational designs, team work relationships, intense focus on the customer, and reliance on partnerships outside of the organization.

The stakeholder business intelligence model depicted in Fig. 14.1 and its related propositions address issues regarding the relationships of business intelligence to those outside of the IT domain. The stakeholder model describes how business intelligence has changed with the new-form organization; it is offered that explicit and tacit knowledge bases will interact within and across organizations. The model is at a preliminary stage and is offered with the intention of promoting research to fill the gap between theory and practice. It fosters the integration of information theories and behavioral theories into a single model, which I believe has the potential to more accurately describe practice. In addition, the interplay between business intelligence and the extra-institutional and institutional forces should be studied. Differences in business intelligence may tend to emerge as the new-form becomes diffused across the globe, reflecting how these forces come to shape and are shaped.

In particular, work is needed on business intelligence integration with communities of practice and customer know-how. Business intelligence will continue to initiate structure to facilitate goal attainment, but it will also foster flexibility and creativity - common characteristics of the new-form organization (Wheatley, 1992). In the 21st century, facilitation of knowledge through the integration of explicit and implicit knowledge bases is replacing the traditionally separate silos of information technology and organizational sciences. While business intelligence remains in part about information technology, it is increasingly about developing social capital by enabling relationships that offer access to other human capital both within and outside the organization. Business intelligence within the new-form organization will encourage interactions and connections, incorporating technological advances, thus entrenching its role within a larger stakeholder model.

References

Adams J (2002) Business intelligence: Getting smart about data, then acting on it. US Banker 112 (December): 26-27

Adriaans P, Zantinge D (1996) Data Mining. Addison-Wesley, Harlow England

Albert, S (1998) Knowledge management: Living up to the hope. Midrange Systems 11 (13): 52

Alexander JR (2002) History of accounting. Association of Chartered Accountants in the United States. (http://www.acaus.org/acc_his.html)

Allison (2001) Targeting ETL success. DM Review Magazine

Altman E (1993) Corporate financial distress and bankruptcy. Second edition John Wiley and Sons, New York

Altman E (1968) Financial ratios, discriminant analysis and the prediction of corporate bankruptcy. The Journal of Finance 23: 589-609

Amer TS (1991) An experimental investigation of multi-cue financial information display and decision making. Journal of Information Systems 5(Fall): 18-34

Anandarajan M, Anandarajan A (1999) A comparison of machine learning techniques with a qualitative response model for auditor's going concern reporting. Expert Systems with Applications 16: 385-392

Anderson JC, Kaplan SE (1992) An investigation of the effect of presentation format on auditors' non investigation region judgments. Advances in Accounting Information Systems 1: 71-88

Anderson JC, Reckers PMJ (1992) An empirical investigation of the effects of presentation format and personality on auditors' judgment in applying analytical procedures. Advances in Accounting 10: 19-43

Anthes G (2003) ROI Guide: Payback period. Computerworld (ROI Knowledge Center) February 17.

Archer N, Wang S. (1993) Application of the back Propagation Neural Network Algorithm with Monotonicity Constraints for Two-group Classification Problems. Decision Sciences 24(1): 60-75

Arinze O (1991) A contingency model for DSS methodology selection. Journal of Management Information Systems 8:149-166

Arinze O, Anandarajan M (2003) An Object-Oriented mapping method for rapidly configuring ERP systems. Communications of the ACM Vol. 46: 61-65.

Arinze O, Banerjee S (1992) A framework for effective data collection, usage, and maintenance for decision support systems. Information and Management 22: 257-268

Arthanassiou N, Nigh D (2000) Internationalization, tacit knowledge and the top management teams of MNCs. Journal of International Business Studies, 31(3): 471-487

Atkinson A, Banker R.D, Kaplan RS, Young SM (1997) Management Accounting. Second edition Prentice Hall, Upper Saddle River NJ

Back B, Sere K, Vanharanta H (1998) Managing complexity in large databases using self-organizing maps. Accounting, Management and Information Technologies 8: 191-210

Bakos JY (1991) Information links and electronic marketplaces: The role of inter-organizational information systems in vertical markets. Journal of Management Information Systems, 8 (Fall): 31-52

Barley, S.R. (1990) The alignment of technology and structure through roles and networks. Administrative Science Quarterly, 35:61-103

Barney JB (1991) Firm resources and sustained competitive advantage. Journal of Management 17(1): 99-120

Barrett S, Konsynski B (1982) Inter-Organization information sharing systems. MIS Quarterly, (Special Issue): 93-105

Bartash Jeffrey & Andrejczak Matt (2003) WorldCom may pay $500 million fine-Deal would aid investors harmed by accounting scandal. CBS MarketWatch.com, May 19

Bassett Gib (2001) Content scorecarding for business process- applying business intelligence to content management portals. Portfolio Management Forum. (http://www.eitforum.com/read.asp?ItemID=1065\)

Bassett Gib (2002) Business Intelligence for corporate information assets. DM Review Magazine

Bell TB, Tabor RH (1991) Empirical analysis of audit uncertainty qualifications. Journal of Accounting Research 29: 350-371

Benbasat I (1986) An investigation of the effectiveness of color and graphical information presentation under varying time constraints. MIS Quarterly (March): 58-81

Benbasat I (1986b) The influence of color and graphical information presentation in a managerial decision simulation. Human-Computer Interaction 2: 65-92

Benbasat I, Dexter AS (1985) An experimental evaluation of graphical and color-enhanced information presentation. Management Science 31(11): 1348-64

Benbasat I, Todd P (1986a) An experimental program investigating color-enhanced and graphical information presentation: an integration of the findings. Communications of the ACM 29 (11): 1094-105

Berardi VL, Zhang GP (1999) The effect of misclassification cost on neural network classifiers. Decision Sciences 30: 659-682

Bertin J (1983) Semiology of graphics. The University of Wisconsin Press, Madison WI

Besser H (2002) Talk on image metadata: Important Recent Activities to the JISC International Image Conference

Betts M (2003) Special Report: Do the math! An ROI Guide. *Computerworld* (ROI Knowledge Center) February 17.

Blackhouse T (2002) Operational risk management - overcoming the hidden dangers. Credit Control 23(5): 28-32

Blank D, Wood AT, Wood CA (2003) A matter of ethics. The Internal Auditor 60(1): 26-31

Blumberg R, Atre S (2003) The problem with unstructured data. DM Review Magazine

Boisot MH (1999) Knowledge assets: securing competitive advantage in the information economy Oxford University Press, New York

Boon C (1998) In pursuit of business intelligence. Document World 3(6): 18-24

Boritz JE, Kennedy DB, de Miranda AA (1995) Predicting corporate failure using a neural network approach. Intelligent Systems in Accounting, Finance, and Management 4: 95-111

Bouwman MJ, Frishkoff P, Frishkoff PA (1995) The relevance of GAAP-based information: a case study exploring some uses and limitations. Accounting Horizons 9 (4): 22-47

Boyns T, Edwards JR (1997) Cost and management accounting in early Victorian Britain: a Chandleresque analysis? Management Accounting Research 8:19-46

Brackett MH (1998) Transforming disparate data. DM Review Magazine

Braverman H (1974) Labour and monopoly capital, monthly review press. New York.

Brockett PL, Cooper WW, Golden LL, Pitaktong U (1994) A neural network method for obtaining an early warning of insurer insolvency. The Journal of Risk and Insurance 61: 402-424

Brown JR, Earnshaw R, Jern M, Vince J (1995) Visualization: using computer graphics to explore data and present information. John Wiley & Sons, New York.

Bryer RA (1993) Double-entry bookkeeping and the birth of capitalism: Accounting for the commercial revolution in medieval Italy. Critical perspectives in accounting 4:113-140

Buchta SA, Banerjee S (2001) Oracle Ultra Search; Unlock your information Assets White Paper. Oracle White paper. (http://otn.oracle.com/products/ultrasearch/pdf/ultrasearch_search_bus_wp.pdf)

Burriesci J, Kestelyn J, Young M (2003). The top 10 trends for 2003. *Intelligent Enterprise* January 1.

Busta B, Weinberg R (1998) Using Benford's law and neural networks as a review procedure. Managerial Auditing Journal 13(6): 356-366

Carbone R, Gorr WL (1985) Accuracy of judgmental forecasting of time series. Decision Sciences 16:153-60

Card SK, Mackinlay JD, Shneiderman B (1999) Readings in information visualization: Using Vision to Think. Morgan Kaufmann, San Francisco, CA.

Cathey JM (1991) Electronic data interchange: What a controller should know. Management Accounting, (November): 47-51

Chandler AD (1990) Scale and scope: The dynamics of industrial capitalism, The Belknap press of Harvard university press, Cambridge Massachusetts.

Chandler, AD (1977) The visible hand: The managerial revolution in American business, Cambridge, Massachusetts, The Belknap press of Harvard University press.

Changeux JP (1986) Neuonal man: The biology of mind. Oxford University Press, Oxford UK

Chen KCW, Church BK (1992) Default on debt obligations and the issuance of going-concern opinions. Auditing: A Journal of theory and practice 11(2): 30-49

Chen SM, Horng YJ, Lee CH (2003) Fuzzy information retrieval based on multi-relationship fuzzy concept networks. Fuzzy Sets and Systems

Chenhall RH, Morris D (1986) The impact of structure, environment, and interdependence on the perceived usefulness of management accounting systems. The Accounting Review, 61(1): 16-35

Chernoff H (1973) The use of faces to represent points in k-dimensional space graphically. Journal of the American Statistical Association 68 (June): 361-68

Chorafas DN, Steinmann H (1995) Virtual Reality: Practical Applications in Business and Industry. Prentice Hall, Englewood Cliffs New Jersey

Cleveland WS (1993) Visualizing data. Hobart Press, Summit,New Jersey

Cleveland WS (1994) The elements of graphing data, Revised Ed. Hobart Press , Summit NJ

Coakley JR (1995) Using pattern Analysis Methods to Supplement Attention-Directing Analytical Procedures. Expert Systems with Applications 9(4): 513-528

Coakley JR, Brown CE (1993) Artificial neural networks applied to ratio analysis in the analytical review process. Intelligent Systems in Accounting, Finance and Management 2: 19-39

Coakley JR, Brown CE (1991a) Neural networks applied to ratio analysis in the analytical review process, Expert Systems Symposium. University of Southern California, School of Accounting: Pasadena, California

Coakley JR, Brown CE. (1991b) Neural networks for financial ratio analysis. In J Liebowitz (Ed.), The World Congress on Expert Systems, Vol. 1: 132-139. Pergamon Press: Orlando, Florida

Coates PK, Fant LF (1992) A neural network approach to forecasting financial distress. The Journal of Business Forecasting 3: 8-12

Cody WF, Kreulen JT, Krishna V, Spangler WS (2002) The integration of business intelligence and knowledge management. IBM Systems Journal 41(4): 697-713

Coffin Z (2001) The top 10 effects of XBRL. Strategic Finance, June.

Cohen E, Hannon N (2000) "How XBRL will change your practice", The CPA Journal, Nov 70:11:36

Colet E, Aaronson D (1995) Visualization of multivariate data: human-factors considerations. Behavior Research Methods, Instruments, & Computers 27 (2): 257-63

Connor D (2003) Data warehouse failures commonplace. Network World 20 (1): 24

Connor K (1991) A historical comparison of resource-based theory and five schools of thought within industrial organization economics: Do we have a new theory of the firm? Journal of Management, 17(1): 121-154

Cook GL, Eining MM (1993) Will cross functional information systems work? Management Accounting, 74(February): 53-57

Cooper C, Taylor P (2000) From Taylorism to Ms Taylor: the transformation of the accounting craft. Accounting, Organizations and Society 25: 555-578

Cooper LA (1990) Mental representation of three-dimensional objects in visual problem solving and recognition. Journal of Experimental Psychology 16 (6): 1097-106

Cooper LA (1995) Varieties of visual representation: How are we to analyze the concept of mental image? Neuropsychologia 33(11): 1575-82.

Cooper R, Kaplan RS, Maisel LS, Morrissey E, Oehm RM (1992) Implementing activity-based cost management: moving from analysis to action, Institute of Management Accountants: Montvale, NJ

Cowan T (2002) Getting a single version of the facts. Financial Executive, Morristown. 18(9): 51-53

Crossan MM, Lane HW, White RE (1999) An organizational learning framework: From intuition to institution. Academy of Management Review, 24(3): 522-537

Daft RL, Lengel RH (1986) Organizational information requirements, media richness and structural design. Management Science, 32(May): 554-571

D'Amico E (2002) Sorting out the facts. Chemical Week New York 164 (41): 22-24

Dasgupta P., Itzkovitz A. and Karamcheti V. (2000) Active files: A mechanism for integrating legacy applications into distributed systems. International Conderence on Distribted Computing Systems (ICDCS-2000)

Davenport (2001) Data to knowledge to results: building an analytical capability. California Management Review 43(2): 117-138

Davenport TH (1998) Putting the enterprise into the enterprise system. Harvard Business Review, 76 (July-August): 121-132

Davidow WH, Malone MS (1992) The virtual corporation. New York: Harper-Collins.

Davis CE, Davis EB, Moore LN (1998) Outsourcing the procurement-through-payables process. Management Accounting, 80 (July): 38-43

Davis JT, Massey AP, Lovell R (1997) Supporting a complex audit judgement task: An expert network approach. European Journal of Operational Research 103 (2): 350-372

DeAngelo H, DeAngelo L, Skinner DJ (1994) Accounting choice in troubled companies. Journal of Accounting and Economics 17: 113-143

Deerwester S, Dumais S T., Landauer TK, Furnas GW, Harshman RA (1990) Indexing by latent semantic analysis. JASIS 41(6): 391-407

DeSanctis G, Jarvenpaa S (1989) Graphical presentation of accounting data for financial forecasting: an experimental investigation. Accounting Organizations and Society 14 (5,6): 509-25

Dictionary.com

Dielman TE, Oppenheimer 1984. An examination of investor behavior during periods of large dividend changes. Journal of Financial and Quantitative Analysis: 197-216

Dijksterhuis MS, Van den Bosch FAJ, Volberda, HW (1999) Where do new organizational forms come from? Management logics as a source of coevolution. Organization Science 10 (5): 569-582

Dillman DA (1978) Mail and telephone surveys: The total design method. New York, NY: Wiley

Doll WJ, Torkzateh G (1988) The measurement of end-user computing satisfaction. MIS Quarterly, 12(June): 259-274

Donaldson T, Preston LE (1995) The stakeholder theory of the corporation: Concepts, evidence, and implications. Academy of Management Review 20 (1): 65-91

Drazin R., Van de Ven AH (1985) Alternative forms of fit in contingency theory. Administrative Science Quarterly, 30 (12): 514-539

Drucker PF (1998) The next information revolution. Forbes: 46-58.

Drucker, P (1968) The age of discontinuity: Guidelines to our changing society, Harper & Row, New York

Dubois Len (2002) Business intelligence: The dirty (and costly) little secret of bad data. DMReview Magazine, September.

Dull RB, Tegarden DP (1999) A comparison of three visual representations of complex multi-dimensional accounting information. Journal of Information Systems 13(2) Fall: 117-131

Dutta S. (1993) Knowledge processing & applied Artificial Intelligence. Butterworth-Heinemann: Oxford, England

dwinfocenter.org

Eakins JP, Graham ME (1999) Technology applications programme report, Content-based Image retrieval. JISC 39

Eisenhardt K, Schoonhoven D (1996) Resource-based view of strategic alliance formation: Strategic and social effects in entrepreneurial firms. Organization Science, 7: 136-150

Elomaa J, Halme J, Hassinen P, Hodju P, Rönkkö J (1999) Nenet -Demo version 1.1a, Vol. 2001. The Nenet Team

Epstein M, Manzoni JF (1997) The balanced scorecard and the tableau de bord: translating strategy into action. *Management Accounting* August: 28-36

Etheridge H, Sriram R (1996) A neural network approach to financial distress analysis. Advances in Accounting Information Systems 4. JAI Press, Greenwich: CT, pp 201-222

Etheridge H, Sriram R (1997) A comparison of the relative costs of financial distress models: Artificial neural networks, logit and multivariate discriminant analysis. Intelligent Systems in Accounting, Finance, and Management 6: 235-248

Etheridge HL, Brooks RC (1994) Neural networks: A new technology. The CPA Journal 64 (3): 36-43

Etheridge HL, Sriram RS, Hsu HYK (2000) A comparison of selected artificial neural networks that help auditors evaluate client financial viability. Decision Science 31(2): 531-550

Evans W (2000) Blown to bits. Boston: Harvard Business School Press.

Fahey MJ (1998) The doorway and the billboard. Marketing Tools Stanford, July

Fanning K, Cogger K (1994) A comparative analysis of artificial neural networks using financial distress prediction. Intelligent Systems in Accounting, Finance and Management 3: 241-252

Fanning KM, Cogger KO (1998) Neural network detection of management fraud using published financial data. International Journal of Intelligent Systems in Accounting, Finance & Management 7(1): 21-41

Fausett L (1994) Fundamentals of neural networks. Prentice Hall, Englewood New Jersey

Fayyad UM, Piatetsky-Shapiro G, Smyth P, Uthurusamy R (eds.) (1996) Advances in knowledge discovery and data mining. AAAI, Menlo Park CA

Feroz EH, Kwon TM, Pastena VS, Park K (2000) The efficacy of red flags in predicting the SEC's targets: An artificial neural networks approach. International Journal of Intelligent Systems in Accounting. Finance & Management 9: 145-157

Finkelstein S, Hambrick D (1990) Top management team tenure and organizational outcomes: The moderating role of managerial discretion. Administrative Science Quarterly 35: 484-503

Fiol CM, Lyles MA (1985) Organizational learning. Academy of Management Review, 10: 803-813

Fisher B (1999) Mellon creates fraud watch to predict and manage risk using neural technology. Journal of Retail Banking Services 21(1): 15-17

Fisher C (1996) The impact of perceived environmental uncertainty and individual differences on management information requirements: A research note. Accounting, Organisations and Society, 21(May): 361-369

Fitzgerald B (2003) Using BI tools to turn information into action. Financial Executive, 19(2): 46-49

Fletcher D, Gross E (1993) Forecasting with neural networks: An application using bankruptcy data. Information & Management 24: 159-167

Foltz PW (1990) Using latent semantic indexing for information filtering. In R. B. Allen (Ed.) Proceedings of the Conference on Office Information Systems, Cambridge, MA: 40-47. (http://www-psych.nmsu.edu/~pfoltz/cois/filtering-cois.html)

Fordham DR (2002) Business intelligence: How accountants bring value to the marketing function. Strategic Finance 83 (11): 24-30

Foster G (1986) Financial statement analysis. Prentice Hall, New Jersey

Fox B, Fox CJ (2002) Efficient stemmer generation. Information Processing & Management 38: 547-558

Fredrickson JW (1986) The strategic decision process and organization structure. Academy of Management Review, 11: 280-297

Freeman RE (1984) Strategic management: A stakeholder approach. Pitman, Boston, MA

Fry LW (1982) Technology-structure research: Three critical issues. Academy of Management Journal, 25(3): 532-552

Fryer B (1996) Visa cracks down on fraud. InformationWeek(594): 87

Funahashi K (1989) On the approximate realization of continuous mappings by Neural Networks. Neural Networks 2: 183-192

Gajpal PP, Ganesh LS, Rajendran C (1994) Criticality analysis of spare parts using the analytic hierarchy process. International Journal of Production Economics 35: 293-297

Galbraith JR (1995) Designing organizations. San Francisco, CA: Jossey-Bass.

Galbraith JR (1994) Competing with flexible lateral organizations. Addison-Wesley, Reading, MA

Gauntt JE, Gletzen GW (1997) Analytical auditing procedures. Internal Auditor, (2): 56-60

Gilson SC, John K, Lang L (1990) Troubled debt restructurings: An empirical study of private reorganization of firms in default. Journal of Financing Economics 27: 315-353

Giovinazzo WA (2000) Object-Oriented data warehouse design: Building a star schema. Prentice Hall PRT, Upper Saddle River, New Jersey

Giroux GA, Wiggins CE (1983) Chapter XI and corporate resuscitation. Financial Executive: 39-41

Giroux GA, Wiggins CE (1984) An event approach to bankruptcy prediction. Journal of Bank Research Autumn: 179-187

Goldstein RC, Story VC (1999) Data abstractions: Why and how? Data & Knowledge Engineering 29: 293-311

Goldwater PM, Fogarty TJ (1995) Cash flow decision making and financial accounting presentation: a computerized experiment. Journal of Applied Business Research 11 (3): 16-29

Goodhue DL (1995) Understanding user evaluations of information systems. Management Science, 41(December): 1827-1844

Govindarajan V, Fisher J (1990) Strategy, control systems, and resource sharing: Effects on business-unit performance. Academy of Management Journal, 33 (June): 259-285

Grant RM (1996) Toward a knowledge-based theory of the firm: Strategic Management Journal 17: 109-122

Grantham C (1993) Visualization of Information Flows: Virtual Reality as an Organizational Modeling Technique. In Virtual Reality: Applications and Explorations, Wexelblat, A. (ed.). Academic Press Professional, Cambridge MA

Graves OF, Flesher DL, Jordan RE (1996) Pictures and the bottom line: the television epistemology of U.S. annual reports. Accounting, Organizations, and Society 21 (1): 57-88

Graziano C (2002) XBRL: Streamlining Financial Reporting, *Financial Executive,* November

Green BP, Choi JH (1997) Assessing the Risk of Management Fraud Through Neural Network Technology. Auditing: A Journal of Practice & Theory 16(1): 14-28

Grinstein G, Ward M (1997) Introduction to Data Visualization. IEEE Visualization Tutorial

Guan T, Wong KF (1999) KPS: a Web information mining algorithm. Computer Networks 31: 1495-1507

Guilding C (1999) Competitor-focused accounting: An exploratory note. Accounting, Organizations and Society 24: 583-595

Gul FA, Chia YM (1994) The effects of management accounting systems, perceived environmental uncertainty and decentralization on managerial performance: A test of a three-way interaction. Accounting, Organisations and Society, 19 (May/June): 413-426

Gurd B, Smith M, Swaffer A (2002) Factors impacting on accounting lag: An exploratory study of responding to TQM. British Accounting Review 34: 205-221

Hage J, Aiken M (1969) Routine technology, social structure, and organizational goals. Administrative Science Quarterly, 14: 368-379

Hamel G, Prahalad CK (1994) Competing for the future. Harvard Business Press,: Boston

Hamel G, Prahalad CK (1989) Strategic intent. Harvard Business Review 67 (3): 63-76

Hamer M (1983) Failure prediction: Sensitivity of classification accuracy to alternative statistical method and variable sets. Journal of Accounting and Public Policy 2: 289-307

Hammer M., McLeod D (1981) Database descriptions with SDM: A semantic database model. ACM Trans. on Database Systems 6(3)

Hannon N (2001) XBRL vendor list, *Strategic Finance*, June

Hannon N (2002) Accounting scandals: Can XBRL help? *Strategic Finance*, August

Hannon N (2003) XBRL: Edgar analyst changes everything. Strategic Finance January

Hansen JV, McDonald JB, Stice JD (1992) Artificial intelligence and generalized qualitative-response models: An empirical test on two audit decision-making domains. Decision Science 23(3): 708-723

Hansotia B (2002) Gearing up for CRM: Antecedents to successful implementation. Journal of Database Marketing 10(2): 121-132

Harding W (2003) BI crucial to making the right decision. Financial Executive 19(2): 49-51

Harris RL (1996) Information graphics: A comprehensive illustrated reference. management graphics, Atlanta Georgia

Hayes DC (1977) The contingency theory of management accounting. The Accounting Review, 52(January): 22-39

Hayes M (2002) "Hershey's biggest treat: No tricks," Information Week, (http://www.informationweek.com/story/IWK20021029S000)

Helleloid D, Simonin BL (1994) Organizational learning and a firm's core competence. In G. Hamel, & A. Heene (Eds.), Competence based competition: Wiley New York, pp 213-239

Heylighen F, Joslyn C, Turchin V (1999) What are cybernetics and systems science. Principia Cybernetica Web.
(http://pespmc1.vub.ac.be/REFERPCP.html.)

Hibbard J (1997) Ernst & Young deploys app for knowledge management. Information Week, July 28: 28

Hitt M, Tyler B (1991) Strategic decision models: Integrating different perspectives. Strategic Management Journal, 12(5): 327-351

Hoadley ED (1990) Investigating the effects of color. Communications of the ACM 33(2): 120-125,139

Hoadley ED (1994) The supplanting function of color in human information processing. In: Carey JM (ed.) Human Factors in Information Systems: Emerging Theoretical Bases. Norwood, NJ: Ablex Publishing

Hoelscher R (2002) Business intelligence platforms boost ERP, Financial Executive, Mar/Apr 2002: 66-68

Hoelscher R (2002) Business intelligence platforms boost ERP. Financial Executive 18(2): 66-69

Honkela, T, Kaski S, Lagus K, Kohonen T (1996) Exploration of full text databases with self organizing maps. International Conference on Neural Networks

Hopwood W, McKeown J, Mutchler J (1994) A reexamination of auditor versus model accuracy within the context of the going concern opinion decision. Contemporary Accounting Research 10: 403-432

Hornik KM, Stinchcombe M, White H (1990) Universal approximation of an unknown mapping and its derivatives using multilayer feed forward networks. Neural Networks 3: 551-560

Hoske MT (2002) How to get the most from a database. Control Engineering 49 (6)

Howell RA (1996) Developing comprehensive competitive intelligence. Hamilton, Ontario: The Society of Management Accountants of Canada

Huber GP (1990) A theory of the effects of advanced information technologies on organizational design, intelligence, and decision making. Academy of Management Review, 15(January): 47-71

Huber GP (1991) Organizational learning: The contribution processes and the literature. Organization Science, 2: 88-115

Hudicka (2003) Bumpy Ride. Intelligent Enterprise Magazine, CMP

Ijiri Y (1982) Triple-entry bookkeeping and income momentum: Studies in accounting research No. 10. American Accounting Association, Sarasota, FL

Ijiri Y (1986) A framework for triple-entry bookkeeping. The Accounting Review 61 (4): 745-59

Ijiri Y (1989) Momentum accounting and triple-entry bookkeeping: exploring the dynamic structure of accounting measurements. Sarasota, FL: American Accounting Association

Ijiri Y (1990) The evolution of bookkeeping to triple-entry systems: multimedia authoring experience. Working paper. Carnegie Mellon University

Inmon WH(1996) The data warehouse and data mining. Communications of the ACM November: 49-50

Inselberg A (1997) Multidimensional detective. Proceedings Information Visualization 1997, John Dill J, Gershon N (eds.). IEEE-CS Press, Los Alimitos CA, pp 100-107

Ives B, Olson MH, Baroudi JJ (1983) The measurement of user information satisfaction. Communications of the ACM, 26(October): 785-93

Janssen P (1988) Model structure selection for multivariable systems by cross validation. International Journal of Control 47: 1737-1758

Jarett IM (1993) Financial reporting using computer graphics. John Wiley and Sons, New York, NY

Jennings (2000) Inside job. Intelligent Enterprise Magazine, CMP

Jensen MC (1983) Organization theory and methodology. The Accounting Review, 53(April): 319-339

Jensen RE, Xiao JZ (2001) Customized financial reporting, networked databases, and distributed file sharing. Accounting Horizons 15: 209-222

Jiang J, Berry MW, Donato JM, Strouchov G, Rady NW (1999) Mining consumer product data via latent semantic indexing. Intelligent Data Analysis 3

John K (1999) Managing financial distress and valuing distressed securities: A survey and a research agenda. Financial Management Autumn: 60-76

Johnson M (1999) ERP trauma ward. ComputerWorld, (http://www.computerworld.com/cwi/story/0,1199,NAV47_STO36452,00.html)

Johnson M (1999) XML for the absolute beginner, available at (http://www.javaworld.com/javaworld/jw-04-xml.html)

Jones CV (1996) Visualization and optimization. Kluwer Academic Publishers, Boston MA

Jones DR, Schkade DA (1995) Choosing and translating between problem representations. Organizational Behavior and Human Decision Processes 61 (2): 214-23

Jones F (1987) Current techniques in bankruptcy prediction. Journal of Accounting Literature 6: 131-164

Kangas J, Kohonen T (1996) Developments and applications of the self-organizing map and related algorithms. Mathematics and Computers in Simulation 41(1-2): 3-12

Kanter RM (1990) When giants learn cooperative strategies. Planning Review 18(1): 15-22

Kaplan R, Norton D (1992) The balanced scorecard – measures that drive performance. Harvard Business Review January/February 71-79

Kaplan R, Norton D (1996) Using the balanced scorecard as a strategic management system. Harvard Business Review January/February 75-85

Kaplan R, Norton D (1997) Translating strategy into action: The balanced scorecard. Harvard Business School Press, Boston MA

Kaplan R, Norton D (1997) Why does a business need a balanced scorecard? *Journal of Cost Management*, May/June, 5-10

Kaplan R, Norton D (2001) The strategy-focussed organization: How balanced scorecard companies thrive in the new business environment. Harvard Business School Publishing Corp., Boston, MA

Kaplan SE (1988) An examination of the effect of presentation format on auditors' expected value judgments. Accounting Horizons 2 (3): 90-5

Keen P, Scott MM (1978) Decision support systems: An organizational perspective, Addison-Wesley, Reading MA

Khotanzad A, Hernandez OJ (2003) Color image retrieval using multispectral random field texture model and color content features. Pattern Recognition 36(8): 1679-1694

Kim KK (1988) Organizational coordination and performance in hospital accounting information systems: An empirical investigation. The Accounting Review, 63(July): 472-489

Kimball (2002) Realtime partitions. Intelligent Enterprise Magazine. CMP

Kimball, Ralph, The data warehouse lifecycle toolkit p. 14

Kimball, Ross (2002) The data warehouse toolkit. John Wiley and Sons, Inc

Klersey GF, Dugan MT (1995) Substantial doubt: Using artificial neural networks to evaluate going concern Advances in Accounting Information Systems 9: JAI Press Inc., Greenwich: CT, pp 267-273

Klose A, Nurnberger A, Kruse R, Hartmann G, Richards M (2000) Interactive text retrieval based on document similarities. Phy. Chem. Earth (A) 25(8)

Kogan A, Nelson K, Srivastava R, Varsarhelyi M, Bovee M (2002) Designing and application of intelligent financial reporting and auditing agent with net knowledge. Working paper, 2002

Kogan A, Sudit EF, Vasarhelyi MA (1997) Management accounting in the era of electronic commerce. Management Accounting, 79(3): 26-29

Koh HC, Tan SS (1999) A neural network approach to the prediction of going concern status. Accounting and Business Research 29(3): 211-216

Kohonen T, Hynninen J, Kangas J, Laaksonen J (1995) SOM_Pak v3.1, Vol. 2001. SOM Programming Team of the Helsinki University of Technology Laboratory of Computer and Information Science

Kohonen T (1997) Self-organizing maps. Springler-Verlag: Berlin

Kolence K, Kiviat P (1973) Software unit profiles and Kiviat figures. Performance Evaluation Review 2(3) September: 2-12

Koskivaara E (2000) Artificial neural network models for predicting patterns in auditing monthly balances. Journal of the Operational Research Society 51(9): 1060-1069

Kosslyn SM (1980) Images and mind. Harvard University Press, Cambridge MA

Kosslyn SM (1994) Elements of graph design. W.H. Freeman and Co, New York NY

Koutsoukis N, Mitra G, Lucas C (1999) Adapting on-Line analytical processing for decision modelling: The Interaction Of Information And Decision Technologies. Decision Support Systems July: 1-30

Krivda CD (1995) Data-mining dynamite. Byte magazine October (http://www.byte.com/art/9510/sec8/art9.htm)

Ladley J (2003) Beyond the data warehouse: Beyond Rows and Columns – Unstructured Information, Part 3. DM Review Magazine, January

Larkin JH, Simon HA (1987) Why a diagram is (sometimes) worth ten thousand words. Cognitive Science (11): 65-99

Latham R (1995) The dictionary of computer graphics and virtual reality, 2nd Ed, New York: Springer-Verlag

Latshaw CA (1999) Fraudulent financial reporting: The government and accounting profession react. Review of Business Jamaica 24(2): 13-15

Lau AH (1987) A five-state financial distress prediction model. Journal of Accounting Research 25: 127-138

Lave J, Wenger E (1991) Situated learning: Legitimate peripheral participation. Cambridge University Press, Cambridge UK

Lebas M (1994) Managerial accounting in France: Overview of past tradition and current practice. *The European Accounting Review* 3(3): 471-487

Lee CY (article in Press) A knowledge management scheme for meta-data: an information structure graph Decision support systems

Legare TL (2002) "The role of organizational factors in realizing ERP Benefits." Information Systems Management 19: 21-42

Lenard MJ, Alam P, Madey GR (1995) The application of neural networks and a qualitative response model to the auditor's going concern uncertainty decision. Decision Science 26(2): 209-227

Leonard-Barton D (1992) Core capabilities and core rigidities: a paradox in managing new product development. Strategic Management Journal, Summer Special Issue 13: 111-125

Lesser EL, Storck J (2001) Communities of practice and organizational performance. IBM Systems Journal 40(4): 831-841

Levy A (1998) Putting semistructured data to practice; Invited speaker. ACM Conference on Information and Knowledge Management

Lewin AY, Long CP, Carroll TN (1999) The coevolution of new organizational forms. Organization Science 10(5): 535-550

Lienhart R, Stuber F (1996) Automatic text recognition in digital videos, in Image and Video Processing IV Proc. SPIE 2666-20

Lienhart R, Wernicke A (2002) Localizing and segmenting text in images, Videos and Web Pages. IEEE Transactions on Circuits and Systems for Video Technology 12(4): 256 -268

Lippermann RP (1987) An introduction to computing with neural networks. IEEE ASSP Magazine 1: 4-22

Littleton AC (1933) Accounting evolution to 1900, Russell and Russell, New York

Lohse GL (1993) A cognitive model for understanding graphical perception. Human-Computer Interaction 8:353-388

Lohse GL, Biolsi K, Walker N, Rueter H (1994) A classification of visual representations. Communications of the ACM 37 (12): 36-49.

Love J (2003) Return to value. Intelligent Enterprise (May 13). (www.intelligententerprise.com/030513/608feat2_1.shtml

Lu G, Hankinson T (1998) A Technique towards automatic audio classification and retrieval. Fourth International Conference on Signal Processing, October 12-16 Beijing

Macintosh NB, Daft RL (1987) Management control systems and departmental interdependencies: An empirical study. Accounting, Organizations and Society, 12: 49-61

MacKay DB, Villarreal A (1987) Performance differences in the use of graphic and tabular displays of multivariate data. Decision Sciences 18: 535-46

Malone TW, Yates J, Benjamin RI (1987) Electronic markets and electronic hierarchies. Communications of the ACM, 30(June): 484-497

Marco D (1999) Metadata and data administration: Advanced metadata architecture. DM Review Magazine

Markham SE (1998) The scientific visualization of organizations: A rationale for a new approach to organizational modeling. Decision Sciences 29(1): 1-23

Martín-del-Brío B, Serrano-Cinca C (1993) Self-organizing neural networks for the analysis and representation of data: Some financial cases. Neural Computing & Applications 1: 193-206

Martini K (1998) Digital archives of engineering images: lessons form the arts. Advances in Engineering Software 29(10): 833-837

Maynor T (2000) Value made visible. CIO Magazine May 1

McCormick BH, DeFanti TA, Brown MD (1987) Visualization in scientific computing – a synopsis. IEEE Computer Graphics and Applications 7(4): 61-70

McGonagle JJ, Vella CM (2002) A case for competitive intelligence. The Information Management Journal (July/August): 35-40

Medsker L, Liebowitz J (1994) Design and development of expert systems and neural networks. Macmillan College Publishing Company, Inc

Meltzer M (2003) The intergalactic data warehouse. DataWarehouse.com (May)

Mia L, Chenhall RH (1994) The usefulness of management accounting systems, functional differentiation and managerial effectiveness. Accounting, Organizations and Society, 19(January): 1-13

Miller GA (1956) The magical number seven, plus or minus two: some limits on our capacity for processing information. Psychological Review (63): 81-97

Miller LL, Honavar V, Barta T (1997) Warehousing structured and unstructured data for data mining. The American society for information science, Annual Meeting 97 IDC. Email Usage to Exceed 60 Billion by 2006. IDC

Moncla B (2000) The rise of the i-Market: The convergence of E-Business and Business Intelligence. DM Review

Moriarty S (1979) Communicating financial information through multidimensional graphics. Journal of Accounting Research 17 (1): 205-24

Mrazek Jan (2003) ETL: The best-kept secret of success in data warehousing. DM Review Magazine (June)
(http://www.dmreview.com/master.cfm?NavID=193&EdID=6802)

Mulqueen JT (1996) Neural nets block fraud. CommunicationWeek(625): 95

Murphy D (2000) XML and XSL: A critical component for content management. DM Review Magazine

Nass C (1994) Knowledge or skills: Which do administrators learn from experience? Organization Science, 5: 38-50

Nelson KM, Kogan A, Srivastava RP, Vasarhelyi MA, Lu H (2000) Virtual auditing agents: the EDGAR Agent challenge. Decision Support Systems 28 (3): 241-253

Nonaka I (1994) A dynamic theory of organizational knowledge creation. Organization Science 5(1): 14-37

Nutt PC (1999) Surprising but true: Half the decisions in organizations fail. The Academy of Management Executive 13(4): 75-87

O'Donnell E, David JS (2000) How information systems influence user decisions: a research framework and literature review. International Journal of Accounting Information Systems 1: 178-203

O'Rounke J (2001) "Creating financial information in XBRL". Strategic Finance June

Odom M, Sharda R (1990) A neural network model for bankruptcy prediction. Paper presented at the International Joint Conference on Neural Networks, San Diego CA

O'Leary D (1998) Using neural networks to predict corporate failure. International Journal of Intelligent Systems in Accounting Finance and Management 7: 187-197

Oram A (2000) The value and Gnutella and Freenet, http://www.webreview.com/pub/2000/05/12/platform/.

Otley DT (1980) The contingency theory of management accounting: Achievement and prognosis. Accounting, Organizations and Society, 5(December): 413-428

Pani JR (1993) Limits on the comprehension of rotational motion: mental imagery of rotations with oblique components. Perception 22: 785-808

Pendley JA, Glorfield LW, Hardgrave BC (1998) Bankruptcy prediction of financially stressed firms: An extension of the use of artificial neural networks to evaluate going concern. Advances in Accounting Information Systems 6: JAI Press Inc., Stamford, CT pp 163-184

Pfeffer J, Salancik GR (1978) The external control of organizations: A resource dependence perspective. New York: Harper and Row

Pfeffer JL (1996) Competitive advantage through people: Unleashing the power of the workforce. Harvard Business School Press, Cambridge MA

Polanyi M (1966) The tacit dimension. Doubleday Anchor, Garden City, New York

Prahalad CK, Hamel G (1990) The core competence of the corporation. Harvard Business Review 68(3): 79-91

Premkumar G, Ramamurthy K, Nilakanta S (1994) Implementation of electronic data interchange: An innovation diffusion perspective. Journal of Management Information Systems, 11(Fall): 157-186

Preston AM, Wright C, Young JJ (1996) Imag[in]ing annual reports. Accounting, Organizations, and Society 21 (1): 113-37

Ragins EJ, Greco AJ (2003) Customer relationship management and E-business: More than a software solution. Review of Business 24(1): 25-30

Rahimian E, Singh S, Thammachote T, Virmani R (1993) Bankruptcy prediction by neural network Neural Networks in Finance and Investing. Probus Publishing Company, Chicago

Ramamoorti S, Bailey ADJ, Traver RO (1999) Risk assessment in internal auditing: A Neural Network Approach. International Journal of Intelligent Systems in Accounting, Finance & Management 8(3): 159-180

Rao R (2002) The secret of unstructured data. E-doc 16(5)

Rasmussen N, Goldy P, Solli P (2002) Financial business intelligence. John Wiley and Sons, Inc., New York

Reed R, DeFillippi RJ (1990) Causal ambiguity, barriers to imitation, and sustainable competitive advantage. Academy of Management Review 15: 88-102

Resnick JT (2002) A matter of reputation. Pharmaceutical Executive 20(6): 74-84

Rezaee Z, Hoffman C (2001) "Standardized financial reporting". *Internal Audit*, August

Rezaee Z, Turner J (2002) *Journal of Government Financial Management*, Summer

Rheingans P, Landreth C (1995) Perceptual principles for effective visualizations. In: Grinstein G, Levkowitz H (eds.), Perceptual issues in visualization (59-74). Springer-Verlag, New York

Ring PS, Van de Ven (1994) Developmental processes of cooperative interorganizational relationships. Academy of Management Review 19(1): 90-118

Roberts J (2000) From know-how to show-how? Questioning the role of information and communication technologies in knowledge transfer

Robinson M (2002) Business intelligence infrastructure, DM Review Magazine May

Romney W, Steinbart S (1999) Accounting information systems. Prentice Hall, Saddle Wells NY

Ross J, Beath C (2002) Beyond the business case: New approaches to IT investment. MIT Sloan Management Review Winter 2002, 51-59

Roth MA, Wolfson DC, Kleewein JC, Nelin CJ (2002) Information integration: A new generation of information technology IBM Systems Journal Armonk

Roussinova D, Zhao J (2003) Automatic discovery of similarity relationships through Web mining. Decision Support Systems 35(1): 149-166

Rudin K, Cressy D (2003) Will the real analytic application please stand up. DM review March 2003 : 1-6

Salchenberger LM, Cinar EM, Lash NA (1992) Neural networks: A new tool for predicting thrift failures. Decision Sciences 23: 899-916

Salton G, McGill M (1983) Introduction to modern information retrieval. New York: McGraw-Hill

Satzinger J, Ørvik TU (2001) The object-oriented approach: Concepts, system development, and modeling with UML, Course Technology, Boston, MA

Saunders C, Gebelt M, Hu Q (1997) Achieving success in information systems outsourcing. California Management Review 39(2): 63-79

Sauter VL(1999) Intuitive Decision Making. Communications of the ACM 42: 109-115

Scapens R, Jazayeri M, Scapens J (1998) SAP: integrated information systems and the implications for management accountants. Management Accounting (UK), 76(September): 46-49

Schaffer JD, Whitley D, Eshelman LJ (1992) Combinations of genetic algorithms and neural networks: A survey of the state of the art in: COGANN-92. IEEE Conference Society Press, Los Alamitos CA, 1-37

Schkade DA, Kleinmuntz DN (1994) Information displays and choice processes: differential effects of organization, form and sequence. Organizational Behavior and Human Decision Processes 57: 319-37

Schneider M (2002) A stakeholder model of organizational leadership. Organization Science 13(2): 209-220

Schroeder W, Martin K, Lorensen B (1998) The visualization toolkit: An object-oriented approach to 3D graphics, 2nd Edition. Prentice-Hall, Upper Saddle River, New Jersey

Seiner RS (1999)A conceptual meta-model for unstructured data; KIK Consulting & Educational Services. TDAN.com (http://www.tdan.com/i024fe01.htm)

Sellers P (1995) So you fail. Now bounce back! Fortune, New York 131(8): 48-58

Senge PM (1990) The fifth discipline: The art and practice of the learning organization. Doubleday, New York

Shacklett M (2001) Data mart may be first step to a comprehensive warehouse strategy, unisysworld.com

Shank JK (1989) Strategic cost management: New wine, or just new bottles? Journal of Management Accounting Research 1: 49-65.

Shepard RN, Cooper LA (1982) Mental images and their transformations. The MIT Press, Cambridge, Mass

Shim JP (2002) Past, present, and future of decision support technology, Decision Support Systems, Jun 2002: 111-126

Silverston L, Graziano KB (1998) Where did that warehouse data come from? DM Review Magazine, February

Simmonds K (1981) Strategic management accounting. Management Accounting (UK): 26-29

Simonin BL (1997) The importance of collaborative know-how: An empirical test of the learning organization. Academy of Management Journal 40(5): 1150-1174

Simons R (1987) Accounting control systems and business strategy: An empirical analysis. Accounting, Organizations and Society, 12(July): 357-374

Sinkkonen J, Lahtinen I (1998) Hermoverkot markkinoinin apuna. Pcmikro(4): 70-74

Smith C, Warner J (1979) On financial contracting: An analysis of bond covenants. Journal of Financial Economics 7: 117-161

Smithers T (1992) Taking eliminative materialism seriously: a methodology for autonomous systems research. Toward a practice of autonomous systems. Proceedings of the First European Conference on Artificial Life. The MIT Press/Bradford Books, Cambridge, MA, pp 31-40

Solomon CM (2001) Managing virtual teams, Workforce, 60-65

Srinivasan K, Kekre S, Mukhopadhyay T (1994) Impact of electronic data interchange technology on JIT shipments. Management Science, 40(October): 1291-1304

Stamps D (1997) Communities of practice: Learning is social. Training is irrelevant? Training. February: 34-42

Steinbach M, Karypis G, Kumar V (2000) A comparison of document clustering techniques. Department of Computer Science and Engineering, University of Minnesota Technical Report #00-034

Stewart GL, Manz CC (1995) Leadership for self-managing work teams: A typology and integrative model. Human Relations 48(7): 747-770

Stimpson J (2003) CRM is Hot! Practical Accountant 36(1): 38-41

Stock D, Watson CJ (1984) Human judgment accuracy, multidimensional graphics, and humans versus models. Journal of Accounting Research 22 (1): 192-206

Sullivan D (2001) Document warehousing & content management: ETL meets content management. DM Review Magazine (October)

Tai X, Ren F, Kita K (2002) An information retrieval based on vector space method by supervised learning. Information Processing & Management 38

Tam KY, Kiang Y (1992) Managerial applications of neural networks: The case of bank failure predictions. Managerial Science 38: 927-947

Tan CM, Wang YF, Lee CD (2002) The use of biagrams to enhance text categorization. Information Processing & Management 38 (4): 529-546

Taylor D, Glezen G (1994) Auditing: Integrated concepts and procedures. John Wiley and Sons, New York

Thierauf RJ (1995) Virtual reality systems for business. Quorum Books, Westport, CT

Thompson JD (1967) Organizations in action: Social science bases of administrative theory. New York: McGraw-Hill

Thomsen E (1997) OLAP solutions: Building multidimensional information systems. John Wiley & Sons, New York, NY

Tower Software (2003), Technology: Unstructured data capture-needle in a haystack

Tufte ER (1983) The visual display of quantitative information. Graphic Press, Cheshire, CT:

Tufte ER (1990) Envisioning information. Graphic Press, Cheshire, CT

Tufte ER (1997) Visual explanations. Graphic Press, Cheshire, CT

Turetsky HF (1997) An empirical investigation of firm longevity: A model of the ex ante predictors of financial distress. Unpublished Phd Dissertation, Virginia: Commonwealth University

Turocy P, Phillips J, Andres B (2002) No more information overload-companies must consider how they classify data so employees can find it fast. Information Week December (16)

Tushman ML, Nadler DA (1978) Information processing as an integrating concept in organizational design. Academy of Management Review, 3(July): 613-624.

Umanath NS, Vessey I (1995) Multiattribute data presentation and human judgment: a cognitive fit perspective. Decision Sciences 25 (5,6): 795-824

Varetto F (1998) Genetic algorithms in the analysis of insolvency risk. Journal of Banking and Finance 22: 1421-1440

Vedder RG (1999) CEO and CIO perspectives on competitive intelligence. Communications of the ACM August: 108-116.

Vellido A, Lisboa PJG, Vaughan J (1999) Neural networks in business: a survey of applications (1992-1998). Expert Systems with Applications 51: 51-70

Venkatraman N (1989) The concept of fit in strategy research: Toward verbal and statistical correspondence. Academy of Management Review, 14: 423-444.

Vessey I (1991) Cognitive fit: a theory-based analysis of the graphs versus tables literature. Decision Sciences, 22(2): 219-41

Vessey I (1994) The effect of information presentation on decision making: A cost-benefit analysis. Information & Management 27: 103-119

Vessey I, Galletta D (1991) Cognitive fit: An empirical study of information acquisition. Information Systems Research, 2(1): 63-84

Visible Decision, Inc. (VDI) (2002) http://www.vdi.com

Volberda HW (1996) Toward the flexible form: How to remain vital in hyper-competitive environments. Organization Science 7(4): 359-374

Wactlar H. D., Christel M. G., Gong Y. and Hauptmann A. G. (1999) Lessons learned from building a terabyte digital video library. IEEE Computer Feb: 66-73

Watson HJ, Goodhue DL, Wixom BH (2002) The benefits of data warehousing: why some organizations realize exceptional payoffs. Information & Management 39: 491-502

Watson HJ, Haley BJ (1997) Data warehousing: a framework for analysis and a survey of current practices. Journal of Data Warehousing 2(1): 10-17

Wegandt, J, Kieso J, Kimmel L (2000) Accounting principles. John Wiley and Sons NY

Wheatley MJ (1992) Leadership and the new science. Berrett-Koehler Publishers Inc., San Francisco CA

Wickens CD, Merwin DH, Lin EL (1994) Implications of graphics enhancements for the visualization of scientific data: dimensional integrity, stereopsis, motion and mesh. Human Factors 36 (1): 44-61

Williams BK, Sawyer SC (2003) Using information technology. Boston, McGraw Hill Irwin. p. 334

Wilson RL, Sharda R (1994) Bankruptcy prediction using neural networks. Decision Support Systems 11: 545-557

Wolff RS, Yaeger L (1993) Visualization of natural phenomena. Springer-Verlag, New York

Wu RC-F (1994) Integrating neurocomputing and auditing expertise. Managerial Auditing Journal 9(3): 20-26

XBRL Progress Report, April 2003. (http://www.xbrl.org/whatisxbrl/currentreport.pdf)

XL Miner software online help; Data reduction and exploration-hierarchical Clustering (http://www.resample.com/xlminer/help/HClst/HClst_intro.htm)

Yu CH, Behrens JT (1995) Applications of multivariate visualization to behavioral sciences. Behavior Research Methods, Instruments, & Computers 27 (2): 264-71

Yu C, Cuadrado J, Ceglowski M, Payne JS (2002) Patterns in unstructured data-discovery, aggregation, and visualization. National Institute for Technology and Liberal Education (NITLE) - Presentation to the Andrew W. Mellon Foundation

Zahedi F (1994) Intelligent systems for business: Expert systems and neural networks. Wadsworth Publishing CA

Zaheer A, Venkatraman N (1994) Determinant of electronic integration in the insurance industry: An empirical test. Management Science, 40(May): 549-566.

Zarowin S (2003) "A napster for financial data? *Journal of Accountancy* January

Zavgren C (1985) Assessing the vulnerability to failure of American industrial firms: A logistics analysis. Journal of Business Finance and Accounting (Spring): 19-45

Zhang G, Patuwo BE, Hu MY (1998) Forecasting with artificial neural networks: The state of the art. International journal of Forecasting 14: 36-62.

Zhu L, Rai A, Zhang A (2002) Advanced feature extraction for keybloack-based image retrieval. Information Systems 27: 537-557

Zimmerman JL (1995) Accounting for decision making and control. Chicago, IL: Irwin

Zmijewski M (1984) Methodological issues related to the estimation of financial distress prediction models. Journal of Accounting Research 22 (Supplement): 59-82

Zu L, Rao A, Zhang A (2002) Advanced feature extraction for keyblock-based image retrieval. Information Systems 27

http://cactus.eas.asu.edu/partha/Papers-PDF/activefiles.pdf
http://dmreview.com/editorial/dmreview/print_action.cfm?EdID=5786
http://fraank.eycarat.ukans.edu
http://javelina.cet.middlebury.edu/lsa/out/cover_page.htm
http://sunsite.berkeley.edu/Imaging/Databases/JISC02-imaging
http://www.cs.washington.edu/homes/alon/cikm98.ppt
http://www.dmreview.com/master.cfm?NavID=198&EdID=5211
http://www.document-manager.com/articles/tech.htm
http://www.nasdaq.com/xbrl
http://www.xbrl.org

Index

List of Contributors

Amobi, Onuora,
  Peoplesoft Technical Project Lead
  Kaiser Permanente
  Oakland CA 94612
  oamobi@amobi.com

Anandarajan, Asokan, Ph.D.,
  Associate Professor of Accounting
  School of Management
  New Jersey Institute of Technology
  University Heights, Newark,
  NJ 07102

Anandarajan, Murugan, Ph.D.,
  Associate Professor of MIS
  Department of Management
  Drexel University
  Philadelphia, PA 19104
  ma33@drexel.edu

Arinze, Bay, Ph.D.,
  Professor of MIS
  Department of Management
  Drexel University
  Philadelphia, PA 19104
  Bay.Arinze@drexel.edu

Devine, W. Patrick
  Doctoral Candidate
  Department of Management
  Drexel University
  Philadelphia, PA 19104
  Patdmis@aol.com

Dull, B. Richard, PhD.,
  Assistant Professor Accounting
  School of Accountancy &
  Legal Studies
  Clemson University
  301 Sirrine Hall, Clemson,
  SC 29634
  rdull@clemson.edu

Hartzel, S. Kathleen, Ph.D,
  Assistant Professor of IT
  Duquesne University
  Schools of Business
  802 Rockwell Hall,
  600 Forbes Avenue, Pittsburgh,
  PA 15828
  hartzel@duq.edu

Hughes, W. Daniel,
  Managing Director
  Claritee Group, LLC
  PO Box 11, Chalfont, PA 18914

Jhaveri, S. Darpan
  General Accounting Department,
  Bristol Myers Squibb Co.,
  Nassau Park, Princeton, NJ

Jones, Ken,
  Managing Director
  Claritee Group, LLC.
  PO Box 11, Chalfont, PA 18914

Jones, H. Trevor, PhD,
  Associate Professor
  School of Business
  Duquesne University
  Pittsburgh, PA 15828
  jonest@duq.edu

Koskivaara, Eija., Ph.D
TUCS Turku Centre for Computer
Science, and Turku School of
Economics and Business
Adminstration,
Lemminkäisenkatu 14 A,
20520 Turku,
Finland
Eija.Koskivaara@tukkk.fi

Lee, Picheng, Ph.D.,
Assistant Professor of Accounting
School of Business and
Administration
Pace University
New York 10570

Nicolaou, I. Andreas, Ph.D.,
Associate Professor of Accounting
Department of Accounting and MIS,
Bowling Green State University
Bowling Green, OH 43403
anicol@cba.bgsu.edu

Simmers, A. Claire, Ph.D.,
Associate Professor
Department of Management
Erivan K. Haub School of Business
St. Joseph's University,
Philadelphia, PA 19131
simmers@sju.edu

Srinivasan, C.A, Ph.D
Emeritus Professor of Accounting
Department of Accounting
Drexel University
Philadelphia, PA 19104

Tegarden, P. David, Ph.D.
Associate Professor
Department of Accounting and
Information Systems
Pamplin College of Business
Virginia Tech, Blacksburg, VA 24061
dtegarde@vt.edu

Trott, C. Valerie, CPA, CIA,
Assistant Professor
Duquesne University
Schools of Business
802 Rockwell Hall, 600 Forbes
Avenue, Pittsburgh, PA 15828
trott@duq.edu

Vasarhelyi, A. Miklos, Ph.D.,
KPMG Professor of AIS
Rutgers University
315 Ackerson Hall, 180 University
Avenue, Newark, NJ 07102
miklosv@andromeda.rutgers.edu

Vinciguerra, M. Barbara, Ph.D.,
Assistant Professor of Accounting
Management Division
Penn State University - Great Valley
Malvern, PA 19355
bvinciguerra@psu.edu

Wu, Jia
Doctoral Candidate
Rutgers University
Department of Accounting and
Information Systems
300v Ackerson Hall,
180 University Ave
jiawu@andromeda.rutgers.edu

Zaman, S Maliha
Doctoral Candidate
Department of Management
Drexel University
Philadelphia, PA 19104
msz26@drexel.edu

Druck: betz-druck GmbH, D-64291 Darmstadt
Verarbeitung: Buchbinderei Schäffer, D-67269 Grünstadt